ParshaNut

ParshaNut

54 Journeys into the World of Torah Commentary

Rabbi David Kasher

QUID PRO BOOKS
New Orleans, Louisiana

Published in 2022 by Quid Pro Books.

ISBN 978-1-61027-444-9 (paperback)
ISBN 978-1-61027-464-7 (hardcover)
ISBN 978-1-61027-463-0 (ePUB)

QUID PRO BOOKS
5860 Citrus Blvd.
Suite D
New Orleans, Louisiana 70123
www.quidprobooks.com

Publisher's Cataloging-in-Publication

Kasher, David.

ParshaNut: 54 journeys into the world of Torah commentary / David Kasher.

p. cm. — mass market paperback edition

Includes biographical references.

1. Bible. Pentateuch. 2. Commentaries. 3. Paraschah. I. Title. II. Kasher, Rabbi David.

BS1225.52 .K46 2022 2022317481

Dedicated to Our Teacher, Nechama Leibowitz, zt"l

מוקדש למורתנו נחמה ליבוביץ, זצ״ל

... and to my dear H.M.

Table of Contents

Acknowledgments

"I will try to clarify from whom I received whatever I have received. First and foremost, there are the Sacred Scriptures, from which I learned how to combine letters. Then there are the Mishnah and the Talmud and the Midrashim and Rashi's commentary on the Torah."
— S.Y. Agnon, Nobel Prize Banquet Speech, 1966

I remember clearly the day I first learned a piece of Rashi's commentary on the Torah. It left my head spinning and my life forever changed. So I am grateful, first and foremost, to Rashi.

From Rashi I learned to be grateful to the *Ba'alei HaMidrash* upon whose work his commentary was based – those rabbis who created the most dynamic form of textual interpretation I have ever encountered.

From Rashi I also learned how to follow a "running commentary" and, in search of others to follow, I went and opened a *Mikraot Gedolot*. The thrill of seeing all those commentaries stacked together on the same page has never left me, and it feels as if I have been living in that book ever since. So I am grateful to Daniel Bomberg, who printed the first Rabbinic Bible in 1517, and I am grateful to all those medieval commentators who appeared in the much-later edition I first came across.

Then came the Achronim, then the Hassidim, then the Moderns, and I am grateful to them all - the march of voices throughout the generations who have participated in and shaped this discourse I love so much.

I am grateful to my own teachers in the Torah and its commentaries. I have been especially influenced by: Rabbi Beryl Gershenfeld – in whose *Gur Ayreh* class I fell in love with the Torah; Rabbi Nathaniel Helfgot – who taught me how to see the divinity of the Torah even without the help of the commentators; Rabbi Avi Weiss – from whom I learned how to live Torah; and my friend David Henkin – from whom I learned how to teach Torah.

I am grateful for two ongoing conversations that have profoundly shaped my relationship with Torah over the years – one with Rabbi

Shmuly Yanklowitz, my spiritual *chevruta* since our yeshiva days; and one with Rabbi Benay Lappe who, within the first hour of meeting her, taught me to see Torah differently all over again.

I am also grateful to those commentators in my own generation whom I have admired from afar – there are many, but Dr. Avivah Gottlieb Zornberg and Rav Elchanan Samet come immediately to mind.

And then, of course, I am grateful to Nechama Leibowitz, to whom we are all indebted for revitalizing the study of *parshanut* in the 20th century. My own rebbe, Rav Avi, often called Nechama his "rebbe in *parshanut*." And I have always seen myself, in this project, following dutifully in her footsteps.

I am grateful to all those who have supported the ParshaNut project along the way. In the beginning, it was a blog on Tumblr, and there I was fortunate to find readers from a much wider range of life experiences than most teachers ever find in a conventional classroom. I began to notice, in particular, that I had a loyal following among young queer and trans folks, and was so inspired by their insights. I am very grateful to them, and to all my readers, for their shared interest and their unique perspectives.

The blog became a full website with the help of the very talented designer Stig Greve. I added a podcast version, which opened with music borrowed from the brilliant composer Nathan Clevenger. I am grateful to them both for the gifts of their artistry.

Then, I had the greatest fortune a blog could hope for when my boss at the time, the visionary Sara Bamberger, offered to fund my work on the project and distribute it under the auspices of *Kevah*, the Jewish Education organization she had started. I will always be grateful to her for that support, and for all of my work with her. At *Kevah*, I was also incredibly grateful to be able to work closely with Dr. Julie Lieber, the greatest professional partner I could have hoped for, and I turned to her often to work out ideas and get feedback when I was writing these essays.

When I took a job as a community rabbi at IKAR, I knew I would no longer be able to keep up the weekly writing project. But I am grateful to my magnificent mentor in the rabbinate, Rabbi Sharon Brous, and to all of my colleagues at IKAR, for supporting the attempt to turn the blog into a book, and for exposing me to a community of learners whose brilliance and passion keeps my own excitement for the material fresh and alive.

This book would never have made it into the hands of a publisher if not for Professor Malcolm Feeley, a dear friend from my days in Berkeley, who connected me with Professor S. Alan Childress at Quid Pro Books. I will be forever grateful to Malcolm for that connection, for it has been an absolute pleasure working with Quid Pro. Alan's wisdom and patience have managed to make publishing feel like a deeply meaningful experience. It is his pure and straightforward love of good books that guides everything Quid Pro does, and they do everything with such integrity.

I am also grateful to Alan for introducing me to Lee Scheingold, the incredible editor who cleaned up the initial manuscript. And I am grateful to the precise and perceptive Hannah Jensen, who did an indispensable final edit. Additional and invaluable editing help has come, over the years, from many others whom I have pestered for access to their keen eyes. I am grateful to them all.

My brother Moshe is the person I trust most in the world, and his opinion has always had the final say in matters of tone and style. I am grateful for his wise counsel, and for his very existence.

I want to sound a special note of gratitude to Rabbi Shlomo Ephraim Lunschitz, author of the *Kli Yakar,* which I have many times called my favorite work of Torah commentary. In one of the *Kli Yakar*'s many beautiful attempts to create a new conceptual framework for a familiar institution, he suggests that the first five of the Ten Commandments are directed toward God, while the second five are directed toward human beings. Neat and tidy. He appears stuck with the fifth commandment, however: "Honor your father and mother," which seems clearly directed to human beings, not to God – but is on the "wrong tablet," so to speak. He resolves this dilemma with a saying from the Talmud (in *Kedushin 30b*): "There are three partners in the formation of a person: The Holy Blessed One, the father, and the mother." And so, he concludes, to honor your parents is also to honor God, their partner in the work of giving you life.

In that spirit, I close with the most eternal gratitude to my father, my mother, and my God, who have together nurtured and nourished me with life, love, and Torah.

ParshaNut

Parshanut

Every week for five years I wrote an essay on the *parsha,* the weekly Torah reading. And every week I tried to take you with me on a journey into the world of *parshanut,* traditional Torah commentary. We would usually begin our weekly investigations – as all good Torah commentary does – with a question in the *parsha,* and then go see what kinds of answers had been given by the great commentators, and how we might put those answers into dialogue with one another.

But I never really explained what I was doing. I just started publishing the essays, as if I were entering a conversation that already existed (which in a sense, of course, I was.) But I never gave you a general overview of how *parshanut* works.

So I want to use this introduction as an opportunity to explain some of the basics of the genre, to introduce you to some of the key players, and to highlight some of the classic styles.

Parshanut is a genre of Jewish literature formed by two seemingly contradictory assumptions: 1.) The text of the Torah is a work of Divine perfection, with infinite levels of meaning embedded in every letter, word, and turn of phrase. 2.) Every oddity or difficulty in the text must be confronted, challenged, and relentlessly scrutinized. (Indeed, it is in the process of doing so that one reveals the truth of assumption #1.) So *parshanut* is a form of discourse that always begins with a question, and one that always presumes there is an answer.

That much is the theory. But for a real understanding of *parshanut,* we need to see how it works in practice. And I can think of no better place to start than at a particular verse in Genesis, Chapter 37.

It is the chapter that begins the Joseph story, a long and dramatic narrative that opens with Jacob settling down in the land of Canaan, presumably to find some peace and quiet after all his years of work and struggle. But he makes one big mistake that will soon upend any hope the family had for tranquility: he loves Joseph more than the rest of his children, and makes his favoritism clear enough (with the famous fancy coat) that, inevitably, the other brothers begin to hate Joseph. Joseph doesn't help matters at all by acting somewhere between arrogant and oblivious, telling the brothers about these dreams he has, in which they all bow down to him. And so "they hated him even more," the text says. It won't be long before they are ready to do him harm.

With all that tension in place, one day Jacob sends Joseph to go check on his brothers, who are out shepherding. Joseph, ever the dreamer, begins to meander, and soon enough finds himself a little lost. And then we read the strangest thing:

A man found him wandering in the field. The man asked him, "Who are you looking for?" He answered, "I am looking for my brothers. Tell me, please, where they are shepherding?" The man said, "They have gone from here. I heard them say, 'Let us go to Dotan." So Joseph went after his brothers, and found them at Dotan. ***(Gen. 37:15-17)***

וַיִּמְצָאֵהוּ אִישׁ וְהִנֵּה תֹעֶה בַּשָּׂדֶה וַיִּשְׁאָלֵהוּ הָאִישׁ לֵאמֹר מַה תְּבַקֵּשׁ. וַיֹּאמֶר אֶת אַחַי אָנֹכִי מְבַקֵּשׁ הַגִּידָה נָּא לִי אֵיפֹה הֵם רֹעִים. וַיֹּאמֶר הָאִישׁ נָסְעוּ מִזֶּה כִּי שָׁמַעְתִּי אֹמְרִים נֵלְכָה דֹּתָיְנָה וַיֵּלֶךְ יוֹסֵף אַחַר אֶחָיו וַיִּמְצָאֵם בְּדֹתָן.

Now, as I said, *parshanut* always begins with a question. There is some problem in the text that needs solving – something missing, or something there that doesn't make sense. And here in this strange back-and-forth, there are plenty of questions we could ask. But the first and most glaring one is this: Who was this anonymous "man"?

This is the kind of thing that sets the commentators on alert: an unnamed figure who plays an important role in the narrative, and even seems to hold secret knowledge. What's going on here? There must be more to this story than meets the eye. This is a job for the *parshanim* – the great interpreters of the Torah.

If you open a book of collected Torah commentary – what's called a *Mikraot Gedolot* – you'll see a big, chunky group of words up at the top. That's the text of the Torah itself. And then, all around the rest of the page, you'll have little blocks of other texts, printed in different fonts and sizes to distinguish one from another. They look almost like columns in a newspaper, or pop-ups on a webpage. And each of these little bubbles of text is the running commentary of a different rabbi, all of them shouting out answers to the questions they have about the Torah text at the top, creating a beautiful cacophony of interpretations, right there on the page.

In these collections, there are some commentators who are more commonly included, and some who are less. But there are three guys who are always there. I call them 'The Big Three' – the most celebrated and studied commentators of the Middle Ages – Rashi, the Ibn Ezra, and the Ramban.

Rashi is the Grandfather of the Commentators, the greatest of them all – his name resonates in yeshivas the way Shakespeare's does in English departments. Abraham Ibn Ezra, an eclectic thinker, and all-around man of letters, was the only commentator other than Rashi to be included in the very first *Mikraot Gedolot* ever published. These two were the standard bearers of the genre, the go-to authorities on the interpretation of the Torah. But when Rabbi Moses Nachmanides came out with his commentary, it was such a clear masterpiece, that he soon rounded out the group and became the third must-see commentary on any question in the Torah.

What's valuable about this trio is not simply that they are all brilliant and prolific, but that they are, each one, very stylistically different from the other two. Getting to know their commentaries, then, means not just familiarizing yourself with the top three works in the genre, but also coming to understand three general approaches to *parshanut*. So let's take a look at what they each have to say to our question: Who was that mysterious man?

1. Rashi *(Rabbi Shlomo Yitzchaki 1040 – 1105)* – The Literary Approach

We begin with Rashi, of course. And we might also have called his style, "poetic," or "homiletic," or even "fantastic." But really what we're trying to say is: "midrashic" – and it's hard to translate what that means exactly. Because what Rashi is most famous for doing is collecting and condensing stories from the Midrash – records of Biblical interpretations by the rabbis of the Talmudic period, roughly the 2nd to 7th centuries. Their style was based on a blend of wordplay, intertextual connections, and imaginative storytelling. They saw the words of the text as embedded with multiple levels of meaning – packed with hidden messages that could be decoded through careful pattern-spotting coupled with creative interpretation. So the Midrash contains some of the wildest, most fantastic answers to our questions – but they are always based on linguistic cues in the text itself. This sensitivity to language, along with a willingness to weave new stories into the old one, make for an approach we'll call "literary."

So let's see what Rashi has to say about our "man":

A man came upon him – **This is Gabriel, as it says (in Daniel 9:21), "the man, Gabriel."**

וימצאהו איש – זה גבריאל, שנאמר והאיש גבריאל (דניאל ב').

The man was Gabriel, meaning – the "man" was actually an angel. For Gabriel is an angel who appears in a vision in the Book of Daniel and, as Rashi says, Daniel refers to Gabriel as, "the man." So that's the connection – the man here, the man there – it must be the same man, who is actually no man at all, but the angel Gabriel.

Now this may sound like a stretch, linking two figures on opposite ends of the Bible with just one word. It's classic midrashic technique. But it isn't the only reason that Rashi is compelled to think of our man as an angel. There's precedent. As a matter of fact, we've already seen a couple of stories in the Torah so far with mysterious "men" who turn out to be angels.

Abraham is sitting by his tent one day when "three men" appear and deliver the message that he and Sarah will have a child in their old age. (*Gen. 18:2*) And not only do these men seem to have this divine knowledge, but they then head on to Sodom (*v. 16*), and when they arrive there, are explicitly called "angels." (*Gen. 19:1*)

And then there is the famous story of Jacob wrestling with an angel. Only his opponent is never actually called an 'angel.' The text merely says: *"A man wrestled with him until the break of dawn." (Gen. 32:25)* And again, this man has some kind of divine message – he gives Jacob a new name. And when the man departs, Jacob says, *"I have seen God face to face!"* Here, too, a mysterious "man" has come to be understood as an angel.

So what appears at first to just be Rashi's penchant for the supernatural is actually an interpretation that builds on the echo of two other stories in the Torah – and then the linguistic connection from the book of Daniel just seals the deal. The "midrashic" style, in other words, is really a kind of literary technique.

2. The Ibn Ezra *(Abraham ibn Ezra 1089 – 1164)* – The Straightforward Approach

But maybe all that textual interweaving feels forced to you. Or maybe you just don't believe that angels are hiding out all over the place. You don't like to think of the Torah as some kind of spiritual ghost story. You just want to take the text at face value. None of that wild speculation –

what is the best reading of the actual words on the page?

In that case, the Ibn Ezra is your man. He is, for the most part, a literalist. He usually doesn't rely on midrashic tradition in his commentary. He is more likely, instead, to give a grammatical or semantic explanation, or a close reading based only on the words in the local context of the story.

So what does the Ibn Ezra make of our mysterious man?

A man came upon him **– The plain meaning is that this was one of the fieldworkers along the road.**

וימצאהו איש – דרך הפשט אחד מעוברי דרך.

That's the straightforward approach for you. He even says it explicitly: "the plain meaning." No angels. No backstory. If we read that Joseph encountered a man while he was on the road, the simplest explanation is that he passed by a field and there was just a random guy working there who happened to have seen his brothers pass by beforehand.

The Ibn Ezra, who traditionally never garnered the kind of esteem accorded to Rashi, has been reclaimed by modern scholars, who also tend to prefer a straightforward, rational interpretation of the Bible. He is seen as an independent thinker, willing to read the text as it is, without the baggage of the midrashic tradition, or the bias of religious dogma.

But if we gain a measure of reasonableness with this approach, we lose something as well. Because this more simplistic interpretation doesn't really help us understand what this scene is doing in the Torah to begin with. Was it really so important to read that Joseph stopped to ask for directions? If he'd met an angel on the road, well then, we'd want to hear about that. But if this was just some guy who happened to be there, then was this conversation really worth recording?

So the straightforward approach is generally excellent for making sense of the verse itself, but less concerned with the big picture. For that, we turn to...

3. Ramban *(Moses Nachmanides 1194 – 1270)* – The Theological Approach

Nachmanides – also known as the Ramban – more than any other commentator, managed to construct an entire theology through his interpretation of the Torah. Each little piece he writes is like a tiny philosophical or mystical treatise on some central matter of Jewish faith.

In the introduction to his commentary, he makes it clear that he sees the Torah as more than just a good story, or even a sacred story, but in fact *the source of all wisdom* – if only we knew how to uncover it. And that uncovering is the job he takes upon himself.

The Ramban often references Rashi and the Ibn Ezra, and is willing to borrow from both of their approaches – but then he usually takes things a step further. And that's just what he does here in our little passage.

Now, so far we have a debate: Rashi said the man was an angel. The Ibn Ezra said it was just a random fieldworker. So which side will the Ramban take?

A man came upon him wandering in the field **– ...This is all to let us know that the divine decree overrides all human strategies, for God prepared for him a guide, who unwittingly led Joseph straight into their hands. And this is what the rabbis meant (in the midrash) when they say that these "men" are angels – that this story is not one of happenstance. It is a way of showing us that 'God's intention will always be fulfilled.'**

וימצאהו איש והנה תעה בשדה – ...ולהודיענו עוד כי הגזרה אמת והחריצות שקר כי זמן לו הקב"ה מורה דרך שלא מדעתו להביאו בידם ולזה נתכוונו רבותינו (ב"ר פד יד) באמרם כי האישים האלה הם מלאכים שלא על חנם היה כל הסיפור הזה להודיענו כי עצת ה' היא תקום.

Notice how the Ramban manages to collapse the debate by redefining what an angel is. An angel is a guide, planted by God, to lead people toward their destiny. But the angel doesn't have to be conscious of what he's doing. In fact, the angel doesn't have to be a supernatural creature at all. The Torah calls these angels, "men," precisely because ordinary men and women can act as angels, or messengers of God.

So everyone is right. Was it an angel? Yes. Was it a fieldworker? Yes. But more importantly, it was a lesson to us that God was watching over Joseph, and that even as he seemed to be wandering aimlessly, he was being taken exactly where he was supposed to go. And that lesson, of course, the Ramban means to be extended to every human interaction. We are all being led, sometimes directly, and sometimes in hidden ways, toward our destiny. The hand of Divine Providence guides us all.

So there you have it. You can see why I called this 'The Theological Approach.' In the Ramban's formulation, this little conversation on the road turns out to be the Torah's way of making a strong statement about

God's role in the world, and how human beings play their parts in the divine plan.

*

Now, maybe you think that this is a little heavy-handed, a little much to read into the appearance of this anonymous man. Perhaps. But I'll tell you who seems to agree with the Ramban.

Joseph.

Joseph's journey has just begun, and before it finishes, he will be sold into slavery, thrown into prison, and appointed leader over Egypt; he will save an entire region from famine, take revenge on his brothers in an elaborate deception, and then reveal himself to them in the dramatic climax. And when they finally realize what has happened – that the brother they thought was dead now stands before them – they are stunned speechless, overcome with guilt. But Joseph says:

Now do not be distressed or blame yourselves because you sold me here. For it was to save life that God sent me ahead of you. It is now two years that there has been famine in the land, and there are still five years to come in which there shall be no harvest. But God sent me ahead of you to ensure your survival on earth, and to save your lives, in a great deliverance. So it was not you who sent me here, but God… ***(Gen. 45:5-8)***

וְעַתָּה אַל תֵּעָצְבוּ וְאַל יִחַר בְּעֵינֵיכֶם כִּי מְכַרְתֶּם אֹתִי הֵנָּה כִּי לְמִחְיָה שְׁלָחַנִי אֱלֹהִים לִפְנֵיכֶם. כִּי זֶה שְׁנָתַיִם הָרָעָב בְּקֶרֶב הָאָרֶץ וְעוֹד חָמֵשׁ שָׁנִים אֲשֶׁר אֵין חָרִישׁ וְקָצִיר. וַיִּשְׁלָחֵנִי אֱלֹהִים לִפְנֵיכֶם לָשׂוּם לָכֶם שְׁאֵרִית בָּאָרֶץ וּלְהַחֲיוֹת לָכֶם לִפְלֵיטָה גְּדֹלָה. וְעַתָּה לֹא אַתֶּם שְׁלַחְתֶּם אֹתִי הֵנָּה כִּי הָאֱלֹהִים וַיְשִׂימֵנִי לְאָב לְפַרְעֹה וּלְאָדוֹן לְכָל בֵּיתוֹ וּמֹשֵׁל בְּכָל אֶרֶץ מִצְרָיִם.

This is Joseph, looking back on his life, and seeing, in retrospect, that the hand of God was always guiding him to this very moment. His brothers, then, were just agents of God – angels, if you will. His father, too, was an angel of God. Even Pharaoh, in this sense, was an angel, a kind of messenger. We are all, Joseph now realizes, agents of Divine Providence.

And maybe, at this very moment, Joseph is thinking back to that day he went looking for his brothers, and remembering the man he met on the way. "Who was that man?" he asks himself – just as we have been asking all along. He considers a supernatural explanation. But no, that's not exactly right. He considers the straightforward explanation. But that's not enough, it doesn't account for everything. So he comes, at last, to the theological explanation. He has heard that beautiful cacophony of possible interpretations of his life, and he has settled on the one that makes most sense to him.

Joseph has learned, in a sense, how *parshanut* works. And now – having followed him down the road a ways – I hope you have, too.

Some Notes on Usage and Translation

I wanted, in this book, not only to familiarize people with the great works of Torah commentary, but also to expose them to the discourse of *parshanut*. I wanted them to hear the sound of a conversation that has been taking place between commentators for centuries and continues today among their inheritors.

So I have tried to follow the norms of discourse I learned in the *Beit Midrash* (the classical Jewish study hall). Well-established customs dictated that some commentators were known by their last names (Ibn Ezra, Abarbanel, Sforno), some by the acronym formed by 'R' (for "Rabbi") and their initials (Rashi, Ramban, Rashbam), and some by the title of their commentary (Kli Yakar, Or HaChayim). We also had the custom of prefacing each of these references with the definite article; so it was not just Ibn Ezra, but *The* Ibn Ezra, and *The* Ramban, and *The* Kli Yakar – as if to say, "The Great Kli Yakar," or perhaps, "The Author of the Kli Yakar." The one exception was Rashi, who needed no grand introduction, and was always just "Rashi."

I have followed all these customs throughout the book – except in the case of Maimonides, who is known in the *Beit Midrash* as "The Rambam" (Rabbi Moshe Ben Maimon), but has become so well-known in the wider world by his Latin name that it seems most accessible to refer to him as such in English (not to mention that it avoids the common confusion between the The Rambam and The Ramban).

A similar consideration led me to refer to all the Biblical figures by their famous anglicized names: so, Moses, not Moshe, and Joshua, not Yehoshua. (If, on the other hand the anglicized name was less well-know – as in Simeon or Balaam – I sometimes used the Hebrew name instead: Shimon, Bilaam.) But it made sense to call all the rabbis of the Talmud – whose are less universally known – by their Hebrew or Aramaic names: so, Rabbi Yehuda, not Rabbi Judah, and Rabbi Akiva, not Rabbi Jacob.

I prefer not to refer to God with gendered pronouns, for theological reasons, so I have avoided doing so in my own writing. But I wanted to faithfully record the literature I am quoting, so I translated my sources as accurately as I could, following the language of the author. I also chose in most cases to translate God's name as 'the Eternal,' but left it as the more traditional 'Lord' in a few places where that better fit the context of the verse.

I have generally deferred to the standards set by the Academy of the Hebrew Language for transliteration – rendering, for example, the *saf* (ת) with a 't' and the *kamatz* (ָ) with an 'a.' However, I have occasionally deviated from their advice, as I did when I transliterated the *tzeirei* (ֵ) with an 'ei,' in order to distinguish it from the 'e' of the *segol* (ֶ) .

Then there are the infamously difficult-to-transliterate letters *chet* (ח) and *khaf* (כ), which produce that engine-grinding sound at the back of the mouth that Hebrew is famous for. There is no English way to render this sound, so these letters are alternately represented as: 'h,' 'ch,' or 'kh,' or as an 'h' or a 'k' with a line or a dot under it. Initially I thought to use the 'h' with a dot, to indicate the unusual pronunciation to the reader. But my publisher warned that those alternative 'h' marks do not always reproduce well in e-readers, and anyhow, he wisely pointed out (on behalf of English-speaking America), "We've all learned what *Chutzpah* is." So I went ahead and used the 'ch,' for (ח), but then a 'kh' for (כ), to distinguish between the two. [Publisher's note: I recognize that telling a rabbi how to transcribe Hebrew is the very definition of *Chutzpah*.]

In each essay you will find I have bolded the names of the commentators to indicate that you can read more about them in the Biographical Notes section at the end of the book.

There are two key words that I have left untranslated throughout the book:

- **The *parsha* (פרשה) – or *parasha*, or *sidra*, or *sedra* – is the reading assigned to a particular week in the yearly cycle of reading through the Torah. There are a total of fifty-four *parshot* (pl.), which are sometimes doubled up into one week, depending on various calendrical considerations. In this book, however, you will find one separate essay for each of the fifty-four *parshot*. In the titles you will see the construct form '*Parshat*,' which is used when the word is joined to the name of the *parsha*.**

- ***Parshanut* (פרשנות), then, is simply, "the study of the *parsha*." The term is also sometimes used to refer to a particular style of textual analysis: a running commentary on the plain Biblical text, from the voice of one thinker, attempting to explain oddities**

and resolve inconsistencies. I have used the word more broadly to refer to the whole genre of Jewish commentary on the weekly *parsha*, beginning with the great masters of Midrash.

On that note, I should say for the record that the wordplay in the title was originally unintentional: I bought the domain name parshanut.com, intending to write on the *parsha*, yes, but more specifically to highlight Torah commentary – *parshanut*. But many more people have heard of the *parsha* than have heard of *parshanut*. So when people saw the name of the website, they started pronouncing it, "parsha nut." I thought that was great and captured well the basic spirit of my loving obsession – so I capitalized the 'N,' got myself a walnut logo, and became The Parsha Nut.

The rest, as they say, is commentary. Now go and learn.

I

Genesis

CHAPTER 1
THE WANDERER – Parshat Bereishit

What ever happened to the first murderer?

It didn't take very long, did it, for the killing to begin? Just four chapters in, just four people on earth, and one of them strikes his brother down in a jealous rage. And when God comes to question him, Cain responds with the famous disavowal:

Am I my brother's keeper? ***(Gen. 4:9)***

הֲשֹׁמֵר אָחִי אָנֹכִי?

The answer, of course, is: yes. What do you think a brother is?! Forget brothers, what do you think a human life is, that you can take it away so easily?

Monster. Butcher. Savage.

How could he?? And what will God do? Surely, just as he killed, so he will be killed. Surely he has forfeited his own life.

And yet, God does not kill Cain. He is to live many years more, in fact. His punishment, instead, will be this:

You shall become a ceaseless wanderer on the earth. ***(Gen. 4:12)***

נָע וָנָד תִּהְיֶה בָאָרֶץ.

A wanderer. Well, that doesn't sound so bad, as punishments for murder go. God even offers Cain protection, when he worries of attacks on the road:

I promise, if anyone kill Cain, sevenfold vengeance shall be taken upon him. ***(Gen. 4:15)***

לָכֵן כָּל הֹרֵג קַיִן שִׁבְעָתַיִם יֻקָּם.

And God places a sign upon Cain – by tradition, a mark on his forehead – a warning to anyone who sees him, to let him be. It seems Cain has gotten away easy, all things considered. He's free to go. And he does:

Cain left the presence of the Eternal, and settled in the Land of Nod, east of Eden. ***(Gen. 4:16)***

וַיֵּצֵא קַיִן מִלִּפְנֵי ה' וַיֵּשֶׁב בְּאֶרֶץ נוֹד קִדְמַת עֵדֶן.

A relatively benign line, it appears at first glance. But wait... does it say that Cain "settled"? That doesn't sound right. This is a man cursed to eternal wandering – and the very first thing he does is settle down? But the verse is stranger still, for he settles "in the Land of Nod," and the word '*nod'* (נוד), in Hebrew, means: 'wandering.'

Here is the richness of ancient Hebrew literature on full display. *"He settled in the Land of Wandering."* That's a phrase you could get lost in for days. What does it mean, he *settled* in Wandering? Was he wandering or did he settle? The great commentators do not miss this paradoxical wordplay, and they offer various interpretations. **Ibn Ezra** says:

He **called it that because he was a ceaseless wanderer.**

קראו כן בעבור שהיה נע ונד.

So it was Cain who named the place after his own wandering, as if to memorialize his journey. **Rashi** offers a similar explanation, suggesting that the city was named for those who ended up there:

The Land of Nod [or, of Wandering] **– the land to which all who were exiled would wander.**

בארץ נוד – בארץ שכל הגולים נדים שם.

This was a home for wanderers, a meeting place for those who had been cast out and had no other place to go. In both of these interpretations, there is a kind of settling. The Land of Nod is a final destination for those who have been wandering for a long time, and it bears a name that represents its vagabond inhabitants.

But it is the **Ramban** who gives us the most textured explanation of Cain's strange mix of wandering and settling:

The reason it was called the Land of Wandering is that he did not go all over the world. He settled in that one place, but was always wandering in it, and never felt any comfort from the place at all.

וטעם וישב בארץ נוד שלא הלך בכל העולם. אבל באותה הארץ ישב נודד תמיד לא ינוח במקום ממנה כלל.

Cain tried to settle down. He tried to escape his cursed fate. But he was restless. He never went anywhere, but he was always wandering. One imagines him pacing the streets at night, circling the town, lost in thought, haunted by memories.

He did his best, the Torah tells us, to build a life for himself. In the next verse we read that:

Cain knew his wife, and she conceived and bore Enoch. And then he was building a city, and named it after his son Enoch. ***(Gen. 4:27)***

וַיֵּדַע קַיִן אֶת אִשְׁתּוֹ וַתַּהַר וַתֵּלֶד אֶת חֲנוֹךְ וַיְהִי בֹּנֶה עִיר וַיִּקְרָא שֵׁם הָעִיר כְּשֵׁם בְּנוֹ חֲנוֹךְ.

He got married, had children. He even began a construction project. This sounds like a man who is getting on with his life. But again, the Ramban provides a psychological account of these details that suggests a very different mentality at work:

He named the city after his son Enoch, because at first he thought he would be childless, because of his sin, but after a child was born to him, he began to build a city so that his son could settle in it. But because he knew he was cursed and his own actions would never succeed, he called the place "Enoch," as if to say that he was not building it for himself, for he could never have a city, or any settlement on the earth, for he was an eternal wanderer.

ויקרא שם העיר כשם בנו חנוך כי מתחילה היה חושב להיות ערירי בעונו ואחרי שנולד לו זרע החל לבנות עיר להיות בנו יושב בה. ובעבור כי הוא ארור ומעשיו לא יצליחו קראו חנוך להגיד כי לא בנאה לעצמו כי הוא אין לו עיר ומושב בארץ כי נע ונד הוא.

Cain knew he could never escape his fate. He knew he was destined to wander the earth forever. But at least, he thought, he could build a home for his child. At least the son would not inherit the sins of the father.

This much the Ramban gets from the name of the city. But then he has an even more penetrating reading, based on the unusual verb tense he notices in the phrase, *"he was building a city"*:

Because it doesn't say, "he *built* the city" ... which shows that he was building the city his whole life, but because everything he did was cursed, he would build a little bit, with great strain and effort, and then he would get restless and wander off for a while, and then come back and build a little more, and he would never complete his tasks.

ומפני שלא אמר 'ויבן עיר' יורה כי היה כל ימיו בונה העיר כי מעשיו ארורים יבנה מעט בטורח ועמל וינוע וינוד מן המקום ההוא ויחזור שם ויבנה מעט ולא יצליח את דרכיו.

The verb is in the present tense because Cain was always building. The city was constantly under construction, but never completed, because Cain could not keep himself in one place long enough to see anything through. And so the Sisyphean task of creating a home for himself and his family stretched on throughout the rest of his days, never yielding any peace or satisfaction. He could not escape the wandering.

And the wandering, says the Italian renaissance rabbi, Ovadiah **Sforno**:

... was a terrible life – like death, or even worse.

נע ונד, שהם חיים רעים כמו המות או יותר ממנו.

Yes, God had spared Cain's life, but only to deliver him into an existence worse than death. He could traverse the earth or he could try to stay in one place, but no matter – he would always be wandering. Because the real wandering took place inside of his mind, as he went over, again and again, the memory of what he had done.

Did this torture ever end? Not for a long time, it seems. But a legend in the Midrash borrows some language from Ecclesiastes to imagine one possibility of what may have finally happened to Cain:

"He would live for many more years... and was never eventually buried..." **but just kept withering away, until the Flood came and washed him away.** ***(Shemot Rabbah 31:17)***

ושנים רבות יחיה...וגם קבורה לא היתה לו, שהיה תלוי ברפיון ובא המבול ושטפו.

If he died in the Flood – that is, in the generation of Noah – that means he kept wandering for hundreds of years. He who first took life could only die himself when all other life on earth ceased.

When the waters finally came upon him, they must have provided some form of relief. Perhaps the rushing torrent even managed to wash the mark off his forehead. He was no longer branded as a killer, for he had served his time. As his body sunk down into the deluge, his wandering had come to an end.

CHAPTER 2
A WAR ON GOD – Parshat Noach

Nine lines long.

The whole Tower of Babel story is just nine lines long. This famous legend, which has captured the world's imagination, and inspired everything from Renaissance paintings to Hollywood films, is deftly contained in nine quick verses. It is a classic example of the remarkable efficiency of Biblical storytelling which, again and again manages to deliver, in very few words, tales that have endured throughout the centuries.

But for all its renown, this is a rather strange tale. After the great flood, the descendants of Noah gather together to build a tower *"with its head in the sky."* God seems to be disturbed by this plan, and so *"confounds their speech"* – which has generally been understood to mean that God made them all speak different languages, so that it would be too confusing to work together. And then God scattered them all over the earth.

What is this story doing here, tucked in between Noah's Ark – which is the main subject of this week's parsha – and our introduction to Abraham in next week's parsha? Many have suggested that this is what's called an 'etiology' – that is, a retrospective attempt to explain a basic human phenomenon – in this case, the diversity of languages and cultures. How did this all come about? The Tower of Babel.

That may be one of the functions of the story, but it doesn't explain what role the story plays in the narrative of the Torah. Why do we have to read this now? It also doesn't explain what these people were doing in the first place. Why are they building a tower to the sky, in this time long before corporate offices in city skyscrapers?

The Torah itself gives an answer:

"Come," they said, "let us build a city, and a tower with its head in the sky, to make a name for ourselves, lest we be scattered all over the earth." ***(Gen. 11:4)***

וַיֹּאמְרוּ הָבָה נִבְנֶה־לָּנוּ עִיר וּמִגְדָּל וְרֹאשׁוֹ בַשָּׁמַיִם וְנַעֲשֶׂה־לָּנוּ שֵׁם פֶּן־נָפוּץ עַל־פְּנֵי כָל־הָאָרֶץ.

"To make a name for ourselves." So maybe this was about glory – the human desire for achievement and the prestige it brings. In which case, this is a moral tale: when humanity becomes obsessed with self-promotion as an end in itself, we will eventually be humbled by forces larger than we can imagine.

But the verse also says, *"Lest we be scattered all over the earth."* That sounds less about pride, and more about fear. They wanted to stick together, to make sure that they would not lose one another. Maybe the tower was meant to act as a kind of locating point, visible to all, to help people gather together around one central city. That is essentially what Rabbi Naftali Tzvi Berlin (or, the "Netziv") suggests in his commentary, **HaEmek Davar**. He says this plan to centralize was:

against the will of God, who said [back in the Garden of Eden] to "spread out over the earth and populate it," which means to migrate throughout the length and width of the globe, and to settle it...

וזהו נגד רצון ה' שאמר שרצו בארץ ורבו בה היינו להתהלך לארכה ולרחבה...

So why would they want to huddle together instead? Remember that this was just after the great flood, the destruction of almost all of humanity. On some level they must simply have been terrified that disaster could strike again at any time – and who would want to be isolated when that happened?

And speaking of the flood, the most obvious reason for a tall tower might just be that it was a good way to get above water level, should God ever decide to flood the world again. This is what the ancient historian Josephus says – that people at the time were generally:

...greatly afraid of the lower grounds on account of the flood, and so were very loath to come down from the higher places... ***(Antiquities 1:4:1)***

In other words, they were shell-shocked, traumatized, and living in constant anxiety, waiting for the next "big one." Frankly, given what the world had just gone through, that mindstate makes a lot of sense. I'd have wanted a tower to run into myself.

But our foremost commentator, **Rashi,** takes up none of these explanations. Instead, he suggests a very different attitude prevailed among the people as they built the tower:

They said, "[God] cannot take the entire upper realm. We will go up to the sky and wage war with God."

ואמרו לא כל הימנו שיבור לו את העליונים, נעלה לרקיע ונעשה עמו מלחמה.

A war against God! How bold! In this interpretation, the tower wasn't a panicked attempt to plan for disaster, but an aggressive move to storm the heavens and dethrone God Almighty.

The Midrash that Rashi has borrowed from adds another detail. In this fuller account, the people said:

Let us make ourselves a tower, and we shall place an idol at the top of it, and we shall put a sword in its hand, such that it will appear to be waging war against Him. ***(Bereishit Rabbah 38:7)***

בואו ונעשה לנו מגדל ונעשה עבודת כוכבים בראשו, ונתן חרב בידה, ותהא נראית כאלו עושה עמו מלחמה.

The tower is literally piercing the heavens with idolatry, as a direct, violent challenge to God's authority as the only deity. We will send another god, they said, to kill God. Or, as yet another Midrash has it, they were willing to do the job themselves:

Let us ascend to the sky, and we will strike God with hatchets. ***(Tanchuma, Noach 18)***

נעלה לרקיע ונכהו בקרדמות.

Imagine, a pack of wild, desert warriors, clambering up the tower, axes in hand, ready to literally murder God. The image is somehow both ludicrous and terrifying, all at once.

So who were these people? What kind of person was willing to engage in hand-to-hand combat with the Creator of Heaven and Earth? What kind of fury could motivate a war on God?

We've already seen suggestions that perhaps they were an arrogant lot, consumed with their own fame and glory. So maybe this was just a kind of megalomania, but taken to a divine scale.

And then there are plenty of midrashim that ascribe all kinds of other terrible crimes to the Babel generation, disturbing traits that might account for their savagery. The most well-known of these is the following depressing description of the building process itself:

If a person fell and died, they wouldn't pay any attention to him, but if a brick fell, they would sit down and cry and say, "How will another take its place?!" ***(Pirkei d'Rabbi Eliezer 24)***

אם נפל אדם ומת לא שמים את לבם עליו ואם נפלה לבנה אחת היו יושבין ובוכין ואומרין אוי לנו אימתי תעלה אחרת תחתיה.

The building had become an obsession. It was all that mattered. They had lost any sense of ethical concern or basic human compassion. They just had to keep going, higher and higher. They wanted to reach the heavens, to achieve greatness, and to conquer.

These are the sorts of interpretations we would expect to see from the commentators. The builders of the tower were terrible people. The worst kind of people. Barbarians, maniacs, idolaters, murderers. These are the kinds of people who go to war with God.

But the **Ibn Ezra** identifies some other folks in the crowd of builders whom we might be surprised to see. *"Do not be astounded,"* he says, *"that Noah and Shem were there."* Noah, that most righteous man on earth, the one person saved from the flood – along with his most righteous son – are now part of this rebellion. The man who built the ark is helping to build the tower. The family who devotedly followed God's command is now openly defying God.

In a way, though, that makes sense. Noah had more reason to be traumatized than anyone, more reason to be angry with God. He was the one who had personally witnessed the destruction of humankind. He was the one who had lost everyone he knew, and had to start to build society again, all alone. Maybe Noah had become bitter at the God who had put him through all this. Maybe Noah was ready for revenge.

But the Ibn Ezra calls out another familiar figure there in Babel, and this one comes as a real shock:

Abraham was one of the builders of the tower... ***(commentary on Gen.11:1)***

היה אברהם מבוני המגדל...

Abraham?! The founder of our faith? The one who walked before God? In next week's parsha, we will begin the story of this man who would become known as the model of perfect faith, the father of nations of believers. Could it be that just a few years earlier, he was part of the greatest revolt against God in human history?

At the least, that would mean that Abraham was one of the fearful, worried that God could destroy the earth again at any moment. Or maybe he was one of the opportunists, looking to make a name for himself, to receive glory for his stunning achievements. Neither of these descriptions seem to fit a paragon of faith.

But it would be even more difficult to imagine Abraham as one of those who wanted to go to war against God. Did Abraham approve of the idol with the sword in its hand? Did Abraham pick up a hatchet, ready to swing it at God? Is it really possible to suggest such a thing?

One of the great questions in Torah commentary is, "Where did Abraham come from?" Why did God choose him? What was his origin story? And there are tons of great answers. The most famous midrash of all tells us that even as a boy, he was destroying idols and preaching the faith. Maimonides describes Abraham on an intellectual quest, like a little scientist, intent on understanding the movement of the planets and the origin of the universe. And there are wilder stories – one says that he was buried underground for thirteen years, and then suddenly emerged, speaking Hebrew and praising the Lord.

But what if Abraham's origin story was not one of faith, but of doubt? What if Abraham came to be this great servant of God only after years of rejecting God, mocking God, fighting God? What if Abraham was, like everyone around him, once a heretic?

If that were so, it would make some sense of the Tower of Babel's placement in the narrative, lodged in between the story of the flood and our introduction to Abraham. This was a period of transition. It was a time when people were either scared of God, or oblivious to God, or even angry with God. And Abraham was no exception. He lived through this phase of human development, and even participated in it, but eventually grew out of it and led humanity toward a new kind of faith – a wiser, more mature faith.

This reading would also offer a whole new understanding of Abraham's personal journey. He was not the golden child, born enlightened, who always intuited the truth, even as everyone around him spouted nonsense. He was not the earnest philosopher, probing the cosmos, desperate for answers. He never smashed his father's idols.

He worshipped them, like everyone else. He went out into the world to seek fame and fortune, like everyone else. And perhaps even, like so many others, he went through a period of doubting God – or believing in God, but hating God. Perhaps Abraham, too, went to war with God.

Would that make Abraham a lesser hero? Would it tarnish his reputation as the founder of Western religion? I don't think so. In some ways, I think it would make him even greater. Because it would mean that he knew what it was like to rage against God, to curse God, to question God's existence or God's righteousness. He felt that kind of doubt that so many of us feel at some point in our lives, and yet – he struggled with it, he worked through it, and he came out on the other side with faith – a faith made stronger by the long and difficult journey.

Sometimes it is only by going to war that one can find peace.

CHAPTER 3

THEN AND THEN – Parshat Lekh Lekha

Here is a verse, said Spinoza, that shakes the very foundations of Jewish theology:

Abram passed through the land up to the place of Sheckem, at Alon Moreh – and the Canaanites were then in the land. ***(Gen. 12:6)***

וַיַּעֲבֹר אַבְרָם בָּאָרֶץ עַד מְקוֹם שְׁכֶם עַד אֵלוֹן מוֹרֶה וְהַכְּנַעֲנִי אָז בָּאָרֶץ.

Wait, was that it? Abraham's travel itinerary?! What's the big deal?

Yet this seemingly benign verse, detailing the first steps on the journey Abraham took after God's famous charge to *"Go forth!"*, was one of the prime examples given by the great Dutch philosopher – and most illustrious of Jewish heretics – Baruch Spinoza, to prove that the Torah could not have been written by Moses through divine revelation. And that premise, that Moses received the Torah – every word of it – from God on Mount Sinai, is perhaps the faith principle upon which the whole of classical rabbinic theology rests.

So what exactly is the problem with the verse in question? It doesn't even mention God – or miracles, or morality, or anything controversial. What could be wrong?

The great challenge, it seems, is to be found in the phrase, *"and the Canaanites were then in the land,"* and in particular, with the past tense. Because it sounds like the line is written by someone who lives at a time when the Canaanites are *no longer* in the land. They were there *then*, but they are not there anymore. But here's the difficulty: Moses presumably wrote the Torah when the Canaanites were still very much in the land, since the story of Moses leading the Children of Israel through the desert culminates in their entering the land to conquer those very Canaanites.

And so, concludes Spinoza: Moses could not have written the Torah. At least not this verse. It must have been inserted later, by someone referring back to Moses' time. And if this line was cut and pasted, who knows what else was edited in or out? More to the point, even if we were to accept that there was a divine revelation, who knows what counts as divine revelation and what is just human addition? The whole notion of a perfect, sacred text has been undermined.

And yet, this Baruch Spinoza wasn't just some angry atheist on a rant. He was a nice, Jewish boy – and he knew his Torah. So he didn't claim that he had come up with this critique on his own; he grounded it in the sources. In fact – in a chapter of his *Tractatus Theologico-Politicus* entitled, "On The Interpretation of Scripture" – he cites none other than Abraham **Ibn Ezra**, one of the greatest of the classical medieval commentators, as the person who first pointed out this same difficulty with our verse.

So, let's go back and see. Here is the Ibn Ezra, in his own words:

and the Canaanites were then in the land **– It is possible that the Land of Canaan was captured by the Canaanites just after Abraham got there.**

והכנעני אז בארץ – יתכן שארץ כנען תפשה כנען מיד אחר

Okay, that is his first answer. Maybe this means: It just so happens, that at the very moment Abraham was crossing through into the land, just then, the Canaanites were conquering it.

But the Ibn Ezra doesn't seem satisfied with that. And so he goes on – but with a shift in tone:

And if that is not the case, then there is a secret here. But the one who understands it, should remain silent.

ואם איננו כן יש לו סוד והמשכיל ידום.

Well now, that's intriguing. A secret?? Spinoza was right, there's *something* going on here! But could it really be that pious Ibn Ezra, back in the 12th century, was saying the same thing that Spinoza, the Enlightenment heretic, would later claim: that this verse was inserted, centuries later, by some post-Mosaic author?

It appears so. For in his comments on the first verse in Deuteronomy – which also seems like it could have been written after Moses' time – the Ibn Ezra *again* refers to a "secret," and says that if you understand it, "then you will recognize the truth." (תכיר האמת). Perhaps the only difference is that the Ibn Ezra thought this ought to be kept "secret," for the good of the faith, whereas Spinoza was finally willing to expose the Torah's imperfections to the world. So Spinoza takes Ibn Ezra to be the proto-Biblical critic, one of the earliest Jewish voices to really admit that the whole Torah was not the word of God.

Now, let's be fair – the Ibn Ezra was only talking about a few verses, here and there, and not some massive editing project that involved pulling together scraps from various documents. Moreover, other comments of the Ibn Ezra's clearly indicate that he was a believer in a Mosaic moment of divine revelation.

Nevertheless, he does seem to allow for a historical analysis of the text that would put our pristine record of that revelation into question. And that, in itself, is a perilous move. For once we allow people to start chipping away, here and there, at the divinity of the Torah we have before us, who knows if anything will be left when they are through. It's no wonder the Ibn Ezra wanted to keep things quiet.

*

There are, of course, many other interpretations of this verse – various attempts to read the grammar this way or that. The one I am most interested in, for the purpose of contrast, is **Rashi's**, not only because he is the other of the two greatest medieval commentators, but also because his interpretive approach is often the exact opposite of the Ibn Ezra's, in that it is distinctly ahistorical – even, in a way, *anti*-historical. That is, he does not read the Torah in the light of what we now know from history, but instead, reads the narrative of the Torah as having laws of its own, that can even transgress the laws of history.

What do I mean? Well, let's take a look at Rashi's comments on the verse. He is interested in why Abraham is journeying to precisely these places. Why does the verse mention 'Shekhem'? Why 'Alon Moreh'?

up to the place of Shekhem **– In order to pray for the Children of Jacob, when they would eventually go and do battle in Shekhem.**

עד מקום שכם – להתפלל על בני יעקב כשיבאו להלחם בשכם.

Alon Moreh **– Which is also in Shekhem. And he was shown Mount Gerizim and Mount Eival, where Israel accepted the Oath of the Torah.**

אלון מורה – הוא שכם, הראהו הר גריזים והר עיבל ששם קבלו ישראל שבועת התורה.

According to Rashi, Abraham is taking a tour forward in time, scanning the land not just for what is there now, but what will be there one day. For Shekhem is, indeed, a city in which Jacob's children will one day wage a bloody battle *(in Genesis 34)*. And Alon Moreh is another place mentioned later *(in Deuteronomy 11)*, said to be near where the Nation of Israel took an oath on Mount Gerizim and Mount Eival.

So before even thinking about how those later mentions might hearken back to Abraham's journey, Rashi already sees Abraham gazing forward, into the future, to see how his descendants will fare in this same land. The connection between the place names gives Rashi license to imagine the two moments in time as connected – and a portal opens between them through which one can move in either direction. The language of the Torah defines the logic of the universe.

Now, what is interesting to think about, given the rest of the verse, is that at the time that Moses and the Children of Israel were taking oaths at Alon Moreh... the Canaanites were in the land. So if we read the verse through Rashi's suggestion that Abraham was looking into the future, then from Abraham's perspective, the Canaanites were indeed in the land during the scene he was witnessing.

"Now wait a minute," you grammarians out there will shout. "That's a very nice metaphysical trick you've played. But remember – the verse is in the past tense! That was the whole point! 'The Canaanites *were* then in the land.' Abraham cannot be seeing something that will happen and reflecting on it as something that already has happened."

And yet, there is a solution to this contradiction. For here is the truly dizzying thing about the verse: the word for 'then' in Hebrew – *az* (אז) – can refer to *either* the past *or* the future.

I'm not making this up. The Brown-Driver-Briggs Hebrew and English Lexicon of the Old Testament – a standard-bearer for Biblical semantics – has these as the first two usage definitions for '*az*':

***az* (אז) – *then*... an adverb, a. Of past time, or, b. Of future time.**

...and then they give many examples of each usage.

And this is not so strange as it might first sound to the reader, for in English, too, the word *then* can point forward or backward: "We did it *then*." "We will do it *then*." So too, the phrase "And the Canaanite was *then* in the land," could also be read "And the Canaanite will *then* be in the land."

So again, following Rashi's transhistorical reading of the journey, Abraham went to Shekhem, saw his great-grandchildren fighting, and prayed for them. And then he went to visit Alon Moreh, and there were his descendants, now a whole people, accepting the Oath of the Torah as they prepared to enter the land. And then he saw, as he peered through this window into the future, that the Canaanites would *then* be in the land. And he knew, already in the first moments after hearing God's command, everything about how that command would echo through the generations. He could see the Torah straight through to the end.

Now, to be clear, that's not how the Brown-Driver-Briggs Lexicon reads this verse. They place this usage of '*az*'/'then' in the first category, referring to past time – as did the Ibn Ezra, as did Spinoza. And even Rashi, after all of his time-traveling interpretations, does not explicitly suggest that perhaps Abraham saw that "the Canaanite *will be then* in the land."

But I have offered both possibilities here because the indeterminacy of it all appeals to me. I like that the very word with which some would disprove the Torah's divnity could also be the word which lends the Torah transcendent metaphysical power. I like that the language of Torah is vague enough, capacious enough, pregnant enough as to offer us two readings which contradict each other in every conceivable way, and are nevertheless both technically correct. For what is this Torah supposed to be, if not infinite?

CHAPTER 4

PLAYING AROUND WITH THE TORAH – Parshat Vayeira

Everybody's wondering what Ishmael did to the baby.

It seemed innocent enough. After little Isaac was born, Abraham and Sarah threw a party, to celebrate the miracle that God had done. They were far too old to have expected a child, after all. So everyone was invited to come share in their joy, with feasting and drinking.

And of course, Hagar and Ishmael were there. They were part of the household now. Sarah's had given her maidservant, Hagar, to Abraham as a concubine, and Hagar had given birth to his first son, Ishmael, who was by now a teenager. And the boy appeared to be right at home, having fun at the party.

But then something happened. At least, Sarah seemed to think so.

Sarah saw the son whom Hagar the Egyptian had borne to Abraham, playing around. ***(Gen. 21:9)***

וַתֵּרֶא שָׂרָה אֶת בֶּן הָגָר הַמִּצְרִית אֲשֶׁר יָלְדָה לְאַבְרָהָם מְצַחֵק.

Playing around? Well, isn't that sweet! Was Ishmael playing with his little brother? Or perhaps he was just horsing around, amusing himself, as boys of that age will do.

But Sarah saw something more. Something that set her into a rage. She turned to Abraham, in the next verse, and exploded:

Cast that slave woman out with her son! For the son of that slave will not share in the inheritance with my son Isaac! ***(Gen. 21:10)***

גָּרֵשׁ הָאָמָה הַזֹּאת וְאֶת בְּנָהּ כִּי לֹא יִירַשׁ בֶּן הָאָמָה הַזֹּאת עִם בְּנִי עִם יִצְחָק.

What?! What has happened? Why is Sarah angry enough to throw a woman and her child out into the desert, presumably to wander off and die? What could she have seen that prompted such a reaction?

It all seems to come down to what exactly this "playing around" was. For the Hebrew word, *metzachek* (מצחק), is rather ambiguous. There is some kind of frisky, sporting feel to it, but it doesn't indicate any particular activity. So the commentators attempt to figure out what Ishmael could have been doing.

Rashi gives us three different possibilities – each of which is, indeed, extreme enough to justify Sarah's outrage.

***Playing around*: this is the language of idolatry ... or, this is the language of incest ... or, this is the language of murder.**

מצחק – לשון עבודה זרה... דבר אחר לשון גילוי עריות...דבר אחר לשון רציחה.

Goodness. So either Ishmael was worshipping idols in the house of these monotheism missionaries, or he was doing something sexually illicit, or he was trying to kill the baby.

Well, that is quite an array of possible sins! Now I begin to have a bit more sympathy for Sarah. If Ishmael was really trying to hurt my infant child, I probably would have thrown him out myself.

Now, these three possibilities were not chosen at random. Rashi brings textual proofs for each one. But more than that, the student of Jewish Law will recognize these as the three cardinal sins, the rare actions for which one should be willing to die rather than committing *(see Babylonian Talmud, Sanhedrin 74a)*. So Rashi is telling us that not only was Ishmael doing something terrible, he was doing the worst possible things you could imagine. Only such grave crimes could have incurred Sarah's swift and severe punishment.

But, as is often the case in *parshanut*, when we solve one problem we create another. Rashi has given us an explanation for Sarah's harsh reaction to what seemed like a harmless moment of fun. But now we have to imagine that not only is Ishmael some kind of burgeoning sociopath, but that the Torah alludes to his most sinister acts with the lighthearted phrase, "playing around."

In fact, in one of the early sources that Rashi is drawing from, Rabbi Shimon bar Yochai critiques the far-fetched nature of this interpretation – which, it turns out, was first given by Rabbi Akiva. The implicit debate between these two Talmudic sages is one of the best explorations I have seen of the question: What are the limits of legitimate *parshanut*? Let's take a look:

Rabbi Shimon ben Yochai said, there are four places where I prefer my words to the words of Rabbi Akiva:

[One of them is upon the verse] "Sarah saw the son whom Hagar the Egyptian had borne to Abraham, "playing around" ***(metzachek).***

Rabbi Akiva interpreted the "playing around" here as none other than Idolatry! As it says, "And the people sat down to eat and drink, and they got up to make merry ***(letzachek)." (Exodus 31) …***

Rabbi Eliezer, son of Rabbi Yossi HaGalili says, "It is sexual perversion! As it says, "The Hebrew slave came upon me to fool around with me (***letzachek bi*****)."** ***(Genesis 39) …***

Rabbi Yishmael says, "It is murder! As it says, "Avner said to Yoav, 'Let the young men come forward and sport before us ***(yisachaku lifneinu)…*****Each one thrust his sword into his opponent's side, and they all fell together.'"** ***(Samuel II 2) …***

But I say: "God forbid that there be, in the house of this righteous man, anyone doing such things!... Rather, this "playing around" had to do with the inheritance… Ishmael was fooling around and saying, "I am the eldest, and so I will take a double portion."

And I prefer my words to the words of Rabbi Akiva. *(Tosefta Sotah 6)*

אמר ר"ש בן יוחאי ארבעה דברים היה ר"ע דורש ודברי נראין מדבריו
דרש ר"ע (בראשית כ"א:ט') ותרא שרה את בן הגר המצרית אשר ילדה לאברהם
מצחק אין צחוק האמור כאן אלא עבודת כוכבים שנא' (שמות לא) וישב העם לאכול
ושתו ויקומו לצחק...
ר"א בנו של ר' יוסי הגלילי אומר אין צחוק האמור כאן אלא גילוי עריות שנא'
(בראשית ל"ט:י"ז) בא אלי העבד וגו' לצחק בי...
ר' ישמעאל אומר אין לשון צחוק אלא שפיכות דמים שנא' (שמואל ב ב':י"ד) ויאמר
אבנר אל יואב יקומו נא הנערים וישחקו לפנינו [וגו'] ויקומו ויעברו במספר [וגו']
ויחזיקו איש בראש רעהו וחרבו בצד רעהו ויפלו יחדיו ...
ואני אומר חס ושלום שיהיה בביתו של [אותו] צדיק ההוא כך... אלא אין צחוק
האמור כאן אלא לענין ירושה....ישמעאל מצחק ואומר ...אני בכור ואני נוטל שני
חלקים שמתשובת הדבר אתה למד [שנאמר] (בראשית כ"א:י') כי לא יירש בן האמה
וגו'
ורואה אני את דברי מדברי ר"ע.

Let us begin by acknowledging that Rabbi Akiva and his colleagues have done some impressive textual work in order to justify their claims. They have taken the word for "playing around," *metzachek,* and found other uses of it in Tanakh (the Hebrew Bible), which – in context – indicate the sin that they then ascribe to Ishmael. This is classic *midrash*, the rabbinic method of Biblical interpretation.

Rabbi Akiva suggests idolatry because, at the worshipping of the Golden Calf, we are told that the people got up "to make merry" (*letzachek* – לצחק). So playing around is associated with idolatry.

Rabbi Yossi HaGalili suggests sexual transgression because when Potiphar's wife tries to seduce Joseph, and then takes revenge on his rejection by accusing him of sexual assault, she says that he tried "to fool around with me" (*letzachek bi* – לצחק בי). So, as in English, playing/fooling around has a sexual connotation.

Rabbi Yishmael – whose name rings especially powerful as he accuses the first Ishmael of murder – suggests violence because when the young soldiers came and sparred with one another, they were told "to sport" (*yisachaku* – ישחקו), and then many of them died. So playing around is associated with violent death.

In this last instance, the interpretive method is already beginning to show cracks, because the verb Rabbi Yishmael uses as a proof, *lesachek* (לשחק), is close to, but not the same as the verb for playing around, *letzachek* (לצחק). One already wonders if these rabbis are getting carried away with their fancy wordplay.

But Rabbi Shimon bar Yochai objects to all of this on different grounds. In a pious exclamation, he says, *"God forbid that there be, in the house of this righteous man, anyone doing such things!"* How dare they suggest that holy Abraham could have allowed idolatry, incest, and murder to take place right under his nose? An unthinkable insult to our patriarch!

We needn't be defending Abraham's honor, however, to agree with Rabbi Shimon that all these explanations stretch credulity. Did this young man, who has given no indication of bad behavior so far, really try to strangle his baby brother? Or commit some terrible act of molestation? Such horrific crimes would surely have merited greater attention than the casual mention of "playing around." And as for idolatry, where exactly did Ishmael find idols and how did he manage to worship them? Another version of the legend *(in Bereishit Rabbah 53:11)* answers that he would catch grasshoppers and sacrifice them on a mini-altar he built. That should give you a sense of how far we have to stretch the imagination to make these interpretations fit into our story...

So what does Rabbi Shimon bar Yochai propose instead? That Ishmael's "playing around" was his teasing Isaac about the inheritance. He stood over the baby, and said, *"I am the eldest, and so I will take a double portion."*

Now this explanation fits nicely into our story, in a number of ways. First of all, it seems much more like the behavior of a fourteen-year-old boy. Mean-spirited perhaps, but just some natural sibling rivalry, born of jealousy. This less egregious transgression, then, also better fits the basic meaning of the word for "playing around."

It also, most importantly, directly matches the words with which Sarah responds to the incident: *"The son of that slave will not share in the inheritance with my son!"* Why was she so triggered to think about inheritance at that moment? Now we have an answer: Ishmael must have mentioned it.

What's more, whether or not he was serious, Ishmael was playing into larger family tensions. For there was a real question over which of Abraham's sons would be considered his *bekhor*, his first-born, and would thus inherit both his wealth and – more importantly – the covenant that God made with Abraham "and his offspring." Sarah, who for so many years, believed she had lost the chance to be the matriarch of this covenant, now finally has an heir ... and any threat to that child's inheritance will send her into a protective, motherly fury.

So Rabbi Shimon's straightforward explanation makes much more sense of the narrative gaps in our story than did Rabbi Akiva's wild interpretive methods. But it also may lead us, finally, to a sense of what the verb *metzachek* (מצחק) might mean here. Because the root of the verb is the same as the root of Isaac's name, in Hebrew – *Yitzchak* (יצחק). He was given this name because both Abraham and Sarah "laughed" when they heard they would have a child. Playing around often involves laughing, so we can see how the two are related.

But in this context, next to Isaac's crib, teasing him about the inheritance, we begin to understand that Ishmael was doing more than just playing around. He was, more precisely, "*Isaac*-ing." In other words, he was trying to *be Isaac* – to take his place, to be the inheritor. In Rabbi Shimon's framework, we can begin to see that what appears to be ambiguous language is actually hinting to us at exactly what was going on, on a psychological level, and why it made Sarah so angry.

Rabbi Shimon bar Yochai is having a serious debate with Rabbi Akiva about the limits of interpretation. He accuses Rabbi Akiva and his fellow interpreters of going too far, of playing fast and loose with the text. It is true, they find amazing connections that reach across the whole of the Biblical narrative and loop two stories together with the hitch of a common verb. Their mastery of the text is remarkable, and their creative powers are virtuosic. But when we return to the local scene, says Rabbi Shimon, we find it distorted, stretching to accommodate this wild new information, and rendering the original story outlandish. Instead, he suggests, we ought to just look at the text in front of us, and try our best to understand it in its own, local context.

But Rabbi Shimon is also proving that this more contained approach, far from being straightforward and boring, has the capacity to release new layers of meaning that are hidden in the text itself. The story in front of us is like a puzzle with a missing piece. If, instead of jamming in something that doesn't fit, we can patiently search for exactly the right bit of information, then when we put it gently into place, the whole picture comes together with greater depth and beauty than we had anticipated.

There is an art to good interpretation. One can still play around with the text without doing violence to it.

CHAPTER 5
THE ECONOMY OF CHARACTERS – Parshat Chayei Sarah

My friend and I have a long-standing debate over what he calls the "Economy of Characters" principle in rabbinic interpretation. That is, when the rabbis of the midrash are confronted with two figures in the Torah who play similar roles, they will often just fold the two characters together into one person. My friend hates when they do this. But I think it's great.

He says that it flattens the story, takes two separate, interesting narratives and shoves them, unnaturally, into one. He sees it as sacrificing complexity for an obsession with harmony.

But I find it exciting, the idea that there are hidden connections between two seemingly separate stories. We are then compelled to take what we know about the earlier story and read it into the later one, and this adds a new layer of meaning – a backstory.

I guess it just depends on what kind of narrative you prefer.

There are two different versions of "economizing characters," actually, and they *both* appear in this parsha. The first version is when you have an unnamed character whom the rabbis identify as an earlier, named character.

So, for example, the bulk of *Parshat Chayei Sarah* follows the journey of the anonymous, "Abraham's servant," to find a wife for Isaac. That's all he's ever called in this chapter: "the servant." But two weeks earlier we read Abraham refer to, *"the one in charge of my household, Eliezer of Damascus." (Gen. 15:2)* And then this week, Abraham's servant is introduced as, *"the one in charge of all that he had." (Gen 24:2)* So there's the connection, and most interpretations then just assume that this servant is Eliezer.

But the other version of the Economy of Characters principle is even stranger.

That is when the rabbis take two different characters, with two totally different names, and claim that they are actually one and the same person. And here, the classic example comes from a story toward the end of this week's parsha when, after Abraham has mourned the death of his wife, and made sure his son was to be married, he finally settles down in his old age and:

Abraham took another wife, whose name was Keturah. ***(Gen. 25:1)***

וַיֹּסֶף אַבְרָהָם וַיִּקַּח אִשָּׁה וּשְׁמָהּ קְטוּרָה.

Okay, so Abraham got married again in his old age. It happens sometimes, people suddenly finding new love again in their golden years. Good for him!

But not so fast. The midrash jumps in and gives us a backstory:

Her name was Keturah **– Rav said: this was Hagar.** ***(Bereishit Rabbah 61:4)***

ושמה קטורה **– רב אמר זו הגר.**

Hagar?? Well, now that changes the dynamics of the story completely! Because Hagar isn't just some new woman Abraham happened to meet at the retirement home. This is his wife Sarah's maidservant. And this is the woman whom Sarah, when she was barren, told him to sleep with instead of her. Abraham did just that, and had a child with Hagar – his first son, Ishmael, whom he apparently loved and expected would be his heir.

But then, predictably, things quickly turned ugly in that complicated love triangle. As soon as Hagar had conceived, Sarah became increasingly angry, feeling that she had become lowered in Hagar's esteem, and began to torture Hagar until she fled into the desert and took refuge beside a well.

But an angel of God called to Hagar, out there in the wilderness, and told her to return, and that she would have a son called Ishmael, *"for the Lord has paid heed to your suffering." (Gen. 16:11)* So she calls out to God in gratitude for having seen her affliction. And that is why, the Torah says, the well was called *Be'er Lechai Ro'i*, the 'Well of One Who Lives and Sees Me.' And she returns to Abraham and Sarah's house and gives birth to Ishmael.

But it doesn't last. When Sarah finally does have a son of her own – Isaac – she drives Hagar and Ishmael out again – this time for good. And this time, Ishmael almost dies of thirst in the desert – until Hagar begins to cry and again, an angel of God hears her and saves them. They head out into the Wilderness of Paran, accompanied by divine promises that they will one day become a great nation, and that is the last we hear of Hagar.

Until now.

Hagar is back. Hagar and Abraham are back together – this time as husband and wife. Abraham, it seems, never stopped thinking about her, all these years. And finally, now that Sarah – whom he also loved dearly – is gone and cannot be wounded by jealousy, Abraham and Hagar can reunite, and spend their last years rediscovering a long-lost love. It's all quite romantic, actually.

But how does the midrash get away with this? It makes for a great story, sure, but what justifies the merging of these two characters, Hagar and Keturah?

Well, there is one connection. Just a few lines before we hear about Abraham's new wife, when Isaac is about to meet Rebecca for the first time, we are told that:

Isaac had just come back from *Be'er Lachai Ro'i*... *(Gen 24:62)*

וְיִצְחָק בָּא מִבּוֹא בְּאֵר לַחַי רֹאִי...

Does that place sound familiar to you? If not, let **Rashi** remind you where you've heard it before:

***From Be'er Lachai Ro'i* – Because he went to bring Hagar to his father Abraham, so he could marry her.**

מבוא באר לחי רואי – שהלך להביא הגר לאברהם אביו שישאנה

So that's the clue the rabbis have that Hagar is back. Because where did we last see *Be'er Lachai Roi*? That was Hagar's well, the one she named when God first saved her. Now suddenly, for no particular reason, we hear that Isaac has come back from *Be'er Lachai Roi*. So what was he doing there? And why do I care what the place was called?

It must be a connection to Hagar. He was going to find Hagar. And when we read a few lines later that Abraham married again – now we know why he wanted Hagar to come back. Now that Isaac's mother was gone, now that he would soon have a wife of his own – he didn't want his father to be all alone. Sarah may not have been able to tolerate Hagar, but Isaac could put the family feud aside and simply wish for his father to be able to live out his last years in happiness, with someone to love – someone Isaac had the sensitivity to realize his father had never stopped loving.

*

But wait, wait, wait, wait, wait. It's all so very sweet, but before we get carried away with this sweet love story... what would my friend – the one who hates all this economizing of characters – have to say about all this?

He would remind us – very simply – that this new woman has a different name!! Keturah, remember?! It's not Hagar; it's Keturah. That's that. The plain words of the text are clear. It's a different woman! Imagine any romantic new beginning you wish, but you can't say this is Hagar when her name is Keturah! There's that old Economy of Characters principle for you, mixing up two stories that ought to be separate.

Now, I don't know. The truth is, there is some precedent for characters in the Torah explicitly having two names. Jacob was also called Israel. Joshua was once Hoshea. Even Abraham and Sarah got small name changes. So why not Hagar? Maybe taking a new name was common practice in those days.

But let's assume my friend is right. Hagar was Hagar, and Keturah is Keturah. They're two different women, with two different stories, and two different relationships with Abraham. Hagar's ended a long time ago, and wherever she is, she's not coming back. So we can get rid of the whole dramatic backstory of long-lost love.

If that's so, there's still one question that we have to answer. What was Isaac doing at *Be'er Lachai Ro'i*? If he wasn't bringing back Hagar, why did he specifically go to the place we only know because of her?

There's only one other reason he might have gone there: to bring back his brother Ishmael.

And that possibility *is* actually borne out by the plain words of the text. After Abraham marries, has more children, and finally *"breathed his last, dying at a good ripe age, old and contented,"* we then read:

His sons Isaac and Ishmael buried him in the Cave of Machpelah, in the field of Ephron... *(Gen. 25:9)*

וַיִּקְבְּרוּ אֹתוֹ יִצְחָק וְיִשְׁמָעֵאל בָּנָיו אֶל מְעָרַת הַמַּכְפֵּלָה אֶל שְׂדֵה עֶפְרֹן...

Where did Ishmael, gone all these years, suddenly come from? Maybe, the text is hinting to us, Isaac brought him back. That was the gift he gave his father in his old age. Not finding him a wife, but reuniting him with his other son, his firstborn son, whom he had not seen for decades. If that is so, Isaac wasn't putting aside his mother's honor – he was putting aside his own. He, who had the place of privilege in the family lineage, brought back the older brother who was once seen as a threat to his birthright.

And why? For his father's happiness, certainly. No wonder Abraham died "old and contented." He was surrounded, finally, by *all* of his children.

But also, perhaps, Isaac did it for himself. He had been raised an only child. But he had a brother, somewhere out there in the wilderness, estranged. And now, his mother was gone. His father would soon be gone. It was Isaac who would be alone in the world. Where was Isaac's family?

At *Be'er Lachai Ro'i.*

So he went there, looking for his brother. He took it upon himself to make the overture, to be the first to extend his hand in peace. And despite what had happened all those years ago, and whatever bitterness had grown in the many years they had been apart, Isaac managed to bring his brother back.

And then, after Abraham had been buried, where did Isaac go from there? The very next line tells us:

And Isaac settled near *Be'er Lachai Ro'i. (Gen. 25:11)*

וַיֵּשֶׁב יִצְחָק עִם בְּאֵר לַחַי רֹאִי.

He was welcome there.

CHAPTER 6

BLIND LOVE – Parshat Toldot

The great modern Torah commentator, **Avivah Gottlieb Zornberg**, in the introduction to her book on Genesis, writes about **Rashi's** "fantastic citations from the midrash," that:

His commentary works as a dreamtext, suggesting many alternative – but not exclusive – facets of reality.

This week, we encounter one of the most fantastic – and most beautiful – of Rashi's midrashic citations, and it will offer us an alternate, dreamlike reading of a classic story.

Our setting is the famous scene in which Jacob pretends to be his twin brother, Esau, in order to steal Esau's blessing from his father, Isaac. Commentators for centuries have struggled to untangle the conflicting moral threads of this story. Because, on the one hand, Jacob (aided and abetted by his mother, Rebecca) is the clear villain: he lies to his aging father and supplants his apparently innocent older brother, all for personal gain. But on the other hand, Esau is generally understood to be the more savage, less responsible brother – a man unfit to carry the Abrahamic covenant and lead the family. Some traditions even suggest that he was violent – a murderer and a rapist. So maybe it's good that Jacob comes along and deposes his unstable brother before he can wreak havoc and ruin the family name.

If that were true, however, why would Isaac be so insistent on blessing Esau to begin with? If Esau is such a known scoundrel, how could Isaac have trusted him to assume the mantle of this sacred family mission? Wasn't Isaac wise enough to sense who is good and who is evil? What was he thinking?

We may have a small clue into Isaac's state of mind in the language at the very beginning of the chapter:

When Isaac was old, and his eyes had dimmed from seeing, he called in his older son Esau... ***(Gen. 27:1)***

ויהי כי זקן יצחק ותכהין עיניו מראת ויקרא את עשו בנו הגדל...

So Isaac is getting old, and going blind. And maybe those details are just meant to tell us that Isaac is increasingly enfeebled, perhaps even losing some mental capacity, and so his judgment is not to be entirely trusted.

But many of the commentators wonder if this blindness represents something more than just the loss of a physical capacity. **HaEmek Davar** puts it this way:

His eyes had dimmed **– It is not that his aging caused this, because he was not at the end of his life. For he lived sixty more years after this. Rather, the cause was from heaven, and many answers are given in the midrash…**

ותכהין עיניו מראות – אין לפרש שהזקנה גרמה זאת שהרי לא הי' זקן כ"כ לפי ערך ימי חייו. שהיה חי עוד ששים שנה. אלא סיבה היה מן השמים. וכמבואר עוד ברבה הרבה טעמים ...

He is assuming there is some spiritual significance to the blindness, that the Torah is telling us something more about what is going on with Isaac than just the loss of sight. And he alludes to various possibilities given in the midrash.

Among these possibilities, the most striking one of all – the one I wanted you to see – is recorded by Rashi:

When Isaac was bound on the altar, and his father wanted to slaughter him, at that moment, the heavens opened up, and the angels saw what was happening, and began to cry. Their tears came down and fell into Isaac's eyes. And that is why his eyes became dim.

כשנעקד ע"ג המזבח והיה אביו רוצה לשחטו, באותה שעה נפתחו השמים וראו מלאכי השרת והיו בוכים, וירדו דמעותיהם ונפלו על עיניו, לפיכך כהו עיניו.

Here we have the power of midrash, in all its fullness. The imagery alone is so rich – and so tragic. But meanwhile, as usual, the midrash is also dealing with a textual problem. The verse that told us about Isaac's blindness said that his eyes had become dimmed *"from seeing."* That phrasing is awkward. From seeing *what*, exactly? Now we have an answer: he saw the angels crying for him.

But the real power of this midrash is that it links Isaac's blindness back to the great horror of his childhood: his being bound on the altar by his father Abraham, to be slaughtered and sacrificed – only to be spared by God at the last moment. This was the defining moment of his life, one that we suspect must have changed him forever. So the image of angels crying into his eyes, and somehow scarring them permanently, gives us a tangible metaphor for some more profound, internal scarring. Whatever happened to Isaac up there on the altar, when he came back he was never the same. Something in his vision of the world had become fundamentally distorted. He would never see things clearly again.

Now this is – thanks to Rashi – a very well-known midrash, and I am not the first to suggest that it can be read on this deeper level, as a metaphor for psychological trauma. But still, we might ask, why this particular imagery? Why does he see, of all things, angels crying into his eyes? And furthermore, to return to our story in the Torah, what does all this have to do with the blessings of Esau and Jacob? Why would his experiences on the altar affect which of his sons he wanted to bless?

Some surprising answers to these questions might be found in an earlier midrash from the same collection, *Bereishit Rabbah*. This one appears back in the Binding of Isaac story itself, which we read a couple of weeks ago. It is less well-known but, as you'll see, the imagery is remarkably familiar:

And Abraham reached out his hand **– He reached out his hand to take the knife, and his eyes dripped with tears, and the tears fell into Isaac's eyes. These came from the compassion of a father. But even so, his heart was happy to do the will of his Creator.** ***(Bereishit Rabbah 56:8)***

וישלח אברהם את ידו, הוא שולח יד לטל את הסכין ועיניו מורידות דמעות ונופלות דמעות לעיניו של יצחק מרחמנותו של אבא, ואף על פי כן הלב שמח לעשות רצון יוצרו.

In this rendition, it was Abraham who cried above Isaac, Abraham whose own tears fell into his son's eyes. And these tears that Isaac felt dripping upon him were the tears of fatherly love. Abraham, caught up in the throes of a terrifying act of violence, suddenly, for just a moment, flashed a face full of compassion for his beloved son. And then, just as quickly as the moment came, it passed, and Abraham recommitted to the task at hand.

But when Isaac looked up, for that one moment, he thought he had seen an angel appear before him. The man who had become his killer was suddenly his father again, eyes full of love and tears, heart full of pity.

He had thought he was about to die. He thought his father had abandoned him, that his father had become some kind of monster. But no.

Look at that. This angelic figure would never harm him. He would be safe. He would be safe.

And then, suddenly, he was.

Then an angel of the Eternal called to him from heaven: "Abraham! Abraham!" And he answered, "Here I am." And he said, "Do not reach out your hand against the boy, or do anything to him…" ***(Gen. 22:11-12)***

וַיִּקְרָא אֵלָיו מַלְאַךְ ה מִן הַשָּׁמַיִם וַיֹּאמֶר אַבְרָהָם אַבְרָהָם וַיֹּאמֶר הִנֵּנִי. יֹּאמֶר אַל־תִּשְׁלַח יָדְךָ אֶל־הַנַּעַר וְאַל־תַּעַשׂ לוֹ מְאוּמָּה...

And Abraham put down the knife. Untied his son. Maybe held him.

It was over.

The angel had saved him. Or was it his father? Yes, that's it – his father. His father had wept over him. Or was that the angels? Now it was all a blur, all a bit jumbled up in his memory ...

... just as the images are all jumbled up in these midrashim. But if we read them together then one thing we get that we didn't have before, is Abraham's compassion. There was trauma, yes. But in the midst of that trauma, there was also an awareness that there was something good and loving in Abraham that never left him. Isaac will never forget those tears. They are a reminder that no one can be fully overtaken by violence. A fundamental human compassion always remains.

So now, he is told that his own son Esau has become a violent man, a bad man. They say he should push him out of the family, bless his younger son instead. Be careful of Esau, they say. He's a killer.

But no. Not his son, whom he loves. His son who loves *him*, who dotes on him, and brings him the food he likes. He's a good boy. Okay, so he can be a little rough sometimes. And some of things we've heard about him are... unnerving.

But he'll be alright. You have to believe he'll be alright. Things always turn out okay, in the end.

Isaac's eyes welled up with tears. And he called out for his son.

CHAPTER 7

THE ROCK OF ISRAEL - Parshat Vayeitzei

It was a watershed moment in religious history.

Jacob went to sleep. He had a marvelous dream, of a ladder, with angels going up and down it. And there, suddenly, was God, standing above him. And God reaffirmed the covenant that had been made with Abraham, promising to give this land to Jacob and his many descendants. And Jacob would be blessed by all the peoples of the earth. And finally, God promised to always protect him.

So Jacob awoke, ecstatic. He had just experienced the presence of God! He had to do something to consecrate the moment. He wanted to praise God, to show his devotion. But what could he do, out there on the road, all by himself? So, creating a new ritual with whatever he had around him, he took the stone he had used as pillow and stood it up, like a pillar, and poured oil on top of it. And with that, Jacob had erected the first religious monument – or, *matzeivah* (מצבה).

*

And yet, it later seems that Jacob may have done something wrong. Jacob is never directly criticized or corrected for his monument. Indeed, he will go on to build three others over the course of the next two Torah readings. Moses, too, seems to have been inspired by Jacob when, after his own great moment of revelation, in the Book of Exodus, he sets up twelve *matzeivot* (pl.) – one monument pillar for each of the tribes of Israel. But when we get to the Book of Leviticus, we come across a line that seems to put all of these religious tributes into question:

You shall not make idols for yourselves or carved images, and do not erect monuments for yourselves, or place figured stones in your land to worship, for I am The Eternal your God. ***(Lev. 26:1)***

לֹא תַעֲשׂוּ לָכֶם אֱלִילִם, וּפֶסֶל וּמַצֵּבָה לֹא תָקִימוּ לָכֶם, וְאֶבֶן מַשְׂכִּית לֹא תִתְּנוּ בְּאַרְצְכֶם,
לְהִשְׁתַּחֲוֹת עָלֶיהָ, כִּי אֲנִי ה' אֱלֹהֵיכֶם.

Some of these prohibitions should not surprise us. Idols, statues, graven images – these are classic Second Commandment violations: *"Do not make for yourself a carved image, or any picture of what is in the heavens above..." (Exod. 20:2)* But, right there alongside them, we are told not to erect a monument – a *matzeivah* – the very thing that Jacob innovated!

And if that wasn't clear enough, the language of a similar prohibition against monuments in Deuteronomy is much stronger:

Do not erect a monument for yourself – for The Eternal, your God, hates such a thing. ***(Deut. 16:22)***

וְלֹא תָקִים לְךָ מַצֵּבָה אֲשֶׁר שָׂנֵא ה' אֱלֹהֶיךָ.

At this point, the commentators start getting uncomfortable. These monuments aren't just forbidden – God *hates* them! If that's true, it's awfully problematic for Jacob. For what had appeared to be a profound form of religious expression, turns out to be despised by God. And if it is problematic for Jacob, it's problematic for us – because this is one of our founding fathers! Were his most classic moments of spiritual inspiration in fact egregious transgressions?

In dealing with this problem, the medieval interpreters basically fall into two camps. On the one side, there is the **Ibn Ezra** and the **Bekhor Shor**, who argue that this prohibition only applies to monuments set up for the wrong reason. So, says Ibn Ezra:

Do not erect a monument for yourself **– for idolatry. To that, the verse declares that** ***God hates*** **it. However, a monument that is not dedicated to idolatry is not forbidden, and the proof of that is Jacob's monument (in** ***Gen. 35:14*****).**

ולא תקים לך מצבה — לע״ז. והעד, אשר שנא. רק מצבה שלא לע״ז איננה אסורה, והעד הנאמן בפרשת וישלח יעקב.

So there are forbidden monuments, to be sure, the idolatrous ones. But Jacob's were dedicated to God, and of course God did not hate *those* monuments. The French commentator, Bekhor Shor, agrees with his Spanish counterpart, and runs through several examples of monuments erected in the Hebrew Bible – by Jacob, by Joshua, and by Avshalom – that were totally permissible (*mutar* – מותר). For both of these commentators, it is important to distinguish between *good* monuments and *bad* ones – and to note that Our Father Jacob did nothing wrong.

On the other side of the debate, we have **Rashi**, the **Rashbam,** and the **Ramban**, who all agree that the prohibition against a stone monument is absolute, and applies even if it is dedicated properly, to the one, true God. In other words, even if one were to set up a monument exactly as Jacob did, God – apparently – would hate it. In which case, we are back to the question of whether or not God actually disapproved of Jacob's own famous monument. And here, Rashi's explanation leads the way, in attempting to distinguish not just between good and bad, but between *then* and *now*:

God hates such a thing **– ... this God hates because it became a religious practice of the Canaanites. And even though it was beloved to God in the days of the Patriarchs, now God hates it, because it has become an idolatrous ritual.**

אשר שנא – ...ואת זו שנא כי חק היתה לכנענים. ואף על פי שהיתה אהובה לו בימי האבות עכשיו שנאה, מאחר שעשאוה אלו חק לעבודה זרה.

So again we find that the commentators are unwilling to say that there was any problem with Jacob's monument. It's true, nowadays all such monuments are forbidden – even despised. But in the days of Jacob and Moses, God was delighted with these stone tributes. It's just that since then, the practice has been misused, and over time, become strongly associated with idolatry. So now, it has gotten to the point where God cannot stand *matzeivot*, and has totally forbidden them, even when they are set up with the right intentions – as they certainly were by Our Father Jacob.

*

However, if one turns back to look at the larger Jacob story itself, one cannot help but wonder if perhaps there was cause for concern even then. For there are signs that Jacob's relationship with these symbolic objects was not entirely healthy.

We began with the revelatory moment in which Jacob first set up a stone pillar and established a new religious ritual. But this was far from the only appearance of stone imagery in Jacob's life. Remember, first of all, that this monument was made from the stone Jacob had used as a pillow that night. We read, just before his famous dream:

[Jacob] took one of the stones from the place and put it under his head, and went to sleep in that place. ***(Gen. 28:11)***

וַיִּקַּח מֵאַבְנֵי הַמָּקוֹם וַיָּשֶׂם מְרַאֲשֹׁתָיו, וַיִּשְׁכַּב בַּמָּקוֹם הַהוּא.

And then...

He awoke in the morning and took that stone that he had put under his head, and placed it as a monument pillar. ***(Gen. 28:18)***

וַיַּשְׁכֵּם יַעֲקֹב בַּבֹּקֶר וַיִּקַּח אֶת הָאֶבֶן אֲשֶׁר שָׂם מְרַאֲשֹׁתָיו, וַיָּשֶׂם אֹתָהּ מַצֵּבָה.

Fine, that we knew. He used what was available to him. We might have begun to suspect that the stone already had special significance for him, since it was upon it that he had the marvelous dream. But then look what he says about the stone, just after he sets up the monument:

This stone which I have placed as a monument will be the House of God... ***(Gen. 28:22)***

וְהָאֶבֶן הַזֹּאת אֲשֶׁר שַׂמְתִּי מַצֵּבָה יִהְיֶה בֵּית אֱלֹהִים...

This stone "will be the House of God"? What does that mean? Is it just loose language meant to emphasize the way the monument marks the place where God appeared. Or does he mean that God dwells, somehow, inside the stone? No, that cannot be...

As we move on to the next episode in Jacob's life, his meeting with Rachel at the well, we soon enough encounter another significant rock:

The stone on the mouth of the well was large. When all the flocks were gathered there, the stone would be rolled from the mouth of the well, and they would give to water the sheep, and then return the stone back to the mouth of the well. ***(Gen. 29:2-3)***

וְהָאֶבֶן גְּדֹלָה, עַל פִּי הַבְּאֵר. וְנֶאֶסְפוּ שָׁמָּה כָל הָעֲדָרִים, וְגָלְלוּ אֶת הָאֶבֶן מֵעַל פִּי הַבְּאֵר,
וְהִשְׁקוּ אֶת הַצֹּאן, וְהֵשִׁיבוּ אֶת הָאֶבֶן עַל פִּי הַבְּאֵר לִמְקֹמָהּ.

Jacob, having just consecrated a stone to mark the most intense religious experience of his life, must surely have noticed this big stone in front of him now. But soon he beholds an even more captivating sight: Rachel arrives, and he immediately falls in love. And how does Jacob respond?

When Jacob saw Rachel, the daughter of his uncle Lavan, with the flock of his uncle Lavan, Jacob went up and rolled the stone off of the mouth of the well and watered the flock of his uncle Lavan. Then Jacob kissed Rachel, and broke into tears. ***(Gen. 29:10-11)***

וַיְהִי כַּאֲשֶׁר רָאָה יַעֲקֹב אֶת רָחֵל, בַּת לָבָן אֲחִי אִמּוֹ, וְאֶת צֹאן לָבָן אֲחִי אִמּוֹ, וַיִּגַּשׁ יַעֲקֹב וַיָּגֶל אֶת הָאֶבֶן מֵעַל פִּי הַבְּאֵר, וַיַּשְׁקְ אֶת צֹאן לָבָן אֲחִי אִמּוֹ. וַיִּשַּׁק יַעֲקֹב לְרָחֵל, וַיִּשָּׂא אֶת קֹלוֹ וַיֵּבְךְּ.

Rashi tells us that he did this to show Rachel that *"his strength was so great,"* that he could roll this gigantic rock off, *"just like taking the cap off a bottle."* One wonders if it was precisely his ardor for Rachel that gave him this sudden burst of strength.

Whatever the case, he has now had another profound moment with a stone as the prominent image. And now he has two strong associations with stones: God and Love – two of the most primary forces in human life.

From then on, Jacob seems obsessed with stones. At the end of our parsha, when he makes a peace agreement with his Uncle, once again:

Jacob took a stone and raised it up as a monument. ***(Gen. 31:45)***

וַיִּקַּח יַעֲקֹב אָבֶן וַיְרִימֶהָ מַצֵּבָה.

And then, as if that one stone was not enough:

Jacob said to his kinsmen, "Gather more stones." So they gathered stones and made a pile. ***(Gen. 31:46)***

וַיֹּאמֶר יַעֲקֹב לְאֶחָיו לִקְטוּ אֲבָנִים. וַיִּקְחוּ אֲבָנִים וַיַּעֲשׂוּ גָל.

More stones. Jacob calls this mound of stones, *"Gal-Ed,"* the Mound of Witness (גלעד), meant to bear witness to the pact between them. But then, just after naming, Lavan says, *"May God be a witness between us."* (ראה אלהים עד ביני ובינך) Well, which is it? Is God the witness, or is the pile of stones the witness? Things are starting to become blurry...

And then more stones, when God appears to Jacob again in Paddan-Aram and blesses him with the new name, 'Israel':

And Jacob set up a monument in that place where God had spoken to him, a monument of stone, and he offered a libation on it and poured oil upon it. ***(Gen. 35:14)***

וַיַּצֵּב יַעֲקֹב מַצֵּבָה בַּמָּקוֹם אֲשֶׁר דִּבֶּר אִתּוֹ, מַצֶּבֶת אָבֶן, וַיַּסֵּךְ עָלֶיהָ נֶסֶךְ וַיִּצֹק עָלֶיהָ שָׁמֶן.

This one, strangely, he also names "The House of God" (*Beit El*) – though it is in a different place than the earlier House of God. Where is God "housed," then? In a place? Or perhaps ... in these stones?

Then, still more stones. When Rachel dies:

Jacob set up a monument pillar over her grave, which is the monument at her grave to this very day. ***(Gen. 35:20)***

וַיַּצֵּב יַעֲקֹב מַצֵּבָה עַל קְבֻרָתָהּ, הִוא מַצֶּבֶת קְבֻרַת רָחֵל עַד הַיּוֹם.

Now this final monument is interesting, because it is the first that does not seem to be associated with God at all. This is a tribute to Rachel, the woman he loved. It is a fitting memorial indeed, since a large stone was present at the moment they met. But is it permissible, now, to use these religious monuments to honor people, instead of God? The power of the pillar seems to have become independent of the deity it honors, and to have taken on a life of its own.

Has this gotten out of hand? Is Jacob beginning to overuse the stone monument, and to invest too much meaning into particular objects? Has he begun to drift into the domain of the Second Commandment, and to see the stone pillar as a statue that does not merely represent, but even *contains* divinity?

God forbid. Not our righteous forefather! Our commentators have all rejected such a possibility.

There is, however, one last little problem. Jacob's story contains one final image of a stone – this one at the very end, as he lies on his death-bed. When he calls over his favored son Joseph, to give him a blessing, Jacob invokes several names for God – and one of them, in particular, will stand out to us:

[Joseph's] bow stayed taut, and his arms were made firm by the hands of the Mighty One of Jacob. There, The Shepherd, The Stone of Israel, the God of your father, who helps you… ***(Gen. 49:24-25)***

וַתֵּשֶׁב בְּאֵיתָן קַשְׁתּוֹ וַיָּפֹזּוּ זְרֹעֵי יָדָיו מִידֵי אֲבִיר יַעֲקֹב, מִשָּׁם רֹעֶה אֶבֶן יִשְׂרָאֵל, מֵאֵל אָבִיךָ וְיַעְזְרֶךָּ...

The Stone of Israel. This is the first time such an appellation has been used to describe the God of our ancestors. It is, after all, not a bad metaphor for God's strength and stability. And it will be used many times again, in the poetry of the Book of Psalms (*"O Lord, my Rock and Redeemer"* – צוּרִי וְגֹאֲלִי) on down through the lofty rhetoric of the Declaration of Independence of the modern State of Israel (*"with trust in the Rock of Israel"* – מתוך ביטחון בצור ישראל).

But in Jacob's case, such imagery is not merely poetic. It evokes all of the most profound spiritual and romantic moments of his life. And it makes reference to a religious practice that he founded and then maintained as the central ritual in his life.

Could it be, then, that Jacob began to lose sight of the line between the ritual and the reason, the difference between the object and the intention? Could it be that the monument to God began to appear to Jacob as the form of God Itself? So that increasingly, whenever he saw a stone, he thought of God, and – far more problematically – whenever he thought of God, he saw the image of the Stone of Israel.

If there was even a trace of that confusion, we can see why God would have come to hate all monuments – even, and maybe especially, Jacob's. For it became clear that the very thing that once was meant to remind people of God could, over time, cause them to forget about God.

Perhaps the lesson of Jacob's stone monuments is that any object invested with religious sanctity can, over time, become a substitute for the real thing. The "Real thing" – the God we believe in – cannot ever be seen or touched. Our God has no form or figure, and does not reside in any place or pillar. The truth of our God must remain mysterious and unknowable.

Several times throughout the Torah, we are told to, *"Tear down their altars, smash their monuments, cut down their sacred posts, and burn their images in the fire." (Exod. 34:13, Deut 7:5, Deut. 12:3)* We generally assume that this applies to the religious sites of the Canaanites, the Amorites, the Hittites, the Girgashites, the Perizzites, the Hivites, and the Jebusites – the seven idolatrous nations that lived in the land before we crossed over. For they were wicked, and we are righteous. They were heretics, and we are pure of faith.

But it may be that the true test of our faith is not whether we are willing to smash the idols of our enemies, but whether we are willing to smash our own.

CHAPTER 8
TIMNA'S STORY - Parshat Vayishlach

I'll tell you the least important line in the Torah:

Timna was a concubine of Esau's son Eliphaz; she bore Amalek to Eliphaz. ***(Gen. 36:12)***

וְתִמְנַע הָיְתָה פִילֶגֶשׁ לֶאֱלִיפַז בֶּן עֵשָׂו וַתֵּלֶד לֶאֱלִיפַז אֶת עֲמָלֵק.

Well, it's either that or one other.

How do I know? I know because Maimonides says there are *no* unimportant lines in the Torah. But the way he says it tells you that there actually are.

Let me explain.

In **Maimonides**' 'Commentary on the Mishnah,' there is a famous section in Tractate Sanhedrin where he first articulates what became known as the "Thirteen Principles of Faith." These are, essentially, thirteen things that he says you have to believe in order to be faithful Jew. Things like: there is a God; there is only one God; God created the world; etc.

Now these propositions, stated in such absolute terms, are somewhat suspect; for Judaism is a religion that famously celebrates debate – even in critical matters of theology. Nevertheless, they caught on, and became the foundation of Jewish orthodoxy. They are now printed in most traditional prayerbooks, so that they can be recited daily.

And the eighth of these Thirteen Principles mandates belief that the Torah, "*is from heaven, that the whole Torah given by Moses, all of it, is from the mouth of the Almighty.*" In other words, God "wrote" the Torah – all of it. And to emphasize the divinity of every single line, Maimonides writes the following:

There is no difference between, *"And the descendants of Ham were Cush and Egypt" (Gen 10:6)*, or, *"Timna was the concubine [of Eliphaz]," (Gen. 36:12)* and, *"I am the Lord your God," (Exod. 20:2)* or, *"Hear, O Israel, [the Lord is our God, the Lord is One]." (Deut 6:4)* For they were all from

the mouth of the Almighty, and they are all a part of God's perfect, pure, holy Torah of Truth.

ואין הפרש בין ובני חם כוש ומצרים ושם אשתו מהטבאל ותמנע היתה פלגש ובין אנכי ה' אלהיך ושמע ישראל כי הכל מפי הגבורה והכל תורת ה' תמימה טהורה וקדושה אמת.

So what he's saying, ostensibly, is that because every word of the Torah was uttered by God, they all have equal stature as Divine Writ. Sure, from our human perspective, this line may seem more interesting or important than another – but on some essential level, every line is as holy as the next. There are no throwaway verses.

That may be so, but if you think for a moment about the verses Maimonides has chosen, you'll see that they certainly aren't arbitrary. "*I am the Lord your God*" is the first of the Ten Commandments. And ""*Hear, O Israel, the Lord is our God, the Lord is One"* is the central pledge of Jewish faith, which we recite twice daily. In other words, these two lines *are* clearly two of the most – if not the two most – important lines in the whole Torah.

And they are clearly being contrasted with the two other verses he cites: *"And the descendants of Ham were Cush and Egypt," and* – the line from our parsha this week – *"Timna was the concubine of Eliphaz."* Which suggests that *these* two lines are – at least on some level – the least important lines in the Torah.

Now what makes these two verses so lowly? Well, for one thing, they both appear in the midst of lineage records. If you've read the Bible before, you've run into these sections – I call them "the begats" – that are just long lists tracing the generations in a family tree. So, "This guy begat this guy, and then this guy begat these other guys, and then they all begat more guys." Begat, begat, begat. And on and on and on. They are, I think it's fair to say, some of the least exciting readings in the Torah.

But besides their just being "begat" lines – there are lots of those, after all – both of these particular lines are also giving over the lineages of men of questionable character: Ham, who was cursed by his father Noah; and Esau, who was denied a blessing by his father Isaac. So these are not just begats – these are *bad* begats. So maybe that's why Maimonides picks them as paradigmatic examples of verses you would think are unimportant or lowly.

The line about Timna, however, may just edge out its partner and claim the title of the Lowliest Verse of All. Because on top of all these other factors, this verse also tells us that Timna was a concubine: a kept woman, of second-class status – not exactly a prostitute, but not quite a wife either. Timna's brief mention in the family tree is a record of her disgrace.

*

So who was Timna? And why mention her at all, if she was so wretched? Doesn't the Torah have better things to do than to detail every sordid affair that our ancestors had, and to highlight the shame of a poor woman?

The rabbis of the Talmud wondered the same thing; and so, they gave us a backstory. According to them, Timna's story is much more complicated than it appears:

Who was she? Timna was the daughter of a king... And she wanted to convert. So she came to Abraham, Isaac and Jacob. But they didn't accept her. So she went and became a concubine to Eliphaz son of Esau, for she said, "Better to be a maidservant to this nation than to be royalty to another nation." ***(Sanhedrin 99b)***

מאי היא תמנע בת מלכים... בעיא לאיגיורי באתה אצל אברהם יצחק ויעקב ולא קבלוה הלכה והיתה פילגש לאליפז בן עשו אמרה מוטב תהא שפחה לאומה זו ולא תהא גבירה לאומה אחרת.

Timna, it turns out, wasn't just a poor girl, forced by economic hardship into terrible circumstances. She was a future queen, probably wealthy and comfortable. But she left everything she had and everyone she knew because she was compelled by the vision of this new nation. She wanted to become one of them, to pledge herself to their faith, and their way of life.

But they turned her away. Why? It seems we don't know; the record is lost. She must have tried for a long time, because look, they say she petitioned three generations of patriarchs. And we know that the family of Abraham was generally open to converts – even sought them out. But in this case, again and again, they shut her out.

They probably had their reasons. Maybe she came from a suspicious land, or was connected to dangerous people. Maybe they doubted her sincerity, or questioned her loyalties. Whatever it was, they didn't trust her. And they turned her away.

So she went elsewhere, trying desperately to get as close as she could to the life she wanted. Struggling to survive, she finally agreed to become the concubine of a powerful man. She had no choice, it seems, but to trade her dignity for a measure of security. And then she was trapped, stuck in a life of subjugation.

And then she had a son.

The Talmud continues:

From her came Amalek, who tortured Israel. And why? Because they should not have driven her away.

נפק מינה עמלק דצערינהו לישראל מאי טעמא דלא איבעי להו לרחקה.

Amalek. Israel's arch-nemesis. The predatory nation that would one day attack the Children of Israel when they were at their most vulnerable, fleeing from slavery. The nation that would reappear in different forms, again and again throughout history, as a force of pure evil, hellbent on destroying Israel.

And why? Because Amalek was born into disgrace. He was the son of a concubine, always aware that he was marked, that he was seen as less than those around him. He had no inheritance. No tribe. He would have to fend for himself. So he took the only power that was available to him: violence. And he used it against the people who had made him this way. The people who had turned his mother away when she was vulnerable.

He would make them pay. He would do everything he could to destroy them.

And so the Children of Israel have had to fight the nation of Amalek *"from generation to generation." (Exod. 17:16)*

Could all of this have been avoided? Looking back, the rabbis of the Talmud seem to wish we had just let Timna in. Perhaps we could have changed the course of history, and spared ourselves centuries of violence. But then again, who knows? It's hard to predict the future of a rewritten history.

One thing we can say, though: Maimonides was right. Every verse in the Torah is important – even the ones that seem insignificant at first. It's easy to recognize the greatness of a line like, *"I am the Lord your God."* That's the centerpiece of our faith, the very essence of who we are.

But a verse like, *"Timna was the concubine of Eliphaz,"* we just gloss over. We keep reading. We forget that the second half of the verse – *"she bore Amalek to Eliphaz"* – may contain the seeds of our destruction.

When we forget Timna's story, we may well be putting our very existence in danger. In that sense, upon this one line rests every other line in the Torah. There is, as Maimonides said, no difference.

So we should read our Torah carefully, all of it. And we should also be very careful whom we turn away from it.

CHAPTER 9

CHAPTER THIRTY-EIGHT – Parshat Vayeishev

Everyone is surprised when they get to Chapter 38.

With Chapter 37, we began the story of Joseph, which will be the longest continuous narrative in the Book of Genesis. We opened with Joseph's bratty teenage years, which he spends infuriating his brothers with descriptions of his dreams – all of which seem to end with some image of them bowing down before him. In fact, the brothers come to hate Joseph so much, they decide to kill him. They throw him into a pit, intending to leave him there to starve to death. But suddenly, Judah, who seems to have taken the leadership role among the brothers, convinces them that they would be better off selling Joseph to the Ishmaelites as a slave – which is exactly what they do, for twenty pieces of silver. Then they take Joseph's famous coat, dip it in goat's blood, and convince their father Jacob that Joseph has been torn apart by a wild animal. Jacob falls into a deep mourning, the family tries in vain to console him, and Joseph – we are told in the last line of the chapter – is sold in Egypt to Potiphar, a eunuch of the Pharaoh.

What next? How will Joseph fare? Will he ever see his family again? The famous story of his improbable but meteoric rise to power in Egypt awaits...

*

But as Chapter 38 commences, we find ourselves on some kind of detour, following the story of a different character:

It was at that time that Judah went down from his brothers and pitched a tent near an Adulamite man whose name was Hirah. *(v. 1)*

וַיְהִי בָּעֵת הַהִוא וַיֵּרֶד יְהוּדָה מֵאֵת אֶחָיו וַיֵּט עַד אִישׁ עֲדֻלָּמִי וּשְׁמוֹ חִירָה.

We will have to wait to find out what happens to Joseph, it seems. For now, instead, we will hear the tale of Judah and Tamar. And it is a strange and tragic one – though with a sort of happy ending. Judah quickly marries, has three sons – Er, Onan and Shelah – and marries the first one off to Tamar. But Er displeases God and is killed; and Judah now marries Tamar to Onan. But Onan also displeases God (by way of a rather popular sin that will come to bear his name), is also killed, and now Tamar stands to be married to Shelah. But Judah has seen the pattern, and doesn't want to lose his last son. So he tells Tamar to go back to live in her father's house, and just wait until Shelah grows up. It is clear, however, that his true intent is to keep her there as a widow, forever.

Time passes, Judah's unnamed wife dies and, after a period of mourning, he travels to Timnah with his friend Hirah, ostensibly to shear their sheep. When Tamar hears that Judah is coming that way, she covers herself in a veil and goes down to the road. As Judah passes, he sees her there, takes her for a prostitute, and turns aside to solicit her services. She asks for payment, and when he promises a goat from his flock, she demands he leave a pledge, which he does: his seal, his cord, and his staff.

And then Tamar disappears. Judah does try to pay the mysterious woman back, but cannot find her.

Three months later, he is told that Tamar is pregnant. She is officially committed to Shelah, so this is an offense to the family, and Judah shows no mercy. "Bring her out," he says, "and let her be burned."

But she then sends him the items of pledge – not outing him directly, but leaving the matter in his hands. And when he sees them, and realizes what has happened, he stops the execution with the words, *tzadkah mimeni* (צדקה ממני), "she is more righteous than me."

And that, dear reader, is the story of Judah and Tamar. Chapter 38 ends, and we are returned, in Chapter 39, to our regularly scheduled programming. The story of Joseph continues:

And Joseph was taken down to Egypt, and Potiphar – a eunuch of Pharaoh, his chief steward, an Egyptian man – bought him from the Ishmaelites who brought him down there.

וְיוֹסֵף הוּרַד מִצְרָיְמָה וַיִּקְנֵהוּ פּוֹטִיפַר סְרִיס פַּרְעֹה שַׂר הַטַּבָּחִים אִישׁ מִצְרִי מִיַּד הַיִּשְׁמְעֵאלִים אֲשֶׁר הוֹרִדֻהוּ שָׁמָּה.

We're picking up right where we left off. The Torah has taken us back to Joseph, and it didn't miss a beat. This first verse in Chapter 39 could have easily followed the last verse in Chapter 37.

So what was the purpose of the great interruption of Chapter 38? This is what all the commentators want to know.

*

The best answers come, as usual, from the great **Rashi**, who, borrowing from a midrash in *Bereishit Rabbah* (85:2), gives us two intriguing explanations. The first:

***And Joseph was taken down* – We now return to the previous topic. But it was interrupted in order to compare Judah's *"going down"* with the sale of Joseph, to tell you that it was because of this that [Judah] was *taken down* from greatness.**

ויוסף הורד – חוזר לענין ראשון. אלא שהפסיק בו כדי לסמוך ירידתו של יהודה למכירתו של יוסף, לומר לך שבשבילו הורידוהו מגדולתו.

We have, at first glance, a straightforward moral message being offered here. Judah encouraged the sale of Joseph – and so, as a punishment (or a consequence), he falls away his from his exalted status in the family into a life of meanness and depravity out on his own.

The midrash, however, is also highlighting an obvious linguistic connection between the two stories. Chapter 38 begins: "*It was at that time that Judah went down.*" And Chapter 39 begins: "*And Joseph was taken down.*" Both brothers are going down, and *"at that time"* – the same time. So yes, we are to understand that because Judah caused Joseph to go down to Egypt, Judah then went downward in his own way. But more than that, it appears that the trajectory of these two figures are linked. When one goes down, the other follows. And so, perhaps, their risings will have to be linked as well.

This link between Judah and Joseph is an important one. It begins here, but it will continue to be significant throughout the history of the tribes of Israel. For not only are these two sons of Jacob going to be the most significant players for the rest of the Book of Genesis, but in fact, their descendants will go on to form the most significant leadership factions in Ancient Israel – the Northern and Southern Kingdoms, sometimes referred to in the Books of the Prophets as "The House of Joseph," and "The House of Judah." *(see: Zechariah 10:6)* There are even, in the eschatological literature of Judaism, legends that the future Messiah will be not one figure, but two: one descended from Judah, and one from Joseph. *(see: Babylonian Talmud, Sukkah 52a-b)*

Okay, this is all getting a little heady, but before we get carried away, let's not forget that Rashi had another reason why Chapter 38 had been inserted here in the middle of the Joseph story:

And further, this all was meant to compare the story of Potiphar's wife to the story of Tamar, in order to tell you that just as this one did it for the Sake of Heaven, so too, that one did it for the Sake of Heaven. For [Potiphar's wife] saw through her astrology that she would one day raise children that came from him. But she did not know whether they were to come from her or from her daughter.

ועוד, כדי לסמוך מעשה אשתו של פוטיפר למעשה תמר, לומר לך מה זו לשם שמים אף זו לשם שמים, שראתה באצטרולוגין שלה שעתידה להעמיד בנים ממנו ואינה יודעת אם ממנה אם מבתה.

Now this is a more surprising comparison. We've just told Tamar's story, and though it included her committing what might have been considered a scandalous act, we left her in good standing: proven "more righteous" than Judah. The tradition remembers Tamar favorably.

Potiphar's wife, on the other hand, is not such a celebrated character. In Chapter 39, she will try desperately to seduce Joseph, and then – when her advances are rebuffed – attempt to force herself on him. When he escapes that attack, she lies in order to present Joseph as the assailant, and lands him in prison. So Potiphar's wife has traditionally been presented as a villain.

Yet here we find an attempt to vindicate both of these women by imputing to them not just noble intentions, but a kind of prophetic knowledge of the lineages they will produce. Tamar knows that she is meant to be a mother to the offspring of Judah. Her first two husbands were taken before that mission could be fulfilled; if she is now unjustly denied Shelah (whose name, by the way, literally means, "hers"), she will instead lure Judah himself into fathering her children. And remember, it is through this line that messianic hopes will one day be charted. So Tamar seems to have known what she was doing.

Just so, in Rashi's equivalency, Potiphar's wife has divine knowledge of a future coupling between her family and Joseph's. She just gets the generation wrong. She thought perhaps *she* was to be the one to bear Joseph a child, but instead it will be her daughter. For indeed, when Joseph is finally released from prison and ascends to Pharaoh's second-in-command, he is married off to none other than Potiphar's daughter, Osnat. (*Gen. 41:45*) And if the legends are true that there will also be a messiah from the line of Joseph, that messiah will descend from this union.

So we have, in Rashi's explanation, two reasons for the interpolation of the Judah story in the middle of the Joseph story: 1.) To join the fate of these two warring brothers – first in descent, and then in ascent as future leaders of Israel. 2.) To highlight, through comparison, the phenomenon of seemingly devious sexual schemes that ultimately result in covenantal offspring.

*

But why does Rashi feel the need to give *both* of these reasons? Is there any connection between them?

Indeed there is. A moment's reflection on the previous stories in Genesis will remind us that both of these themes – sibling rivalry and sexual scheming – were once dominant tropes in the life of Jacob, the father of Judah and Joseph.

First of all, Jacob was, almost from the moment of his birth, locked in a power struggle with his twin brother Esau. It is the ultimate brotherly conflict in the Torah: one that begins as Jacob grabs Esau's heel on the way out, continues through Jacob's crafty purchase of Esau's birthright and outright theft of Esau's family blessing, and is never fully resolved.

And then, Jacob also finds his most intimate relationships negotiated through acts of deception and manipulation. He falls in love with Rachel, asks her father Lavan for her hand in marriage, and intends to consummate the marriage with her after seven years of work... only to wake up next to Leah! Lavan has tricked Jacob into marrying his eldest daughter first. But then, Lavan consents to allow Jacob to marry Rachel as well. Jacob is incensed, but the first marriage stands, and through it come seven of his children – including Judah. With Rachel, meanwhile, he will have two other beloved children – including his favorite, Joseph. It is a strange, almost perverse arrangement, being married to two sisters, and it only gets stranger when he takes their maidservants as third and fourth wives. Along the way, there is plenty of bitterness, infighting, and even some exchange of currency for the right to sleep with Jacob (placing *him* in the role of the prostitute). But in the end, all seems justified, for – unlike in previous generations – all of Jacob's children are to be included in the covenantal destiny, and together they will make up the twelve tribes of Israel.

So Joseph and Judah's stories, taken together, serve to work out some of the lingering tensions in their father's legacy. These two favored sons will again deal with sibling rivalry, as they contend with one another for the ultimate place of privilege in the family and, one day, the nation. And they will each reckon with illicit sexual advances, unsavory or unwanted, that nevertheless lead, through twists and turns, to desired (or even divinely ordained) offspring.

*

The question remains, other than continuing established family patterns, what do the Joseph/Judah stories *do* with these motifs? Are the heroes of this generation simply destined to replay the same traumas that their ancestors set in motion, or are they meant, somehow, to resolve them?

There may be the beginning of an answer to these questions in material that Rashi kept hidden from us. For though he took his two explanations for the appearance of Chapter 38 from a midrash in *Bereishit Rabbah*, he left one out. When we turn back to the midrash itself, we find still a *third* reason for connecting the Joseph and Judah stories:

Why are these two chapters placed together? Rabbi Elazar said: In order to compare one "going down" to another "going down." Rabbi Yochanan said: In order to compare one "recognition" to another "recognition." Rabbi Shmuel bar Nachman said: In order to compare the story of Tamar to the story of Potiphar's wife.

ומפני מה הסמיך פרשה זו לזו? רבי אלעזר ורבי יוחנן רבי אלעזר אמר: כדי לסמוך ירידה לירידה. רבי יוחנן אמר: כדי לסמוך הכר להכר. רבי שמואל בר נחמן אמר: כדי לסמוך מעשה תמר, למעשה אשתו של פוטיפר.

We have already discussed the first and last answers. But what are these two "recognitions" that Rabbi Yochanan speaks of? There is, first, a technical answer. Joseph's brothers, in Chapter 37, bring the bloody coat to their father and ask him:

Please recognize this coat. Is it your son's, or not? *(v. 32)*

הַכֶּר נָא הַכְּתֹנֶת בִּנְךָ הִוא אִם לֹא

And Jacob does recognize it (וַיַּכִּירָהּ), and so assumes that Joseph had been killed.

In Chapter 38, Tamar sends the pledged items to Judah and asks:

Please recognize whose seal and cord and staff are these? *(v. 25)*

הַכֶּר נָא לְמִי הַחֹתֶמֶת וְהַפְּתִילִים וְהַמַּטֶּה הָאֵלֶּה

And Judah does recognize them (וַיַּכֵּר יְהוּדָה), and so confesses that he must be the father of Tamar's child.

There is the same language in both scenes – *haker na*, "Please recognize" – and these are the only two times that this phrase is used in the Torah. So there it is – another connection between the two stories.

But the significance of these 'recognitions' is not just technical or linguistic – it is much greater than that. For recognition is exactly what has been missing from all of these stories, from Jacob on down.

- In Jacob's struggles with Esau it was unclear who deserved the birthright, and each parent identified a different son as the heir.

- On Jacob's wedding night he did not recognize the woman in his bed, and ended up marrying the "wrong" sister.

- Now it is again unclear who is the heir apparent to Jacob: Judah or Joseph?

- Judah does not recognize Tamar on the road, nor does he recognize that she is supposed to bear children to his family.

- Potiphar's wife *does* recognize Joseph as the father to her descendants, but does not recognize, in her divinations, who is supposed to be the mother.

So much confusion in this family – and from confusion, so much pain.

But now we have two recognitions. That's a start.

Though the language is the same, however, they are actually very different moments. Jacob does recognize his son's coat, but he still misreads the situation. He is fooled again, this time into thinking his living son is dead. Like so many of the moments in Jacob's life, this one lacks real clarity.

Judah, however, truly sees things as they are. He not only recognizes the items placed before him, he also recognizes that he is in the wrong, and that Tamar must be set free. His recognition is a profound one, for it causes him to see himself differently, and to redirect his actions based on new information. He gains control of his fate, in this moment, by discovering humility. This same humility will allow him to take responsibility for his role in the sale of Joseph, and to finally reconcile with the brother who was to be his adversary. Judah's moment of recognition, then, is the beginning of a process that will rescue his whole family from a tragic fate, unify the embittered siblings and welcome *all* of their descendants into the covenant.

Fitting, then, that Chapter 38 ends with a scene that seems to bookend the contentious moment of Jacob's birth. For Tamar and Judah *also* have twins – the only other pair in Tanach. And these, too, seem initially to be struggling for first position:

While she was in labor, one of them put out his hand, and the midwife tied a crimson thread on that hand, to signify: 'This one came out first!' But just then, he drew back his hand, and out came his brother, and she said, "What a breach you have made for yourself!" So he was named Peretz. Afterward his brother came out, on whose hand was the crimson thread, and he was named Zerach. ***(vv. 28-30)***

וַיְהִי בְלִדְתָּהּ, וַיִּתֶּן-יָד; וַתִּקַּח הַמְיַלֶּדֶת, וַתִּקְשֹׁר עַל-יָדוֹ שָׁנִי לֵאמֹר, זֶה, יָצָא רִאשֹׁנָה. וַיְהִי כְּמֵשִׁיב יָדוֹ, וְהִנֵּה יָצָא אָחִיו, וַתֹּאמֶר, מַה-פָּרַצְתָּ עָלֶיךָ פָּרֶץ; וַיִּקְרָא שְׁמוֹ, פָּרֶץ. וְאַחַר יָצָא אָחִיו, אֲשֶׁר עַל-יָדוֹ הַשָּׁנִי; וַיִּקְרָא שְׁמוֹ, זָרַח.

This time, it is clear who is who. For, despite a moment of struggle and confusion, we recognize the red string on the one who first put out his hand. There is no need for heel-grabbing. And there is no need for a birthright, a good twin or an evil twin. Both of these children will be blessed.

*

Where, then, is the bookend for the other great moment of confusion in Jacob's life, the night he woke up with an unexpected bride?

For that, we will have to wait many centuries, until the Book of Ruth. This is the tale of Ruth the Moabite, who attempts to enter the Jewish people, but must secure a place in some established family to do so. She and her guardian, Naomi, hatch a plan to seduce Boaz (a man of the tribe of Judah!) into sleeping with her by sneaking into his makeshift bed in the fields. More deception, more manipulation! How will Boaz react?

In the middle of the night, the man gave a start and pulled back – and behold, there was a woman lying at his feet! ***(Ruth 3:8)***

וַיְהִי בַּחֲצִי הַלַּיְלָה וַיֶּחֱרַד הָאִישׁ וַיִּלָּפֵת וְהִנֵּה אִשָּׁה שֹׁכֶבֶת מַרְגְּלֹתָיו

This *"behold"* is the same language we found on Jacob's wedding night:

When morning came, behold, Leah! ***(Gen. 29:25)***

וַיְהִי בַבֹּקֶר וְהִנֵּה הִוא לֵאָה

Jacob was then confused and angry, and demanded, *"Why did you deceive me?!"*

But Boaz's reaction to being startled in the night is very different, when he asks:

"Who are you?" and she replied, "I am your handmaid, Ruth. Spread your robe over your handmaid, for you are a redeemer."

He exclaimed, "You are blessed before the Eternal, daughter! Your latest deed of kindness is greater than the first, for you have not turned to younger men, neither poor nor rich. And now, daughter, have no fear. I will do on your behalf whatever you ask, for all of my people know what a woman of valor you are!" ***(Ruth 3:9-11)***

וַיֹּאמֶר: מִי אָתְּ? וַתֹּאמֶר: אָנֹכִי רוּת אֲמָתֶךָ. וּפָרַשְׂתָּ כְנָפֶךָ עַל אֲמָתְךָ, כִּי גֹאֵל אָתָּה. וַיֹּאמֶר: בְּרוּכָה אַתְּ לַה בִּתִּי הֵיטַבְתְּ חַסְדֵּךְ הָאַחֲרוֹן מִן הָרִאשׁוֹן, לְבִלְתִּי לֶכֶת אַחֲרֵי הַבַּחוּרִים, אִם דַּל וְאִם עָשִׁיר. וְעַתָּה, בִּתִּי אַל תִּירְאִי. כֹּל אֲשֶׁר תֹּאמְרִי אֶעֱשֶׂה לָּךְ. כִּי יוֹדֵעַ כָּל שַׁעַר עַמִּי, כִּי אֵשֶׁת חַיִל אָתְּ.

Boaz does not reject the woman whom fate has brought to him, but instead seems to praise his good fortune. Despite her deception, despite even her questionable Moabite lineage – Ruth is in. For Boaz, a true descendant of Judah, recognizes her righteousness.

And with that, all of the great personal struggles that were inherited from Jacob have finally been resolved. It took a long time, and a lot of pain, but there is a happy ending. Boaz and Ruth have a child, Oved, and the Book of Ruth ends with a lineage that traces itself back to none other than Peretz, the child of Judah and Tamar:

This is the line of Peretz. Peretz begot Hetzron; Hetzron begot Ram; Ram begot Aminadav; Aminadav begot Nachshon; Nachshon begot Salmah; Salmah begot Boaz; Boaz begot Oved; Oved begot Jesse; and Jesse begot David. ***(Ruth 4:18-22)***

וְאֵלֶּה תּוֹלְדוֹת פָּרֶץ, פֶּרֶץ הוֹלִיד אֶת חֶצְרוֹן. וְחֶצְרוֹן הוֹלִיד אֶת רָם, וְרָם הוֹלִיד אֶת עַמִּינָדָב. וְעַמִּינָדָב הוֹלִיד אֶת נַחְשׁוֹן, וְנַחְשׁוֹן הוֹלִיד אֶת שַׂלְמָה. וְשַׂלְמוֹן הוֹלִיד אֶת בֹּעַז, וּבֹעַז הוֹלִיד אֶת עוֹבֵד. וְעֹבֵד הוֹלִיד אֶת יִשָׁי, וְיִשַׁי הוֹלִיד אֶת דָּוִד.

That last figure, take note, is David, King of Israel, the anointed one, uniter of the Northern and Southern Kingdoms – the House of Joseph and the House of Judah – and the heir to the messianic lineage of Judah. Ruth the Moabite, whose place among the people of Israel was at first not even recognized, found her own unconventional way in (like Tamar before her), and went on to become the Mother to the Messiah. Or to one of them, at least...

And it all begins with Chapter 38.

Everyone was surprised to find it here, but, dear reader, this might just be the most important chapter of them all.

CHAPTER 10

AN OCEAN OF TEARS – Parshat Mikeitz

Joseph can't stop crying.

He has been toughened by years in prison. He has swiftly risen to power in a country he entered as a slave. He now controls the resources of an entire region; by his word starving people will live or die.

And yet, more than once in our parsha, this commanding figure suddenly breaks down in tears.

Now, crying isn't unusual in the Book of Genesis. The first person we see crying is Hagar, Sarah's maidservant, after she has been driven out into the desert with her infant son and left to die of thirst. *(Gen. 21:16)* Next comes Abraham, who cries over the death of his wife. *(23:2)* Then Esau cries when he realizes he's been tricked out of his father's blessing. *(27:38)* Jacob gives us one of the strangest crying episodes when he first meets the woman he loves. He *"kissed Rachel, and then burst into tears."* *(29:11)* Esau and Jacob both cry when then they finally reconcile after years apart. *(33:4)* And Jacob cries again when he believes his son Joseph has been torn apart by wild animals. *(37:35)* Yes, tears flow freely in this family.

But no one in the Torah cries more than Joseph. Before the Book of Genesis is over, he will weep eight times. He cries when he first sees his older brothers again, after years of estrangement. He cries again when he first sees his youngest brother Benjamin. He cries three times when, after a long deception, he finally reveals to his brothers that he is Joseph. He cries when he sees his father again. He cries when his father dies. And he crie one last time when his brothers ask, on behalf of their dead father, to be forgiven.

There is something beautiful in witnessing a Biblical character so wrapped up in emotion, so delicately on the verge of being overwhelmed. But why? Why is Joseph such a crier? What is it about him that makes him so much more prone to weeping than anyone we have encountered so far?

I think the key to answering that question can be found in the first two of his cries, both of which appear in this week's *parsha*. Joseph is involved in an intricate game of deception, hiding his identity from his older brothers as he accuses them of treachery. He forces them to bring their youngest brother as proof of their story, and frames that brother for a crime and threatens to keep him prisoner. But in the midst of all this action, twice, Joseph is overcome with an uncontrollable fit of tears – sudden outbursts that briefly interrupt the flow of a longer dialogue. The volatility of these eruptions is itself significant. But the language that describes them is especially telling. Here, first, when Joseph hears his brothers beginning to panic:

He turned away from them and wept. Then he returned and spoke to them, and he took Shimon from them and had him tied up before their eyes. ***(Gen. 42:24)***

וַיִּסֹּב מֵעֲלֵיהֶם וַיֵּבְךְּ, וַיָּשָׁב אֲלֵהֶם וַיְדַבֵּר אֲלֵהֶם וַיִּקַּח מֵאִתָּם אֶת שִׁמְעוֹן וַיֶּאֱסֹר אֹתוֹ לְעֵינֵיהֶם.

He first turns away. As **Rashi** says, "He went a distance from them, so they would not see him cry." That's not too surprising. After all, he is trying to hide his identity from them. Perhaps he worried that any display of emotion would tip them off. So he turns aside, to quickly hide the tears, and then turns back and gets on with business.

But the second instance contains an even more extreme retreat. This is when he first lays eyes on Benjamin. There, we read:

He hurried out, for he was overcome with feeling for his brother, and had to cry. And he went into a room and wept there. Then he washed his face and took control of himself, and said, serve the bread. ***(Gen. 43:30-31)***

וַיְמַהֵר יוֹסֵף, כִּי נִכְמְרוּ רַחֲמָיו אֶל אָחִיו, וַיְבַקֵּשׁ לִבְכּוֹת. וַיָּבֹא הַחַדְרָה וַיֵּבְךְּ שָׁמָּה. וַיִּרְחַץ פָּנָיו וַיֵּצֵא, וַיִּתְאַפַּק, וַיֹּאמֶר שִׂימוּ לָחֶם.

Again he is struck with a sudden, uncontrollable need to cry. Again he feels he must hide his tears. But this time, he actually leaves the scene to go take refuge in another room. And then, again, he returns to the dialogue only to proceed immediately with some decisive action, as if nothing had happened. What a strange man, they must have thought. Where did he go so abruptly, only to reappear moments later?

Where exactly *did* he go, we might well ask? What kind of room is so immediately available to a crier in the grand vizier's palace?

The 19th century commentary of the Netziv, **HaEmek Davar**, wonders the same thing, and speculates that:

In this house, deep inside, there was a small room that no man could come into, save him alone.

באותו בית פנימי היה חדר קטן שאין איש בא לשם זולתו.

Joseph's inner sanctum. A hidden little room – as if tucked behind some secret panel – that no one was allowed to enter but Joseph. For all we know, this was his designated "crying room," used for no other purpose than to make these escapes when Joseph was feeling overwhelmed.

This is how Joseph cried. He cried alone. He cried in hiding. He kept his tears far away from the public eye, and away from the public persona he had carefully cultivated. That person was a ruler, an Egyptian, a man of power and mystery. That man was to be feared, respected, obeyed. That man didn't cry.

So Joseph kept his crying inside. In public he was stoic, inscrutable. And if there were times when he could not maintain the cool exterior, he would turn away, even take retreat if he needed to. He would shut the world out. No one would ever hear his sobs.

Until the third of Joseph's cries. This is the great climax of the Joseph story, the moment when he is confronted by his brother Judah, who tells him of his father's years of grief and mourning. The story moves him, and something shifts inside of him. The facade he has been maintaining suddenly drops. The game of revenge is over.

And Joseph could not control himself. To all those standing in attendance, he cried out, "Take every man away from me!" So there was no one else standing there when Joseph made himself known to his brothers. And his sobs were so loud that all of Egypt could hear, and they were even heard in the House of Pharaoh. ***(45:1-2)***

וְלֹא יָכֹל יוֹסֵף לְהִתְאַפֵּק. לְכֹל הַנִּצָּבִים עָלָיו, וַיִּקְרָא, הוֹצִיאוּ כָל אִישׁ מֵעָלָי! וְלֹא עָמַד אִישׁ אִתּוֹ בְּהִתְוַדַּע יוֹסֵף אֶל אֶחָיו. וַיִּתֵּן אֶת קֹלוֹ, בִּבְכִי וַיִּשְׁמְעוּ מִצְרַיִם, וַיִּשְׁמַע בֵּית פַּרְעֹה.

This cry is different. He is not seeking to be alone. He does not turn away. He does try to send his attendants out – but no matter, they will hear him anyway. Everyone will hear him. He is making himself known. He lets out a wail that thunders throughout the land, a primal cry that shakes the earth. And when this inarticulate howl finally trails off, when he finds words again, this is what he says:

"I am Joseph." *(45:3)*

אֲנִי יוֹסֵף.

He is Joseph again. He has been two men for so long. One went by the official name, Tzafnat-Paneach, the Egyptian leader who appeared before the people and commanded legions. The other was Joseph – the humiliated Hebrew slave, the dungeon prisoner, the boy with no family – who could only come out in the seclusion of his tiny room (whether we say that was really a physical room, or just a space in his heart). He has kept these two men separate, but he cannot do it any longer.

As the Torah puts it, he "could not control himself." And French medieval commentator, Rabbi Samuel ben Meir – the **Rashbam** – offers an interpretation of these words that succinctly summarizes Joseph's long psychological struggle:

Joseph could not control himself any longer **– for up until now, everything he did was so that he could control himself in his heart.**

לא יכול יוסף להתאפק עוד – כי עד עתה היה עושה כל מעשיו ע"י שהיה מתאפק בלבו.

Joseph has been trying, all these years, to control himself. Everything he did, says the Rashbam, was to this end. To keep his identity concealed, and his power secure, he has had to keep his emotions in check. He has been trying not to reveal his inner pain. He has been trying not to cry.

And now that he finally lets go, it all comes out:

He embraced his brother Benjamin around the neck and cried. *(45:14)*

וַיִּפֹּל עַל צַוְּארֵי בִנְיָמִן אָחִיו וַיֵּבְךְּ.

He kissed all his brothers and cried upon them. *(45:15)*

וַיְנַשֵּׁק לְכָל אֶחָיו וַיֵּבְךְּ עֲלֵהֶם.

He appeared before [his father], and fell upon his neck, and cried on his neck for a long time. *(46:29)*

וַיֵּרָא אֵלָיו, וַיִּפֹּל עַל צַוָּארָיו, וַיֵּבְךְּ עַל צַוָּארָיו עוֹד.

Joseph flung himself upon his father's face and cried over him, and kissed him. ***(50:1)***

וַיִּפֹּל יוֹסֵף עַל פְּנֵי אָבִיו וַיֵּבְךְּ עָלָיו, וַיִּשַּׁק לוֹ.

And Joseph cried as [his brothers] spoke to him. ***(50:17)***

וַיֵּבְךְּ יוֹסֵף בְּדַבְּרָם אֵלָיו.

Joseph cries and cries and cries and cries. And he no longer turns away and hides his face, no longer washes away his tears. He cries openly and without restraint.

This is why Joseph, of all the characters in the Torah, cries so very much: he is making up for lost time. Joseph has been muffling his cries for over twenty years.

Now that the dam has broken, an ocean of tears comes rushing out.

CHAPTER 11

RESUSCITATION – Parshat Vayigash

When he heard the news, his heart stopped.

For twenty-two years Jacob has been without his beloved son Joseph. Twenty-two years he presumed Joseph was dead. Now his sons come back from Egypt and tell him that not only is "Joseph still alive" but he is also the "ruler over the whole land of Egypt." What was it like for Jacob to hear these words? Could he even process what they were saying? The Torah describes the moment like this:

His heart went numb, for he did not believe them. *(Gen. 45:26)*

וַיָּפָג לִבּוֹ, כִּי לֹא הֶאֱמִין לָהֶם.

The language of "numbness" here comes from an unusual Hebrew word – *vayafag* (ויפג). The commentators give various definitions for it, but the **Ramban**, in a particularly vivid piece of commentary, says that it indicates a stopping:

His breathing ceased and the movement of his heart broke off, and he was like a dead person. And this is a well-known phenomenon, when joy comes suddenly. It is recorded in medical books that the weak and elderly cannot bear it, and many of them faint when happy news comes so suddenly.

שנתבטל לבו ופסקה נשימתו כי פסקה תנועת הלב והיה כמת וזה הענין ידוע בבוא השמחה פתאום והוזכר בספרי הרפואות כי לא יסבלו זה הזקנים וחלושי הכח שיתעלפו רבים מהם בבוא להם שמחה בפתע פתאום

Jacob was 130 years old and, the Ramban is saying, his frail heart couldn't take this overdose of joy.

But was it really joy he felt in that moment? "He was like a dead person," the Ramban says. That doesn't sound so happy. And the verse tells us he "did not believe them." Maybe he was just stunned by the surprise. But perhaps he could not accept what they were saying because if it were true, it would mean that something strange and terrible had happened to

Joseph all those years ago – something that led him to abduction and trapped him, somehow, in a foreign land… and Jacob was the last person to see him before he disappeared.

Indeed, it was Jacob who had sent him off to see how his brothers were doing out in the pastures. That was the last time he had ever seen Joseph. As far as he understood, Joseph had been torn apart by a wild animal. A tragic end, to be sure – but an unpredictable act of nature. But now, Jacob wonders: maybe he had let his son wander into enemy territory all alone, and delivered him into evil hands, when he could have been there to protect him. And if this is so, what kind of father was he? He had already spent years grieving the loss of his son. But could it be that he was *responsible* for whatever had happened to Joseph?

That he could not accept. He could not believe them – would not believe. His heart could not bear it.

And then, something mysterious happens in the next line that changes his mind:

They told him all that Joseph had said to them, and when he saw the wagons that Joseph had sent to transport him, the spirit of their father Jacob revived. "Enough!" said Israel. "My son Joseph is still alive! I must go and see him before I die." ***(Gen. 45:27)***

וַיְדַבְּרוּ אֵלָיו אֵת כָּל דִּבְרֵי יוֹסֵף אֲשֶׁר דִּבֶּר אֲלֵהֶם, וַיַּרְא אֶת הָעֲגָלוֹת אֲשֶׁר שָׁלַח יוֹסֵף לָשֵׂאת אֹתוֹ, וַתְּחִי רוּחַ יַעֲקֹב אֲבִיהֶם. וַיֹּאמֶר יִשְׂרָאֵל, רַב! עוֹד יוֹסֵף בְּנִי חָי! אֵלְכָה וְאֶרְאֶנּוּ בְּטֶרֶם אָמוּת.

The question is, what was it that suddenly convinced Jacob that they were telling the truth, that Joseph was really alive? What was it that revived his spirit? **Rashi** has an answer, but it's a strange one. It will take us on a twisted *parshanut* journey, but if you follow me, I promise it will be worth it.

Here's what Rashi says:

[Joseph] gave them a sign, that alluded to the topic he was studying when he left [Jacob] – the section dealing with the Beheaded Calf (עגלה ערופה – *eglah arufah*). This is why it says, "and he saw the wagons (עגלות – *agalot*) that *Joseph* had sent," and not, "that Pharaoh sent."

סימן מסר להם במה היה עוסק כשפרש ממנו – בפרשת עגלה ערופה, זהו שנאמר וירא את העגלות אשר שלח יוסף, ולא נאמר אשר שלח פרעה

Okay, there's a lot to explain here. First of all, Rashi is saying that it wasn't what the brothers told Jacob that convinced him. It was seeing the wagons. Now, that might just have been because this was proof that Joseph was in a position of power, that he could send royal carriages. But no, Rashi is saying that the Hebrew word for wagon – *agalah* – sounds just like the Hebrew word for calf – *eglah* – and so Joseph was using the wagon as a coded reference to a certain section of the Torah that discusses the ritual of the Beheaded Calf. That, as it happens, was the last thing that Joseph and Jacob had studied together, so Jacob suddenly had proof that Joseph was still alive – because only Joseph would have known this.

Now, this is a bizarre suggestion – not just because of the notion that Joseph would send an object that suggested a kind of wordplay that was meant to remind Jacob of some obscure memory – but *also* because it suggests that Jacob and Joseph learned Torah together... before there *was* a Torah. This "beheaded calf" section, mind you, appears in the Book of Deuteronomy, the last book of the Torah, and we're still in Genesis, the first book of the Torah. So how could they have studied something that was only written hundreds of years later?

But you'll have to just take that at face value for now. The rabbis have this theory they keep playing with that somehow the great patriarchs kept and studied the Torah even before it was given. They just can't bear the idea that these holy men lived without Torah, so instead they propose some kind of primordial Torah that was secretly passed down from the days of Adam – or, perhaps, that men like Jacob could just intuit. Anyway, for now, the important thing is not just that Jacob and Joseph might have studied this section together, and that Joseph might have referenced it as a secret signal to his father, but what it is that this section is actually about. Because the rabbis who imagine this scene aren't choosing the law of the Beheaded Calf at random.

So the case in Deuteronomy is as follows: A person is found dead, out in the fields, away from any town, and no one knows who killed him. So the elders of the nearest town perform a ritual. They take a calf – which appears to be some kind of sacrifice or substitute – and they break its neck. Then they wash their hands over the calf and make the following declaration:

"Our hands did not shed this blood, nor did our eyes see it done. Absolve, O Lord, Your people Israel, whom you redeemed, and do not let guilt for the blood of the innocent remain among Your people Israel." ***(Deut. 21:7-8)***

יָדֵינוּ לֹא שָׁפְכוּ אֶת הַדָּם הַזֶּה, וְעֵינֵינוּ לֹא רָאוּ. כַּפֵּר לְעַמְּךָ יִשְׂרָאֵל אֲשֶׁר פָּדִיתָ ה', וְאַל תִּתֵּן דָּם נָקִי בְּקֶרֶב עַמְּךָ יִשְׂרָאֵל.

And then, the Torah says, they are absolved of guilt.

But what guilt did they have, really? What are we worried they might have done? Rashi asks that question also:

Would it enter one's mind that the elders of the court are actually murderers?! Rather, they are saying: We ourselves did not see him and let him depart without food or escort.

וכי עלתה על לב שזקני בית דין שופכי דמים הם? אלא לא ראינוהו ופטרנוהו בלא מזונות ובלא לויה.

No one really thinks that the elders actually killed this person. But perhaps they didn't really take care of him as they should have; perhaps they were negligent. When this stranger wandered into town, all alone, they didn't take him in and feed him. They regarded him suspiciously, and they kept to themselves. And when he drifted on to the next town, they didn't see him safely on his way. They just let him go.

And if that were true, they would bear some responsibility for his death. That is what they are here to deny. They offer this sacrifice and wash their hands over it, as if to say, "Our hands are clean. We did all we could."

It is a strange ritual indeed. But what does this have to do with Jacob and Joseph, their past, and their impending reunion? Well, the case is not an exact replay of their story, by any means, but there are some striking similarities. This corpse is discovered all alone in the fields, just as Joseph was alone in the fields, and then presumed dead. No one knows what happened here, just as no one quite seemed to know what happened to Joseph. And the nearest elders must account for the last sighting of this dead man, just as in Joseph's story, it is the nearest elder – Jacob – who was the last to see Joseph before he left.

The question, then, is: Was Jacob negligent somehow? Did he do all he could to prepare Joseph for his journey? And did he walk down the road with Joseph, and stand for a while and watch him go, to make sure he was safely on his way?

If not, then the implication of this law is that Jacob bears some responsibility for all that happened to Joseph. So maybe that is what Joseph is hinting to his father with these wagons: You abandoned me. You sent me out into danger without any clue of what I was getting myself into. You just let me go, and soon I was lost. And I have been lost now for twenty-two years.

No wonder Jacob's heart stopped.

But Rabbi Shabtai Bass, of 17th century Prague – in his super-commentary on Rashi, the **Siftei Chachamim** – saves us from this depressing possibility. In his commentary on Rashi, he goes back and does a careful rereading of the Jacob and Joseph story, and catches an important detail:

When Joseph left Jacob, Jacob escorted him up to the Valley of Hebron, as Rashi notes back in that verse, which reads, *"and he sent him from the Valley of Hebron." (Gen. 37:14)* Joseph said to him, *"Go on back."* But Jacob replied, *"No, I cannot go back yet. A person is obligated to escort his fellow, as it says in the section of the Beheaded Calf..."* And that is how they learned about the beheaded calf. So when it says that Jacob *"saw the wagons,"* it means, he saw and understood.

כשיוסף פירש מיעקב היה יעקב מלוה אותו עד עמק חברון כדפי' רש"י לעיל בפרשת וישב (לז יד) בפסוק וישלחהו מעמק חברון ויוסף אמר לו חזור בך ואמר לו יעקב איני רשאי לחזור שחייב אדם ללות חבירו כדכתיב בפרשת עגלה ערופה... ומתוך כך למדו אותו פ' עגלה ערופה. ויהיה פירוש וירא את העגלות לשון הבנה.

The Siftei Chachamim brilliantly accomplishes two things here. First, he explains what it might have meant for Jacob and Joseph to have "learned Torah" together. It wasn't that they sat and read from a book that didn't yet exist. Instead, Jacob would teach life lessons as they came up, in real time, and put them into a conceptual framework – and this was *as if* they were reading something like the section of The Beheaded Calf.

Second, by noting the special mention of the Valley of Hebron, which is not where Jacob and Joseph lived, the Siftei Chachamim is able to suggest that Jacob *did* escort Joseph part of the way, did the best he could to ensure Joseph's safety, and made special note of it.

So now, when Joseph sends wagons to his father, alluding to the section of The Beheaded Calf, he is not accusing Jacob. He is exonerating him. Knowing that the shocking news might send Jacob into a panic, forcing him to relive the tragedy, and worrying about his own part in it, Joseph is saying to his father: Do not hold yourself responsible for what happened to me. You did all you could. I remember that day. I remember you tried to keep me safe. If you ever felt guilty for what happened to me, know that you are absolved. Your hands are clean. As the town elders say, in the Book of Deuteronomy:

Absolve, O Lord, Your people Israel, whom you redeemed, and do not let guilt for the blood of the innocent remain among Your people Israel.

When he saw the wagons, his heart started beating again.

CHAPTER 12

THE SECRET CODE - Parshat Vayechi

On his deathbed, Joseph kept mumbling the same phrase, over and over.

... pakod yifkod ... pakod yifkod ...

We have reached the end of the Book of Genesis, and the final scene is Joseph's death. Before he goes, he gathers his brothers and speaks to them one last time, in a tone that sounds almost prophetic. These are the very last lines of the book, so we're listening carefully – and out of the twenty-five Hebrew words he says, one of them he repeats four times, almost like a mantra:

Joseph said to his brothers: "I am about to die. God attends, God will attend to you, and bring you up from this land to the land that God swore to Abraham, Isaac and Jacob... When God attends, God will attend to you, and you will carry my bones up from here." *(Gen 50:24-25)*

וַיֹּאמֶר יוֹסֵף אֶל אֶחָיו: אָנֹכִי מֵת, וֵאלקים פָּקֹד יִפְקֹד אֶתְכֶם, וְהֶעֱלָה אֶתְכֶם מִן הָאָרֶץ
הַזֹּאת אֶל הָאָרֶץ אֲשֶׁר נִשְׁבַּע לְאַבְרָהָם לְיִצְחָק וּלְיַעֲקֹב. וַיַּשְׁבַּע יוֹסֵף אֶת-בְּנֵי יִשְׂרָאֵל
לֵאמֹר: פָּקֹד יִפְקֹד אֱלֹהִים אֶתְכֶם, וְהַעֲלִתֶם אֶת-עַצְמֹתַי מִזֶּה.

Attends, God will attend. Attends, God will attend. The phrase in Hebrew is *pakod yifkod* (פקוד יפקוד). This is a difficult word to translate, but it is some combination of remembering, visiting, and taking note of – so we'll call it, "attending to." The point is, Joseph is promising – with emphasis, as if he wants them to remember just how he said it – that God will deliver them from Egypt.

And that, of course, is exactly what God does. That deliverance will be the central story in the next book of the Torah, aptly called: Exodus.

So okay, Joseph predicted it, or somehow knew it would happen. We already knew Joseph was a skilled dream interpreter, but his final message leaves us wondering if Joseph had greater powers than we suspected, if he was secretly receiving divine messages. Intriguing...

But there is something even more remarkable about Joseph's last words. That is, they appear again, once the actual Exodus is afoot – but this time, in the mouth of the Almighty.

When God first calls upon Moses to lead the people out of Egypt, Moses is reluctant, worrying that he will not be up to the task and that the people will not believe him. So God tells him this:

Go and gather the elders of Israel, and say to them: the Eternal, the God of Abraham, Isaac and Jacob, has appeared to me and said, 'Attend, I have attended to you and what has been done to you in Egypt. And I have said, I will take you out of the misery of Egypt to the land of the Canaanites…' They will listen to your voice... ***(Exod. 3:16-18)***

לֵךְ וְאָסַפְתָּ אֶת זִקְנֵי יִשְׂרָאֵל וְאָמַרְתָּ אֲלֵהֶם ה' אֱלֹהֵי אֲבֹתֵיכֶם נִרְאָה אֵלַי אֱלֹהֵי אַבְרָהָם יִצְחָק וְיַעֲקֹב לֵאמֹר, פָּקֹד פָּקַדְתִּי אֶתְכֶם וְאֶת הֶעָשׂוּי לָכֶם בְּמִצְרָיִם. וָאֹמַר אַעֲלֶה אֶתְכֶם מֵעֳנִי מִצְרַיִם, אֶל אֶרֶץ הַכְּנַעֲנִי... וְשָׁמְעוּ לְקֹלֶךָ...

There it is again! That phrase. "Attend, I have attended..." *Pakod pakadti* (פקוד פקדתי). The tense is different, but it's the same verb, and it has the same unusual doubling that we saw in Joseph's farewell speech. It's as if God is quoting Joseph!

That, says **Rashi**, is exactly what's happening. He says that this is what God means by *"They will listen to your voice."* Moses won't have to convince them.

They will listen to your voice **– Because you will speak to them using this wording, they will immediately listen to you, as this sign has been passed down from Jacob and Joseph – that with this wording they will be redeemed.**

ושמעו לקלך – מכיון שתאמר להם לשון זה, ישמעו לקולך, שכבר סימן זה מסור בידם מיעקב ומיוסף, שבלשון זה הם נגאלים.

Rashi is saying that Joseph wasn't just telling his brothers *what* would happen; he was giving them a code word they could use to know *when* it was truly about to happen. The one who came to them and uttered the secret phrase – *pakod yifkod* – that one would lead them out of Egypt.

And remember, it isn't just the word – it's the *way* he says it. As the **Ramban** explains, picking up on Rashi's comments:

That is why Joseph kept saying ***pakod yifkod*****, with the doubling, to tell them that this was a tradition from his father. And in** ***Midrash Shemot***

Rabbah **it says: And why will they listen to your voice? Because they had a tradition regarding the redemption, that if a redeemer should come and speak to them with the double *pakod*, this would be the true redeemer.**

כי יוסף אמר פעמים פקד יפקוד, להגיד שהיתה מסורת בידו מאביו. ובאלה שמות רבה (ג יא) מיד ושמעו לקולך, למה, שמסורת גאולה היא בידם שכל גואל שיבא ויאמר להם פקידה כפולה הוא גואל של אמת.

But wait a minute. Isn't that a little too easy? All it takes to be recognized as the true redeemer is to say the password... but everybody knows the password! So anyone could come along and claim to be a messenger from God. What's so impressive about Moses uttering these words when they are part of a long-standing tradition? The Ramban considers this question, and gives a brilliant answer:

You may ask, why would they believe him? Maybe Moses had heard this tradition just as they had! ...Now, if he had grown up in his father's house and come and said these things, they would not have believed him, because they would have said, "His father taught him this! Joseph passed it to Levi, and Levi to Kahat, and Kahat to Amram [Moses' father]." Therefore, he was taken from his father's house, so that when he went and said these things to Israel, they would believe him.

ויש עליך לשאול, ומנין להם שיאמינו, שמא שמע משה במסורת הזאת כמות ...שאלו גדל בבית אביו ובא ואמר להם המעשים, לא היו מאמינים בו, שהיו אומרים אביו מסרם לו, לפי שיוסף מסרה ללוי ולוי לקהת וקהת לעמרם, ולכך נתלש מבית אביו, וכשהלך והגיד לישראל כל הדברים, לפיכך האמינו בו.

The Ramban is reminding us that Moses wasn't just any Israelite. He was the boy sent down the river and drawn out by Pharaoh's daughter, to be taken into the palace and raised as an Egyptian. He had been separated from his own people and from his culture, and he had no knowledge of their traditions. He wasn't one of them; he was, as the movie calls him, the Prince of Egypt.

So when that man comes before them and says, *pakod yifkod*, 'Attend, God will attend to you' – the sacred phrase, a phrase he could not have known – then they knew. He was the one. The time had finally come. Redemption was at hand.

And God had orchestrated this whole thing. God had either given Joseph a secret code or, even more remarkable, God had borrowed Joseph's words and turned them into a secret code. And then God had taken Moses out of his house and had him sent to live among the Egyptians, all so that when Moses returned as an outsider, and pronounced the right words, he would be recognized as the one they had been waiting for.

Now this is a dazzling bit of *parshanut*. The rabbis have constructed an elaborate mythology by carefully noting the recurrence of this unusual phrase. We might have overlooked this echoing, just read past it. But once they have pointed it out, it seems so clear and deliberate, as if the Torah itself were encoding hidden messages, and waiting for us to decipher them.

But why? This secret code certainly adds a layer of mystery and excitement to the story; it heightens the drama of the Exodus, the epic moment of Moses' return. But is all of this linguistic interconnectedness just there in the service of good storytelling?

We have not fully cracked the code without considering the meaning of the word itself. It wasn't just repetition itself that Joseph passed on, after all, but the repetition of this particular word – *pakod*, Attending to. So what is the significance of that word?

To understand that, the best place to turn is to the first place this word is used in the Torah. That is back in the Book of Genesis, Chapter 21:

The Lord attended to Sarah, as God had promised, and the Lord did for Sarah as God had spoken. And Sarah conceived and bore Abraham a son… ***(vv. 1-2)***

וַה' פָּקַד אֶת שָׂרָה, כַּאֲשֶׁר אָמָר, וַיַּעַשׂ ה' לְשָׂרָה, כַּאֲשֶׁר דִּבֵּר. וַתַּהַר וַתֵּלֶד שָׂרָה לְאַבְרָהָם בֵּן...

This is probably the most well-known usage of *pakad*, "attended to," and it describes the miraculous conception of Sarah and Abraham in their old age. These two had lived a life of great meaning and purpose, and had shared a partnership for decades – but there was always something missing. They were, to their great sorrow, unable to have a child.

And then, in what seemed like the twilight of their lives, when all chances of conceiving had long passed, God suddenly announces that they will have a son.

And at first, they do not believe it. They just laugh. Such things are not possible. Their time has passed. They've given up.

But then it happens. The Lord *attended* to Sarah. And she conceived, and gave birth to Isaac. In her joy, she exclaims:

Who would have said to Abraham that Sarah would nurse children! Yet I have borne a son in his old age. ***(Gen. 21:7)***

מִי מִלֵּל לְאַבְרָהָם הֵינִיקָה בָנִים שָׂרָה. כִּי יָלַדְתִּי בֵן, לִזְקֻנָיו.

Who would have thought it possible? Who would have believed such a thing could happen? Yet here it is. Anything can happen when God attends to it.

That is the message that Joseph leaves his brothers. And that is the message that Moses delivers to the people. This is a people, remember, who have been enslaved for hundreds of years. They have no power, no weapons. They have nowhere else to go. There is no reason to believe that they will ever be free.

Yet Moses says to them:

The Eternal, the God of Abraham, Isaac and Jacob, has appeared to me and said, 'Attend, I have attended to you…'

And they believe him. Because this is more than just a secret code he has pronounced. This is an invocation of the God who attended to Sarah, the great matriarch from whom they are all descended. That story they know. They have never witnessed God delivering an entire nation. How could they be expected to believe such a thing could happen? But they do believe in a God that answers personal prayers, a God who attends to human suffering, and a God who makes the impossible, possible.

Attend, I have attended...

Just as I have attended to your Mother Sarah, so will I attend to you. Just as I brought forth the birth of your forefather Isaac, so will I bring forth the birth of a nation. The One who has delivered, shall deliver again.

...pakod yifkod... pakod yifkod...

And they listened to his voice.

II

Exodus

CHAPTER 13
A NEW KING – Parshat Shemot

This week, all watchful eyes are fixed on one verse:

A new king arose over Egypt, who did not know Joseph. *(Exodus 1:10)*

וַיָּקָם מֶלֶךְ חָדָשׁ עַל מִצְרָיִם אֲשֶׁר לֹא יָדַע אֶת יוֹסֵף.

It is an ominous line, suggestive of all the terror that is about to envelop the Israelite people as the Book of Exodus begins. It will begin with a fear of the growing immigrant population, move quickly into slavery, and lead eventually to state-sponsored murder.

We left the Book of Genesis with the family of Israel comfortably settled in Egypt, having secured a fertile plot of land, thanks especially to Joseph's close relationship with the Pharaoh. But this new Pharaoh, quite pointedly, does "not know Joseph." How is this possible? Can he really have forgotten the man who served as the right hand to the previous king, and who saved all of Egypt from famine?

There is a debate in the midrash, recorded by **Rashi**, over exactly what kind of new administration this was, and how authentic was their "forgetting":

"A new king arose" **– Rav and Shmuel debated. One said it was truly a new king. While the other said, it's just that his laws were new, and that** ***"he did not know Joseph,"*** **meant that he acted** ***as if*** **he did not know Joseph.**

ויקם מלך חדש – רב ושמואל, חד אמר חדש ממש, וחד אמר שנתחדשו גזרותיו. אשר לא ידע – עשה עצמו כאלו לא ידעו.

The latter opinion is that this was not simply a gap in some new leader's historical memory, but a feigned ignorance by the old Pharaoh, played out for political purposes. Here we have hints of a dangerous psychological profile: a person who could shift personalities at will, and speak lies with total conviction. A sociopath with unlimited power – this was truly a man to fear.

But he did not do it alone. We see him, just after his inauguration, turn to his people and whisper:

Come, let us deal shrewdly with them, so that they do not increase... *(Exodus 1:10)*

הָבָה נִתְחַכְּמָה לוֹ, פֶּן יִרְבֶּה...

But who was he talking to? What team of advisors sat in his inner circle? One of the richest midrashim in all of *Shemot Rabbah* fills the scene with a cast of notable characters:

Rabbi Chiya said in the name of Rabbi Simon, "Three people were there to advise: Bilaam, Job, and Jethro. Bilaam, who affirmed the plan, was killed. Job, who was silent, was punished with suffering. Jethro, who fled, merited children who sat on the High Court of Israel." *(Shemot Rabbah 1:9)*

אמר רבי חייא אמר רבי סימון, שלשה היו באותה עצה, בלעם, ואיוב, ויתרו. בלעם שיעץ, נהרג. איוב ששתק, נדון ביסורין. יתרו שברח, זכו בניו וישבו בלשכת הגזית.

Now this is rabbinic storytelling at its creative best. Three figures, plucked from various side stories across *Tanakh* (the Hebrew Bible), and inserted into Pharaoh's coterie of trusted advisors. Then, each of their imagined responses is used to explain their eventual destinies. Bilaam the prophet is indeed killed, in the war with Midian *(Numbers 31:8)*. Job is the famous epitome of human suffering, a righteous man tested by God with the death of his children, the destruction of all his property, and the agony of a terrible disease. And Jethro is Moses' father-in-law, who will thereby become an ancestor to future leaders of Israel. Three men with three very different fates.

There is one thing, however, that these three men all have in common: they are all non-Israelites. It isn't too common for stories in the Hebrew Bible to feature outsiders so prominently, and when it happens, the rabbinic interpreters are confused as to how to regard them. Are they friends or enemies, righteous or wicked? This midrash, rather than painting over that question with a broad brush, gives the range of possible answers: Bilaam was a bad man, Jethro was good, and Job was somewhere in between. Their characters are measured by how each responds to an unjust government, and together they present us with three possibilities: 1.) Support the ruling power. 2.) Keep quiet and hope for the best. 3.) Defect.

In this relatively simple moral schema, the midrash suggests, everyone will get their just deserts. Consenting to oppression, whether actively or passively, will eventually incur divine punishment. Refusal to participate in the plot of the wicked, though it may require dangerous sacrifice, will be rewarded in the long run.

*

The picture is complicated, however, by a remarkably parallel story we find in the Talmud. The setting is entirely different: centuries later, in the Land of Israel, recently conquered by Roman authorities. And our characters are now not rabbinic reimaginings of Biblical figures, but the rabbis themselves. Yet they are presented with the same basic dilemma that confronted Bilaam, Job, and Jethro: How does one respond to oppressive state power? And look at how similar their responses are:

Rabbi Yehudah, Rabbi Yossi, and Rabbi Shimon were sitting together, and Yehudah ben Gerim was sitting near them. Rabbi Yehudah opened by saying, "How fine are the works of these people! They have made markets, they have built bridges, they have built bathhouses." Rabbi Yossi was silent. Rabbi Shimon bar Yochai said, "All that they have made, they have only made for themselves; they built marketplaces to put whores in them, bathhouses to pamper themselves, and bridges to levy tolls for them." Yehudah ben Gerim went and told what they said, and it was heard by the government. They said: Yehudah, who exalted us, shall be exalted. Yossi, who was silent, shall be exiled to Tzipori. Shimon, who slandered us, shall be killed. So he and his son went and hid... ***(Babylonian Talmud, Shabbat 33b)***

יתבי רבי יהודה ורבי יוסי ורבי שמעון ויתיב יהודה בן גרים גבייהו פתח רבי יהודה ואמר כמה נאים מעשיהן של אומה זו תקנו שווקים תקנו גשרים תקנו מרחצאות רבי יוסי שתק נענה רבי שמעון בן יוחאי ואמר כל מה שתקנו לא תקנו אלא לצורך עצמן תקנו שווקין להושיב בהן זונות מרחצאות לעדן בהן עצמן גשרים ליטול מהן מכס הלך יהודה בן גרים וסיפר דבריהם ונשמעו למלכות אמרו יהודה שעילה יתעלה יוסי ששתק יגלה לציפורי שמעון שגינה יהרג. אזל הוא ובריה טשו...

The basic responses here, at first glance, seem in many ways to be exactly the same as those we saw in our original midrash. Rabbi Yehudah plays the role of Bilaam, supporting the ruling authorities. Rabbi Yossi, like Job, is quiet. And Rabbi Shimon is the Jethro of the tale, refusing to sanction the government, and consequently having to run away to save his life.

Yet there are also some important differences between the two stories:

- First of all, these rabbis are not direct advisors to the Roman government. They are not in positions of power at all. In fact, they are members of the conquered population. They will not merely be witnesses to oppression, but potentially its targets. And so the question of how one responds to a ruthless state power is very different here, when the consequences of that power will have an effect on one's own people.
- Secondly, we are given an extra option for response by Rabbi Shimon: protest. It is true that, like Jethro, he ends up having to flee for his life. But before then, he does something that we never saw Jethro do. He speaks out against the government. Rabbi Shimon is the only figure in either tale that engages in actual resistance.
- Finally – and most troublingly – the recompense for the rabbis' actions is very different than the kinds of rewards and punishments we saw in the midrash. For Bilaam, who supported the Pharaoh, was killed; but Rabbi Yehudah, who praises the Romans, is elevated in status. Instead, it is Rabbi Shimon, who denounced the regime, who is sentenced to death. And while he does manage to flee, like Jethro, and eventually survive, there is no mention of any clear reward for his righteousness. Rabbi Shimon, the lone voice of protest in these narratives, will have to live in hiding for years, and will suffer great afflictions all the while.

What are we to make of all this?

Are there different methods for dealing with dictatorships, depending on whether or not one is in the ruling class? If so, then it is strange that in our two cases, it is those with less power, the rabbis under Roman rule, who produce the strongest voice of resistance. But perhaps that is always the way. The powerful rarely participate in acts of rebellion. We might celebrate Pharaoh's cabinet members for resigning, but we do not expect them to march in the streets against him.

Or, perhaps, the difference between the two stories is simply that God is more present in one than in the other. In the world of Exodus, God intervenes in history – the wicked are punished, and the righteous are saved. Everyone gets exactly what they deserve. By the time we get to the Roman conquest of Jerusalem, it no longer seems clear to the rabbis that this is the case. Forces of violence and oppression are able to seize victory without restraint, and the most vulnerable are left unprotected. Where is the God of Justice when we call out? Why have we been so abandoned? Perhaps these are the questions the rabbis are grappling with.

Then again, maybe the rewards and punishments of our protagonists are not as easily categorized as we have so far suggested. Yes, we heard that Rabbi Yehudah was to be "exalted." But what does that mean, really? It is so vague. And can we trust the Romans to make good on their word? Rabbi Shimon, meanwhile, was sentenced to death – but he does manage to escape. And while his life is not easy afterwards, he does seem to be protected by God, is able to raise his son, and goes on to become one of the most revered scholars of his generation. Is that so different, after all, from the fate of Jethro, whose greatest honor was that his descendants were judges on the Great Sanhedrin? Perhaps righteousness is its own reward.

One thing, however, is consistent between the two stories. Those who stay silent do not fare well. Both Job and Rabbi Yossi decide to say nothing, presumably in hopes that while they may not curry government favor, they will at least go unharmed. We might have expected this strategy to work. Protest is dangerous, but so, too, is colluding with an evil empire. Silence might seem to be the only safe option. Yet the quiet are not rewarded for their restraint. Rabbi Yossi is sent into exile, and Job will go on to suffer as no man ever has – not for his active support of Pharaoh, but for the cowardice of his tacit consent.

It is not at all clear what to do when a wicked king arises. But we will not get away with doing nothing.

CHAPTER 14

THE SERPENT AND THE ROD – Parshat Va'eira

Does the God of Heaven and Earth do party tricks?

That's what it seems like, in this week's parsha, when Moses and Aaron are told to go before Pharaoh and wow him with a miracle. Now, the Book of Exodus will be full of miracles: the ten plagues, the parting of the Red Sea – the kinds of epic, nature-altering miracles that testify to the unlimited power of God. But what God proposes here, in this very first display of divine might, seems a little...less than epic. God says:

When Pharaoh speaks to you and says, 'Produce your marvel,' you shall say to Aaron, 'Take your rod and cast it down before Pharaoh.' It shall turn into a serpent. (*Exod. 7:9*)

כִּי יְדַבֵּר אֲלֵכֶם פַּרְעֹה לֵאמֹר: תְּנוּ לָכֶם מוֹפֵת, וְאָמַרְתָּ אֶל אַהֲרֹן: קַח אֶת מַטְּךָ וְהַשְׁלֵךְ לִפְנֵי פַרְעֹה, יְהִי לְתַנִּין.

Okay. So God can turn sticks into snakes.

That's ... pretty cool, I guess. I mean, it *is* supernatural. But it isn't exactly the kind of mind-blowing miracle you'd expect from the Almighty God. It feels more like a magic trick – like something you'd see on a stage in Vegas. And so when Aaron does cast down the rod, and it does indeed turn into a serpent, Pharaoh is wholly unimpressed. In fact, the Midrash has a particularly vivid account of Pharaoh's reaction:

He began to tease them, and to cluck at them like a chicken, and he said, "These are the kinds of wonders that your God does?! People generally bring merchandise to a place where they don't already have it! Do they bring fish to Akko [a fishing town]?! Don't you know that all the magic arts are in my domain? He immediately called for children to be brought from their schools, so they could perform the same trick. And then he called in his wife, and she did it, too! *(Shemot Rabbah 9:6)*

באותה שעה התחיל פרעה משחק עליהם ומקרקר אחריהם כתרנגלת, ואומר להם, כך אותותיו של אלהיכם, בנהג שבעולם בני אדם מוליכין פרקמטיא למקום שצריכין להם, כלום מביאין מורייס לאספמיא, דגים לעכו, אין אתם יודעין שכל הכשפים

ברשותי הן, מיד שלח והביא תינוקות מן אסכולי שלהם, ועשו אף הם כך, ולא עוד אלא קרא לאשתו ועשתה כך.

This midrash is just picking up on what actually does happen in the next line of the Torah, just after Aaron's little miracle:

Pharaoh then called in his wise men and sorcerers, and the Egyptian magicians did the same thing with their spells: each cast down his rod, and the rods all turned into serpents... ***(Exod. 7:11-12)***

וַיִּקְרָא גַּם פַּרְעֹה לַחֲכָמִים וְלַמְכַשְּׁפִים וַיַּעֲשׂוּ גַם הֵם חַרְטֻמֵּי מִצְרַיִם בְּלַהֲטֵיהֶם כֵּן. וַיַּשְׁלִיכוּ אִישׁ מַטֵּהוּ וַיִּהְיוּ לְתַנִּינִם...

So the Torah itself makes it clear that there was nothing special about this so-called "wonder." Pharaoh seems to have seen this kind of thing before. And his own magicians have no trouble replicating it. The midrash just takes it a step further and says that even little children could do this! And then his wife walks in, and she does it, too – just like that! Looks like *everyone* knows the old stick-to-snake trick! This is no great proof of the one, true God. This is just common parlor magic.

If that is true, then why does God choose this move as the opening gambit? Why begin this announcement of God's power with what appears to be a standard sorcerer's spell? God must have known that Pharaoh would have been underwhelmed, and that he would never have let the people go after a move like this. So what was the point of this meager display? Why the snake trick?

Now, we always turn to the classical commentators for answers to questions like these, but this week, our first "commentator" is a lot more classic than usual. Because one of the most brilliant expositions of this scene is given by none other than the Prophet Ezekiel.

Every *parsha* in the Torah has a designated accompanying reading from the prophets – called the '*Haftarah*.' These selections are not chosen randomly; they always have some thematic link to the passage from the Torah that's just been read. Often, they offer a new spin on that theme, and serve as a subtle way of reflecting on and reinterpreting the original story. *Parshat Va'eira*'s *haftarah*, taken from the Book of Ezekiel, seems to be subtly referencing our incident with the snakes and the sticks. First the snake:

Thus said the Lord Eternal: I am going to deal with you, O Pharaoh, King of Egypt, The Great Serpent, slithering through his rivers, who said, "My Nile is my own; I made it for myself." ***(Ezek. 29:3)***

דַּבֵּר וְאָמַרְתָּ כֹּה אָמַר אֲדֹנָי ה' הִנְנִי עָלֶיךָ פַּרְעֹה מֶלֶךְ מִצְרַיִם הַתַּנִּים הַגָּדוֹל הָרֹבֵץ בְּתוֹךְ יְאֹרָיו אֲשֶׁר אָמַר לִי יְאֹרִי וַאֲנִי עֲשִׂיתִנִי.

And then, two verses later, the stick:

Then all the inhabitants of Egypt shall know that I am The Eternal. Because you were a staff of straw to the House of Israel. When they grasped you with their hands, you would splinter, and wound all their shoulders, and when they leaned on you, you would break, and make all their legs unsteady. ***(vv. 6-7)***

וְיָדְעוּ כָּל יֹשְׁבֵי מִצְרַיִם כִּי אֲנִי ה' יַעַן הֱיוֹתָם מִשְׁעֶנֶת קָנֶה לְבֵית יִשְׂרָאֵל. בְּתָפְשָׂם בְּךָ בַכַּף תֵּרוֹץ וּבָקַעְתָּ לָהֶם כָּל כָּתֵף וּבְהִשָּׁעֲנָם עָלֶיךָ תִּשָּׁבֵר וְהַעֲמַדְתָּ לָהֶם כָּל מָתְנָיִם.

Here Ezekiel is launching into a tirade against a latter-day Egypt, but he uses all the language of our scene back in Exodus. Except that now Pharaoh is both the serpent and the rod. He appears to be menacing, like a snake, but will soon be incapacitated. And he appears to be strong, like a staff, but he will soon crumple beneath you, like a flimsy reed.

If we read this interpretation back into our story in Exodus, then, this alchemy of sticks and snakes is not meant so much as a display of power, but as a message – one written in the language of symbols. It is a warning, first to Pharaoh, but also to everyone around him. Do not trust this fork-tongued man who tells you he is all-powerful. He is like the snake before you: a little scary at first, but easy enough to trap, or to trample. And do not lean on him for support, for anyone who relies on his power will be thrown to the ground, like this staff.

Ezekiel's striking imagery becomes the foundation for a highly symbolic approach to this episode that is then taken up by the midrash, the **Ba'al HaTurim**, and the **Kli Yakar**, all of whom reference Ezekiel directly in their commentary on these verses. Later, in the Hassidic literature of the 18th and 19th centuries, the symbolic analysis continues, with all kinds of new, mystical interpretations of the serpent and the rod. And all of these commentaries are able to sidestep the question of why God would choose such a lowly miracle, so easily replicable. For the point of this trick was not to overwhelm or impress Pharaoh, but to communicate something to him.

The problem with the symbolic approach, however, is that it isn't at all clear that Pharaoh would have understood the symbolism. Sure, Ezekiel can provide us with a reading of this imagery – he's a prophet! But why would we expect Pharaoh or anyone else standing there in his court, to be able to read the hidden nuances in this mysterious language of sticks and snakes? Moses certainly doesn't explain it. Pharaoh doesn't seem to react to it with any sense of comprehending a deeper level of meaning. In fact, when he calls his own sorcerers to perform the same trick, it suggests that he understood the act as a challenge in the game of magic – and one that he easily met. These symbols may speak to us, years later, but when we turn back to the confrontation itself, Pharaoh is still there laughing at Moses and Aaron, and bringing in little children to show them up.

*

There is one final detail, however, that does give Aaron's performance a slight edge.

Just after Pharaoh's magicians have come in and reproduced the snake trick with ease, we get one last bit of magic:

Each cast down his rod, and the rods all turned into serpents. But Aaron's rod swallowed their rods. ***(Exod. 7:12)***

וַיַּשְׁלִיכוּ אִישׁ מַטֵּהוּ וַיִּהְיוּ לְתַנִּינִם וַיִּבְלַע מַטֵּה אַהֲרֹן אֶת מַטֹּתָם.

Okay, so that's a minor victory for Aaron. But really, isn't it just more of the same? We're still dealing with party tricks – just better party tricks. "Sure you can turn a rod into a serpent, but then my serpent eats your serpents! So my serpent is the most powerful! Ha-ha!"

Except that it doesn't say that Aaron's *serpent* swallowed their serpents. It says, "Aaron's *rod* swallowed their rods." Now, maybe it just means the same thing; the serpent was made from the rod, so you can call it a serpent or a rod – whatever, the language is imprecise. But **Rashi** doesn't think the Torah would be so careless in its wording. He notices this switch back to the language of rods, and he says something I think is just brilliant:

Aaron's rod swallowed their rods **– After it returned and became a rod again, then it swallowed them all.**

ויבלע מטה אהרן **– מאחר שחזר ונעשה מטה, בלע את כלן.**

Now so far we've just been dealing with "presto-chango" transformations – "watch as I turn this lifeless staff... into a snake!" – classic stage magic. But this is different. If Rashi is right, it isn't just that Aaron charmed his snake into eating the other snakes. No, suddenly, something happens that makes no sense. Aaron's serpent turns back into a rod, and *then* it swallows the others.

Now a rod doesn't swallow anything. It doesn't have a mouth. So what's going on here?

I think what Rashi's comment suggests is that the real power of this moment lay in a kind of parody of magic. At the very moment when it seemed that nothing more than a simple illusion was happening here, something that any magician could perform – suddenly something totally absurd happens, something that defies the logic of the situation itself, and makes a mockery of the whole performance, and the whole concept of magic.

The Talmudic passage that Rashi is borrowing from (*Shabbat 97a*) says that when Aaron's rod did the swallowing, this was *"a miracle inside of a miracle"* (נס בתוך נס) That is, the trick was never about turning a stick into a serpent. That's just a silly bit of smoke and mirrors. The trick was to get inside of the trick, reconfigure it, and somehow use its variables to produce an outcome that was actually impossible, but somehow happening. That only God could do.

*

There's an old theological question that seems to undermine the concept of God's unlimited power: "Could God create a boulder so heavy that God could not pick it up?" This is called the 'Omnipotence Paradox,' because if God can do anything, God should be able to create something so heavy that God cannot pick it up; but, if God cannot pick it up, then God is not omnipotent.

Most of the classic answers to this question attempt some kind of redefinition of the terms. Maybe omnipotence, for example, doesn't mean being able to do *anything* at all, but being able to do anything that is actually possible.

But I think Rashi's logic in this description of the staff doing the swallowing suggests a different answer to the Omnipotence Paradox. Could God create a boulder so heavy God could not pick it up? God could... and then God could pick it up.

Let go of all your logic, and your laws of nature, Rashi is saying. God is beyond all of those things. Forget about your silly magic tricks. Forget about what you thought a miracle looked like. The Creator of All Being has more in store than just burning bushes and splitting seas. You are soon going to witness the melting of reality as you know it, and the shattering of all your concepts. You are leaving the land of the known, and entering into the realm of the impossible, where the only law is God.

Get ready, O Pharaoh, King of Egypt. The Exodus is about to begin.

CHAPTER 15
THE SILENT CHILD – Parshat Bo

Any fan of midrash has got to love 'The Four Children.'

This well-known section of the Passover Haggadah considers four types of children who might be sitting there at the Passover Seder: the wise one, the wicked one, the simple one, and the one who does not know how to ask. Each one forms a distinct personality archetype, and as we begin to tell the Passover story, we imagine each one asking a different kind of question, and each receiving their own unique answer. It is often celebrated as a record of the pedagogic wisdom of the rabbis, an early articulation of the principle of Personalized Learning.

It is also a masterpiece of midrashic technique, a careful collection of verse fragments from across the Torah, reordered and strung together to form a new narrative. (I say "across the Torah," but really, most of the source material comes from right here in our *parsha*; only the wise child is found elsewhere, over in the Book of Deuteronomy.) The midrash brilliantly picks up on the fact that there are four separate instances in the Torah which make mention of the obligation to tell the Passover story – each one phrased slightly differently, which the rabbis take to mean that they indicate four different kinds of telling.

The Haggadah spells out exactly how all this is done, so we might as well just read the section through. The version we have is actually a synthesis of two appearances of this midrash, one found in the *Mekhilta,* and one in the Jerusalem Talmud. But let's take the classic Haggadah text as our starting point, and we'll interrupt along the way to explain things:

The Torah speaks referring to four children: One is wise, one is wicked, one is simple and one does not know how to ask.

כנגד ארבעה בנים דברה תורה: אחד חכם, ואחד רשע, ואחד תם, ואחד שאינו יודע לשאול.

The wise one, what does he say? *"What are the testimonies, the rules and the laws which the Lord, our God, has commanded you?" (Deuteronomy 6:20)*

חכם מה הוא אומר? מה העדות והחקים והמשפטים אשר צוה ה' אלהינו אתכם.

What a question! Look at how wordy and knowledgeable this kid is! So this is clearly the smart child. And what do we do? The midrash continues...

So you shall instruct him in the laws of Passover, up to 'one is not to eat anything after the Passover lamb.'

ואף אתה אמור לו כהלכות הפסח: אין מפטירין אחר הפסח אפיקומן.

Okay, instruct him in the laws. Moving on...

The wicked one, what does he say? *"What is this service to you?" (Exodus 12:26)*

רשע מה הוא אומר? מה העבודה הזאת לכם.

Uh-oh. The rabbis are not going like the tone of that question. Especially that last part: What's it *'to you'*?

He says 'to you,' but not to him! By excluding himself from the community he has denied that which is fundamental. You, therefore, blunt his teeth and say to him: *"It is because of this that the Lord did for me when I left Egypt" (Exodus 13:8)*; 'for me' – but not for him! If he had been there, he would not have been redeemed!

ולפי שהוציא את עצמו מן הכלל כפר בעקר. ואף אתה הקהה את שניו ואמור לו. "בעבור זה עשה ה' לי בצאתי ממצרים". לי ולא־לו. אלו היה שם, לא היה נגאל.

Yikes. He wouldn't even have made it out. That's a strong statement. Then comes the simple child.

The simple child, what does he say? *"What is this?" (Exod. 13:14)*

תם מה הוא אומר? מה זאת?

That's it. That's all he says. Just "what is this?" This child is confused by the whole ceremony. He really has no idea what's going on. So the rabbis recommend starting from the beginning:

Thus you shall say to him: *"With a strong hand the Lord took us out of Egypt, from the house of slaves."(Exod. 13:14)*

ואמרת אליו "בחוזק יד הוציאנו ה' ממצרים מבית עבדים".

Okay – wise, wicked, and simple. Three question, three answers. But then there's one more child. A child without a question:

As for the one who does not know how to ask, you must open the topic for him, as it is said: *"You shall tell your child on that day, 'It is because of this that the Lord did for me when I left Egypt.'" (Exod. 13:8)*

ושאינו יודע לשאול ,את פתח לו, שנאמר, והגדת לבנך ביום ההוא לאמר, בעבור זה עשה ה' לי בצאתי ממצרים.

Now that last one is a little surprising. If the working assumption of the midrash is that each Passover question recorded in the Torah refers to a different child, and we find three different questions, why not just leave it at three children? Why read in a fourth, silent child?

Now you might say, well, since there's another verse that speaks of telling the Passover story to children, that telling also has to be accounted for, and since there's no prompting question there, that child must not have asked one. So that child must not have known how to ask.

But there are several problems with that logic. First of all, from a midrashic perspective, we don't need to create a silent child for the *"You shall tell your child on that day"* verse, because that particular verse has another function. It is from this very line that the rabbis derive the actual commandment to tell the story of Passover to our children. So this is the primary verse, from which we learn that we tell the story altogether. It's the other storytelling verses that are extra – and so they can be used to describe how we tell the story.

But more perplexing still is the nature of this child. "The one who does not know how to ask"? That doesn't seem like a classic personality archetype. A smart kid, sure, we know that type. A naughty kid – not unusual. And yes, some children are a little slow. But what does it mean that this child doesn't know how to ask? If it were just a question of intelligence, we'd have already covered that with the simple child. No, there's some other disconnect happening for this child.

As is so often the case, **Rashi**'s commentary on this verse hints obliquely at a deeper level of psychological insight into what might be going on. He says:

Here, "You shall tell your child," speaks about the child who does not know how to ask. And the verse is teaching you that you should open for him with words of *Aggadah*, that draw forth the heart. ***(appears in Rashi's comments on v. 5)***

וכאן "והגדת לבנך" בבן שאינו יודע לשאל, והכתוב מלמדך, שתפתח לו אתה בדברי אגדה, המושכין את הלב.

Open with "words of *Aggadah.*" The word, *Aggadah,* itself is significant here. For one thing, it is the Aramaic cognate of the Hebrew, *Haggadah*, both of which mean 'telling' – or, in this case, 'story-telling.'

But more than that, Aggadah always stands, in rabbinic literature, opposite Halakhah – or, Law – as the other major area of traditional study. These are the two basic categories of rabbinic writing: Halakhah and Aggadah, Law and Narrative.

And yet (though it is never officially stated) it always seems that of the two, it is Law which takes the place of primacy. Law has historically been the major focus of Jewish study. The Talmud, the most famous rabbinic work, is primarily thought of as a legal text (though it contains plenty of narrative as well). Indeed, in many yeshivas, standard practice is to spend weeks carefully analyzing every line of halakhic discussion in the Talmud... and then to gloss quickly through the aggadic sections. In the land of traditional Jewish learning, Law reigns supreme.

For an affirmation of this truth, we need look no further than our midrash here in the Haggadah. Who is the "wise child," after all? It is the one who asks, "what are the testimonies, rules, and laws, which the Lord your God has commanded you"? This child is not just knowledgeable – but knowledgeable about the *laws*. And so we answer with a catalog of laws, detailing the Passover rituals, from beginning to end. The standard-bearer of Wisdom is Law.

And yet, something is wrong with this equation. For on Passover, of all times, the reason we are gathered together, is to tell a story. The very name of the book we read from is the Haggadah – literally, 'The Story-telling.' Rattling off a list of rules and regulations will not do. We are here to tell the story of the Exodus.

The Book of Exodus, after all, is itself an epic narrative. Yes, there are many laws in it; but those laws are embedded in a larger story, and they only find their meaning and their authority through their placement in that story. Who would follow the commandments of the Torah if they were presented abruptly, with no context? Who would be there to stand at

Sinai if the Israelites had not been freed from Egypt? That is the whole point of the Book of Exodus: Revelation depends on Redemption. Law depends on Narrative.

The great 20th century legal philosopher, Robert Cover, in his essay, *'Nomos and Narrative,'* puts it this way:

No set of legal institutions or prescriptions exists apart from the narratives that locate it and give it meaning. For every constitution there is an epic, for each decalogue a scripture. Once understood in the context of the narratives that give it meaning, law becomes not merely a system of rules to be observed, but a world in which we live.

And the great 20th century Jewish philosopher, Abraham Joshua Heschel, expresses a similar sentiment in the language of rabbinic discourse:

Halakhah **deals with the law;** ***Aggadah*** **with the meaning of the law.** ***Halakhah*** **deals with subjects that can be expressed literally;** ***Aggadah*** **introduces us to a realm that lies beyond the range of expression.** ***Halakhah*** **teaches us how to perform common acts;** ***Aggadah*** **tells us how to participate in the eternal drama.** ***Halakhah*** **gives us knowledge;** ***Aggadah*** **gives us aspiration.**

The wise child is asking for knowledge – for *Halakhah.* But there is another type of child who is seeking meaning. This one does not know how to ask, because questions are the language of analysis and investigation. Instead this child is listening. Listening for something that lies beyond the range of expression.

How will we know what to say to this silent child? Rashi tells us. We will open with *Aggadah,* with story, because, Rashi says, words of *Aggadah* draw forth the heart. This is not the simple child. This child holds a complexity, there behind the silence. But this is someone who processes the world not with the mind, but with the heart. So we must learn to speak to the heart, to the emotions, to the intuitions.

We must learn to tell the story of the Exodus. This is the child who will teach us how.

CHAPTER 16

THE THINGS WE CARRIED - Parshat Beshalach

This is it. Time to go.

The Exodus is actually happening. The plagues are over, the Pharaoh has relented. The Israelites are packed and ready, carrying everything they own on their backs. They have even stuffed Egyptian gold and silver into their bags – whatever they could grab.

And now they are beginning to stream out, bursting open blood-stained doors, heading for the sea. Everyone running – old men, mothers with little children, tribal leaders...

But in the midst of this torrent of bodies all rushing out of Egypt, one man seems to be scrambling in the wrong direction. A closer look reveals this is not just any man. It is their leader, Moses. Yet he is not, as we might expect, out leading the charge of the Exodus. Instead, he is busy, looking for something... looking...

And then he finds it:

Now the Israelites went up armed out of the land of Egypt. And Moses took the bones of Joseph with him, for Joseph had them swear, saying, "God will surely attend to you, and then you should carry my bones up from here with you." *(Exod. 13:18-19)*

וַחֲמֻשִׁים עָלוּ בְנֵי יִשְׂרָאֵל מֵאֶרֶץ מִצְרָיִם. וַיִּקַּח מֹשֶׁה אֶת עַצְמוֹת יוֹסֵף עִמּוֹ כִּי הַשְׁבֵּעַ הִשְׁבִּיעַ אֶת בְּנֵי יִשְׂרָאֵל לֵאמֹר פָּקֹד יִפְקֹד אֱלֹהִים אֶתְכֶם וְהַעֲלִיתֶם אֶת עַצְמֹתַי מִזֶּה אִתְּכֶם.

Joseph's bones.

It's true – this is the last thing Joseph said before he died, at the very end of the Book of Genesis: Take my bones with you. *(Gen. 50:25)*

But why make special mention of the bones now? And why is it Moses, of all people, who goes and gets them? Doesn't he have better things to do at this particular moment? Shouldn't he be leading the people out of Egypt? Surely they can find someone else to do the bone-carrying!

Over in his commentary on a verse Book of Proverbs *(10:8)* that describes the "wise-hearted one, who takes up the commandments," **Rashi** sees an allusion to Moses:

While the rest of Israel was busy looting Egypt, Our Teacher Moses was attending to sacred obligations – as it says, *"and Moses took the bones of Joseph…" (Exod. 13:19)*

משה רבינו שכל ישראל היו עוסקין בביזת מצרים והוא היה עוסק במצות שנאמר ויקח משה את עצמות יוסף וגו' (שמות י״ג:י״ט)

Now, Rashi is quoting from one of the most amazing rabbinic stories ever written, and we're going to spend our time this week tracing through it. It appears in at least six collections of Midrash, with slight variations, but the version we're going to quote appears in the Talmud, Tractate Sotah (*13a*). It starts off with these same praises of Moses, but the story is really more about how Moses found the bones to begin with.

And the first part of that answer involves a mysterious old woman:

How did Moses know where Joseph was buried? They say that Serach bat Asher was the only one who remained from that generation, and Moses went to ask her, "Do you have any idea where Joseph is buried?"

ומנין היה יודע משה רבינו היכן יוסף קבור אמרו סרח בת אשר נשתיירה מאותו הדור הלך משה אצלה אמר לה כלום את יודעת היכן יוסף קבור

Serach bat Asher is surely one of the most fascinating figures in rabbinic literature. She first appears back in the book of Genesis, in the list of Jacob's family members who went down to Egypt – the only granddaughter mentioned. But then, in the book of Numbers, there is a census taken of all those who escaped Egypt, and Serach appears again, in the midst of a long list of names, with a separate verse all to herself:

The name of Asher's daughter was Serach. *(Num. 26:46)*

וְשֵׁם בַּת אָשֵׁר שָׂרַח.

That's over two hundred years later! So the rabbis do the math, and figure something supernatural is going on with this woman. Serach begins to take on the legend of an immortal. She never dies, and appears again and again in their stories at critical moments to deliver important messages. She was the one who first told Jacob that Joseph was still alive, singing the message to him gently, so that he wouldn't have a heart attack. She was the one who first confirmed that Moses' prophecy was legitimate. She is even reported to have appeared to the rabbis themselves, over a thousand years later.

So the first thing we learn about the search for Joseph's bones is that Moses had to consult a wise elder. Now what did she tell him?

She said, "The Egyptians made a metal casket for him, and sunk it into the Nile, so that its waters would be blessed by him."

אמרה לו ארון של מתכת עשו לו מצרים וקבעוהו בנילוס הנהר כדי שיתברכו מימיו.

That sounds like bad news for Moses! The bones are encased in iron, at the bottom of the Nile. And there's no time to spare. Moses will never get them out! So what did he do?

Moses went and stood on the bank of the Nile and shouted out, "Joseph! Joseph! The time has come about which the Holy One swore, "I will redeem you." And so it is time to fulfill the oath you imposed on Israel. If you will show yourself, well and good! If not, we are hereby released from your oath.

הלך משה ועמד על שפת נילוס אמר לו יוסף יוסף הגיע העת שנשבע הקב"ה שאני גואל אתכם, והגיעה השבועה שהשבעת את ישראל. אם אתה מראה עצמך מוטב אם לאו הרי אנו מנוקין משבועתך.

Imagine the silence of the water, flowing along, the absurdity of Moses' declaration echoing through the air. Far away, in the background, is the rumbling of a slave revolution underway. And here stands the leader of that revolution, all alone, speaking his desperate demands into thin air.

Moses, just go already! It's hopeless! It's okay, there's no way to fulfill this dying wish, and it's not that important anyway. There's an entire nation that needs you now. Get out of here!

Still, he stands there.

And then... a great rumbling...

And suddenly, Joseph's casket shot up and floated to the top!

מיד צף ארונו של יוסף.

And Moses grabbed it and ran. The oath would be fulfilled. Joseph was finally going to leave Egypt.

It's an incredible tale, full of magic and suspense. High drama, worthy of a Hollywood blockbuster.

But still, we might ask: Why? What's the big deal? Why does the Torah, and then the Talmud, go through all of this trouble to highlight the story of Joseph's bones? What is so significant about them in the larger context of the Exodus story?

The Talmud has a kind of answer, just a bit further down on the same page:

All those years that Israel was in the desert, there were two arks – one with the dead body and one with the Divine Presence [hovering over the tablets]. They proceeded side by side. And passersby would ask, 'What is in these things?' And they would be told, 'One has a dead body in it, and one has the Divine Presence hovering over it.' And they would ask, 'But is it right for the dead to proceed alongside the Divine Presence?!' And they would be told, 'This one, [Joseph], fulfilled everything written by this One – [God].''

וכל אותן שנים שהיו ישראל במדבר היו שני ארונות הללו אחד של מת ואחד של שכינה מהלכין זה עם זה והיו עוברין ושבין אומרים מה טיבן של שני ארונות הללו אמרו אחד של מת ואחד של שכינה. וכי מה דרכו של מת להלך עם שכינה? אמרו קיים זה כל מה שכתוב בזה.

These aren't just bones, the Talmud is saying. And Joseph isn't just a dead body. Joseph led a life of righteousness which was the very embodiment of the Divine Will. So his bones are as sacred to us as the very Tablets of the Covenant.

But more than that, this second ark is a reminder that death is as much a part of this story as is life. The purpose of the Exodus is to release the forces of life – the liberation that will allow former slaves to live fully in the world as free people. But this freedom has not been achieved without death along the way. The death of our ancestors. The death of those slaves who never made it out. The death of the children drowned in the Nile.

So while we celebrate life, we honor death, and we never forget those who have come before us. They are as much a part of our story as we are.

This is what Moses was modeling for the Children of Israel. While they were preparing to leave, looking forward into the future, Moses was looking backward, into their past. It's not that Moses was so busy with his own personal obsession that he was too distracted to lead the Israelites out of Egypt. This was his way of leading them. He showed the people not only where to go, but where they had been.

For there is no future that does not emerge out of the past. There are no children without parents, and no parents without grandparents. There is no life without death.

*

For all of Moses' efforts, however, when Joseph's bones finally make it into the ground, at the end of the Book of Joshua, Moses himself goes unmentioned:

The bones of Joseph, which the Children of Israel brought up from Egypt, were buried at Shechem, in the piece of ground that Jacob had purchased... ***(Joshua 24:32)***

וְאֶת עַצְמוֹת יוֹסֵף אֲשֶׁר הֶעֱלוּ בְנֵי יִשְׂרָאֵל מִמִּצְרַיִם קָבְרוּ בִשְׁכֶם בְּחֶלְקַת הַשָּׂדֶה אֲשֶׁר קָנָה יַעֲקֹב...

The "Children of Israel" brought them up? What about Moses?! *He's* the one that brought them up. He's the one that went to all the trouble to get them!

But then, Moses never made it into the Land of Israel. He died before he could bury the bones. So it was the Israelites who actually completed the fulfillment of Joseph's oath. Rabbi Hama bar Hanina, in the Talmud, reflects on this transfer as follows:

When one person does something, but does not finish it, and another comes along and finishes it, that second person is described as having done it themselves.

כל העושה דבר ולא גמרו ובא אחר וגמרו מעלה עליו הכתוב על שגמרו כאילו עשאו.

When Moses met his own death, the Children of Israel took Joseph's bones from him, and kept moving forward. And they buried those bones in land purchased by Jacob, Joseph's father. Everyone played a part. Everyone carried their share of the journey.

It is worth noting here that the word for "bones" in Hebrew, *atzamot* (עצמות), is spelled the same as the word for "essence," *atzmut*. And the words are related – getting to the "essence" of something is like getting "down to the bone." So was it really bones Moses took out of Egypt? Or was it Joseph's essence he passed along?

Then we took from Moses the essence of Joseph – which itself was infused with the essence of Jacob and Rachel, and the essence of Isaac and Rebecca, and the essence of Abraham and Sarah. And we took with us the essence of Moses as well. We carried all of them with us when we left. Inside of us. In our blood, in our bones.

We are all walking around with the bones of Joseph. One day, we, too, will hand them over.

CHAPTER 17

TO BREAK OPEN THE EAR – Parshat Yitro

Nobody reads the Torah literally.

Some may claim they do – that every word of the Torah is to be understood exactly as it is written. But they don't really believe that. What they are really trying to say is that they accept the basic claims of the Torah, no matter how metaphysically bold: that God created the world in seven days, split the Red Sea, and revealed the Law on Mount Sinai. Those things, yes, many people do believe.

But nobody actually believes that every word of the Torah is literally true. That is, quite simply, because the Torah, like any great piece of writing, employs the language of simile, metaphor, idiom, and personification. We recognize these devices when we come across them, and we intuitively switch to a figurative mode of reading. So, for example, when we read that God took us out of Egypt, "with a mighty hand" *(Deut. 26:8)*, no serious interpreter has ever suggested that God has an actual, five-fingered hand. Or when God promised Abraham "I am a shield to you" *(Gen. 15:1)*, no one thought that God would become a protective piece of metal, or even some invisible force field of defense. We know that these are just ways of saying that God is mighty and that God will protect us.

So, too, in this week's *parsha*, as the Revelation at Mount Sinai is about to begin, we know not to take things too literally when we read that:

Mount Sinai was all in smoke, for the Eternal had come down upon it in fire, and the smoke rose like the smoke of a furnace (כעשן הכבשן), and the whole mountain trembled greatly. ***(Exod. 19:18)***

וְהַר סִינַי עָשַׁן כֻּלּוֹ מִפְּנֵי אֲשֶׁר יָרַד עָלָיו ה' בָּאֵשׁ וַיַּעַל עֲשָׁנוֹ כְּעֶשֶׁן הַכִּבְשָׁן וַיֶּחֱרַד כָּל הָהָר מְאֹד.

Now there we have a "simile," a standard figure of speech used to compare one thing to another, different thing. The smoke rose *like* the smoke of a furnace. That doesn't mean it *was* the smoke of a furnace. That seems pretty obvious, right? You don't really need that explained to you.

Well, **Rashi** seems to think that you do. Here's his (rather extended) commentary on this verse:

Could it really have been just like a furnace, and nothing more?! Rather, we learn later *(in Deuteronomy Ch. 4)* that *"the mountain was burning with a fire up to the heart of the heavens."* So then why did the Torah say, *"like a furnace"*? It was in order to break open the ear with something it can hear, the Torah gives people an image they recognize.

Similarly, *(in Hosea Ch. 11)*, it says, *"[God] will roar like a lion!"* Who but God gave strength to the lion in the first place! Yet the Torah compares God to a lion? Rather, we compare and liken God to God's creatures in order to break open the ear with something it can hear.

And similarly again, *(in Ezekiel Ch. 43)*, *"[God's] voice is like the sound of many waters."* Who but God gave waters sound in the first place! Yet you identify God by likening God to God's creation, in order to break open the ear.

יכול ככבשן זה ולא יותר, ת"ל בוער באש עד לב השמים (**דברים ד'**), ומה ת"ל כבשן? לשבר את האזן מה שהיא יכולה לשמע, נותן לבריות סימן הנכר להם.

כיוצא בו כאריה ישאג (**הושע י"א**), וכי מי נתן כח בארי אלא הוא? והכתוב מושלו כאריה, אלא אנו מכנין ומדמין אותו לבריותיו כדי לשבר את האזן מה שיכולה לשמע.

כיוצא בו וקולו כקול מים רבים (**יחזקאל מ"ג**), וכי מי נתן קול למים אלא הוא? ואתה מכנה אותו, לדמותו לבריותיו, כדי לשבר את האזן.

Very carefully, Rashi explains to us that the mountain wasn't really smoking like a furnace. We know from a later verse that the flames were much greater than that, and that this verse is just using a figure of speech to help us enter into the scene. We are being given a simple image, one we can easily grasp, in order to begin to understand the basic idea of what's really happening. As he puts it, "to break open the ear with something it can hear."

In other words, Rashi is taking this opportunity to explain to us the way a simile works, and to make it painstakingly clear that the Torah sometimes uses this kind of linguistic device to communicate ideas. Then, if that weren't enough, he goes on and gives two more examples of this technique in action: God roars like a lion, but God's not really a lion; God sounds like rushing water, but God's not really water!

Okay, thank you for the grammar lesson, Rashi. We get it. The Torah sometimes uses poetic or colloquial language, and we shouldn't take these images at face value. In fact, there is a well-known phrase in Jewish literature for this concept: דיברה תורה כלשון בני אדם – "The Torah speaks in the language of people."

So why is he telling us this now? Why is this the moment he chooses to break down the concept of metaphorical speech? If we really needed this clarification, there have been so many other places in the Torah where Rashi might have jumped in to provide it. In fact, one of the most glaring examples came just a bit earlier in this very same chapter, when God says to Moses:

You have seen what I did to Egypt, and that I carried you on the wings of eagles and brought you to Me. ***(Exod. 19:4)***

אַתֶּם רְאִיתֶם אֲשֶׁר עָשִׂיתִי לְמִצְרָיִם וָאֶשָּׂא אֶתְכֶם עַל כַּנְפֵי נְשָׁרִים וָאָבִא אֶתְכֶם אֵלָי.

On the wings of eagles? I don't remember seeing any eagles during the Exodus! And why did God use a team of eagles to carry us out of Egypt when we could have just walked?!

But of course, this, too, is just a figure of speech. The idea is that God brought us out swiftly and majestically, *as if* we soared out on the wings of an eagle. It's just a metaphor. And yet there, Rashi doesn't feel the need to elucidate the concept of figurative language.

So why now? To understand that, take note of what else is happening in our furnace verse. The mountain was in smoke, we read, because:

...the Eternal had come down upon it in fire...

יָרַד עָלָיו ה' בָּאֵשׁ

And two verses later, again we read this remarkable image:

The Eternal descended upon Mount Sinai, down to the top of the mountain... ***(Exod. 19:20)***

וַיֵּרֶד ה' עַל הַר סִינַי אֶל רֹאשׁ הָהָר

This is the real wonder! Not that the mountain was on fire, but that God Almighty somehow came down from the heavens and appeared on the top of a mountain. This is, in fact, the most audacious claim in all of the Torah – more than the creation of the universe, more than the plagues and miracles. The idea that the Infinite and Incomprehensible God manifested in some tangible way here on earth – was perched on a mountain-top, for all to see – this contradicts everything we believe about God. In fact, it contradicts the very first thing God will say on that very mountain: *"I am the Lord your God... you shall not make any image or picture [of Me]."* And yet here, in the Torah, in this very moment, is an image of that God! God came down onto the mountain? It's heresy!

But wait. This, too, is just a figure of speech, isn't it? God didn't really come down to earth, like some kind of gigantic spaceship. Rashi jumps in again, to make sure we don't get the wrong idea:

Could it be that [God] really "descended"? Rather, we read further on that, *"From the heavens I spoke to you..." (Exod. 20:19)*

יכול ירד עליו ממש, ת"ל כי מן השמים דברתי עמכם (שמות כ')...

Again, Rashi is incredulous at the possibility of a literal reading. And again he proves from a later verse that we cannot understand this image exactly as it is written. Just as the mountain wasn't really a furnace, so God is not really sitting there on top of it.

And that is why Rashi picks the description of a furnace as the moment to stop and remind us that the Torah speaks in the language of human beings, that these images are chosen to "break open our ears" and make the scene come alive for us, but that we cannot understand them straightforwardly. The stakes are high for Rashi in these verses. If we don't notice the usage of metaphor early on, then we are in danger of understanding the whole revelation as a simple matter of a big sky god who has flown down to say hello to the creatures on the ground. That is not Rashi's theology, it is not consistent with the Torah's own theology, and it must be severely guarded against – even at the risk of overstating the case. So, just to be clear, God is NOT a lion, God is NOT the rushing waters, and God does NOT come down onto mountains. Just as the mountain is NOT a furnace.

*

So that explains the "why now?" But there still remains the question of "why this?" That is, once we understand that Torah indeed speaks figuratively, the more interesting question is: Why does the Torah choose this particular image to describe the moment of revelation? Why does the Torah describe the mountain as smoking "like a furnace"? What is it about the furnace, and how is it meant to "break our ears open"?

One way to search for an answer is to look for the other places where this word is used. And it turns out that in the whole Bible, outside of the Book of Exodus, there is only one other place where the word appears: back in the Book of Genesis, in the aftermath of the destruction of Sodom and Gomorrah. Those two cities were notoriously wicked, and God had decided to wipe them out. But before God does this, God shares the fate of Sodom and Gomorrah with Abraham, who famously pleads with God to spare them. That seems not to work, and the destruction is carried out, in fire and brimstone. Everything in the cities is annihilated. And when it's all over, we read this:

Abraham got up the next morning, and went to the place where he had stood before the Lord, and, looking down toward Sodom and Gomorrah and all the land of the plain, he saw smoke rising up from the land like the smoke of a furnace. *(Gen. 19:27-28)*

וַיַּשְׁכֵּם אַבְרָהָם בַּבֹּקֶר אֶל הַמָּקוֹם אֲשֶׁר עָמַד שָׁם אֶת פְּנֵי ה'. וַיַּשְׁקֵף עַל פְּנֵי סְדֹם וַעֲמֹרָה וְעַל כָּל פְּנֵי אֶרֶץ הַכִּכָּר וַיַּרְא וְהִנֵּה עָלָה קִיטֹר הָאָרֶץ כְּקִיטֹר הַכִּבְשָׁן.

The smoke of the furnace here is a sign of devastation, the eerie remains of a city in ashes. The furnace, in its very first usage, becomes fixed in our imagination as a haunting image, a symbol of destruction. What, then, does it mean when that image is evoked once again at Mount Sinai, at the moment of revelation?

Some connection is being forged between this appearance of God and that earlier, terrifying one. There is something about revelation that is akin to destruction, something about encountering the presence of God – even in its most glorious form – that is so overwhelming, it threatens to annihilate one's very being.

The connection between Sinai and Sodom is even more pronounced when we remember that there, too, God "descended" to the earth:

The Lord said, "The outcry of Sodom and Gomorrah is so great, and their sin so grave! I will go down to see whether they have acted according to the outcry that has reached me. If not, I will take note." *(Gen. 18:20-21)*

וַיֹּאמֶר ה' זַעֲקַת סְדֹם וַעֲמֹרָה כִּי רָבָּה וְחַטָּאתָם כִּי כָבְדָה מְאֹד. אֵרְדָה נָּא וְאֶרְאֶה הַכְּצַעֲקָתָהּ הַבָּאָה אֵלַי עָשׂוּ כָּלָה וְאִם לֹא אֵדָעָה.

I will go down. I will descend. I will see. Does God really do all these things? Does God really descend to earth? Does God really reveal Godself?

Does God really destroy?

By now we know the answer to these questions. Yes, and no. Yes, but in a way that we cannot possibly comprehend. So we use these words, this language, because they are the only tools we have to describe something indescribable: Revelation.

We will speak of a mountain on fire. We will speak of a God who came down upon it. We will even tell you what God said to us. But you must know that we cannot ever really describe what it was like.

It was magnificent. But it was terrifying. It was sublime. But it was devastating. We wanted more. But we couldn't handle it.

When we saw the thunder and lightning, the blast of the horn, and the mountain smoking, we fell back and stood at a distance. And we said to Moses:

You speak to us, and we will obey. But let not God speak to us, lest we die. ***(Exod. 20:16)***

וַיֹּאמְרוּ אֶל מֹשֶׁה דַּבֵּר אַתָּה עִמָּנוּ וְנִשְׁמָעָה וְאַל יְדַבֵּר עִמָּנוּ אֱלֹהִים פֶּן נָמוּת.

We saw the mountain on fire and we thought we would die, would be incinerated, like ashes in a furnace.

We did not die. But we were broken open, revealed, by the words of revelation.

CHAPTER 18

WITCH HUNTING – Parshat Mishpatim

Wandering through a dense forest of laws, we come upon a witch.

Parshat Mishpatim, sometimes referred to as the 'Covenant Code,' is a long list of laws given to Moses directly after the revelation at Mount Sinai. Unlike the grand moral statements of the Ten Commandments, these are mostly nitty-gritty case laws meant to regulate a well-functioning civil society. So we have, for example: laws governing marital obligations, restitution for physical assault, punishments for theft, and fines for various forms of damage – including the oft-cited case of one ox goring another ox. These are the sorts of classic cases first-year students still study in law schools today.

And then, out of nowhere, comes a pronouncement that reads more like a sign on the road to a haunted house:

Do not let a witch live! ***(Exod. 22:17)***

מְכַשֵּׁפָה לֹא תְחַיֶּה!

A witch? I didn't think Jews even believed in witches – and now we have to kill them?! This eerie command seems out of place in a body of laws meant to guide basic social conduct. What is it doing here?

If the appearance of witches in the Torah wasn't surprising enough in itself, there are some other oddities in this verse. For though in the Hebrew it is only three words long, at least two of them are unusually phrased:

1. A *makhshefa* is specially a *woman* who practices witchcraft. But why does the verse focus only on female witches? A man can be a witch, too – and in fact, when the prohibition against witchcraft is repeated in Deuteronomy *(18:10)*, the verse there mentions a male witch, a *mekhashef*. Frankly, as a matter of grammar, Hebrew defaults to the male noun form as a base; so if our witch is a woman, it is pointedly so. Why?

2. Then, we are told *lo tichayeh* (לא תחיה) – "do not let her live." That is not the typical way that the Torah invokes the death penalty. We would

have expected it to say *tumat* (תומת), "she shall be put to death." In fact, the *very next verse* – a prohibition against bestiality – takes exactly that form: the perpetrator, "shall be put to death." So why, with our witch, is the verse phrased in the negative: "do *not* let her live"?

Let's try to answer the first question first. Why specifically a female witch? It is true that witches are almost always female in the popular imagination. But is that an assumption that the Torah carries as well? **Rashi** seems to think so. He writes:

***Do not let a witch live* – ...this could refer to male or female witches. But the verse speaks as things usually are, and women are more often engaged in witchcraft.**

מכשפה לא תחיה – ...ואחד זכרים ואחד נקבות, אלא שדבר הכתוב בהווה, שהנשים מצויות מכשפות.

So Rashi notes that the verse deliberately chose the case of a female witch, but he assumes – like most literature and movies on the subject – that this is simply because witches are almost always women.

The trouble with that answer is that in the literature of the Hebrew Bible, this does not seem to be the case. In fact, the only people actually named as witches in the Torah and the later books of the prophets and writings – are men! Pharaoh has a team of *"wise men and witches"* whom he summons to combat Moses and Aaron *(Exod. 7:11).* Nebuchadnezzar, in the Book of Daniel *(2:2)*, also turns to *"sorcerers, magicians, and witches"* to interpret his dreams. All of these figures are male.

It is true that Queen Jezebel, a generally wicked character, is accused of practicing, *"much witchcraft," (II Kings 9:22)*, but it would be a stretch to call her "a witch," and we certainly have no record of her conjuring.

The only woman in the Tanakh who actually seems to engage in forbidden divinations – though she is never explicitly called a witch – appears in a strange story in the Book of Samuel.

King Saul, we are told there, had outlawed all manner of sorcery and witchcraft, in accordance with the laws in the Torah. But now he finds himself in a terrible dilemma, battling both David and the Philistines, and he has no idea how to proceed. So he calls on his men to, *"Find me a woman who is a master of spirits, so that I can go to her and seek answers through her."* Saul now wants to commune with the very forces he has outlawed. But he knows that if he shows up as himself, she will think it is a test of her fidelity to the law and refuse to perform her services. So, he puts on a disguise, goes to her door, and says:

"Please conjure me up a spirit. Bring up for me the one I will name to you." But the woman answered him: "You know what Saul has done, how he has banned consultation with spirits and ghosts throughout the land! So why are you laying a trap for me, to get me killed?" But Saul swore to her by the Eternal, "As the Eternal lives, you will not get into trouble over this." And so the woman asked, "Whom shall I bring up for you…?" ***(I Sam. 28:8-11)***

קָסֳמִי נָא לִי בָּאוֹב וְהַעֲלִי לִי אֵת אֲשֶׁר אֹמַר אֵלָיִךְ. וַתֹּאמֶר הָאִשָּׁה: אֵלָיו הִנֵּה אַתָּה יָדַעְתָּ אֵת אֲשֶׁר־עָשָׂה שָׁאוּל אֲשֶׁר הִכְרִית אֶת הָאֹבוֹת וְאֶת הַיִּדְּעֹנִי מִן הָאָרֶץ. וְלָמָה אַתָּה מִתְנַקֵּשׁ בְּנַפְשִׁי לַהֲמִיתֵנִי? וַיִּשָּׁבַע לָהּ שָׁאוּל בַּה׳ לֵאמֹר חַי ה׳ אִם יִקְּרֵךְ עָוֹן בַּדָּבָר הַזֶּה. וַתֹּאמֶר הָאִשָּׁה: אֶת מִי אַעֲלֶה לָּךְ...?

What a strange story! At first Saul seems to actively promote the ban against witchcraft, and even – judging from the woman's fear – to impose the death penalty for it. But when he *personally* wants to make use of a witch, he hides his identity and goes off to do it in secret. It is *she* who resists and cites the law. But he reassures her, promising the protection of his power, and coaxes her into using the dark arts. He is both the condemner and the consumer of witchcraft.

If this is the only Biblical example we have of actual female witchcraft, how can it be reconciled with our original law in the Torah? Is King Saul a faithful follower of that commandment, or does he secretly disregard its validity? Or is he just a hypocrite – moralizing to everyone else, but willing to bend the rules for himself?

This confusing story seems to have brought us no closer to answering our question about why the Torah speaks of witches in the feminine – not to mention why it was so concerned with witches to begin with.

The key to understanding all of this, I believe, can be found in a clue from the brilliant commentary of the **Ibn Ezra** on our verse in Exodus. He writes:

The reason for mentioning [the Case of the Witch] after the Case of the Virgin is that those who lust after [young women] will use witchcraft to seek fulfillment of their desires.

טעם להזכיר זה אחר הבתולה כי המתאוים יתאוו דרך כשפים למלאת תאוותם והזכיר הנקבה כי היא הנמצאת בכשוף יותר מן הזכרים

The Ibn Ezra tries to see the witch law in the context of its neighboring cases, and he reminds us that the one just previous speaks of a man who seduces an unmarried young virgin. So he presumes there is some relationship between the two cases.

What is remarkable here, however, is the way the Ibn Ezra draws a link between coercive male sexual desire and the attempt to engage women in covert acts of sorcery. In both cases, it is men who attempt to draw women into dangerous acts of transgression, flaunting social norms that they might publicly affirm, in order to fulfill their own personal, private needs.

The King Saul case, then, becomes a perfect illustration of how this kind of abuse of social power might work. A man institutes a public prohibition, condemning women who practice some illicit act. Then, the same man solicits that very act from a woman, thereby drawing her into a vulnerable situation where she might suffer degradation or even violence.

The Torah includes the prohibition on witchcraft, then, along with the case of the seduced virgin, not so much out of an anxiety around occultism, but as one of a series of cases that illustrate the way men lure women into illicit, secret agreements, even as they might publicly condemn such behavior. That explains the Torah's choice to describe the witch as female.

It also helps us makes sense of the other linguistic oddity in the verse: the wording of the command to, "not let her live," rather than to, "put her to death." For if the verse is speaking to men in positions of social power, the primary concern is not so much with the punishment of the women who practice witchcraft as it is with the men who, like Saul, call it forth, and thus "let it live." The Torah is calling out the hypocrisy of a society of men who would openly denounce certain kinds of behavior, but are in fact the very reason such practices exist.

If these men truly wish to live in a society without witchcraft, then rather than going out and hunting down the sins of others, they ought to work on controlling the spirits within themselves that give these forces life.

CHAPTER 19

STRUCTURAL INTEGRITY - Parshat Terumah

Where did they get all that lumber?

That's what everyone wants to know as this week's parsha opens with the commandment to build the Tabernacle – the portable altar the Israelites carried through the desert – and specifically states that they are to build it with "acacia wood." That applies to the ark, its poles, the table, and to the outer structure of the Tabernacle itself. They're going to need a lot of wood! But where will they get it? They're in the desert, after all.

That's exactly what our chief medieval commentator, **Rashi**, asks; and his answer is, as usual, particularly inventive:

Acacia Trees **– Where did they get them in the desert?! Rabbi Tanchuma explained: Our Father Jacob foresaw, through the holy spirit, that in the future Israel would need to build a Tabernacle in the desert. So he brought acacia trees to Egypt and planted them. And he commanded his children to take them with them when they left Egypt.**

ועצי שטים – ומאין היו להם במדבר? פרש רבי תנחומא: יעקב אבינו צפה ברוח הקדש שעתידין ישראל לבנות משכן במדבר, והביא ארזים למצרים ונטעם, וצוה לבניו לטלם עמהם כשיצאו ממצרים.

Well. That is very fortunate indeed. Jacob could see into the future, it seems. And so he began preparing, hundreds of years in advance, for the eventual journey through the desert. These trees were first hauled from the land of Canaan down to Egypt, replanted there, and then chopped down and hauled out of Egypt during the Exodus and dragged through the desert for miles – just for this very special purpose!

And mind you, this was no small load. Later in our *parsha*, we read that:

You shall make the planks for the Tabernacle of acacia wood, upright. The length of each plank shall be ten cubits, and the width of each plank a cubit and a half. ***(Exod. 26:15-16)***

וְעָשִׂיתָ אֶת הַקְּרָשִׁים לַמִּשְׁכָּן עֲצֵי שִׁטִּים עֹמְדִים. עֶשֶׂר אַמּוֹת אֹרֶךְ הַקָּרֶשׁ וְאַמָּה וַחֲצִי הָאַמָּה רֹחַב הַקֶּרֶשׁ הָאֶחָד.

A Biblical cubit is roughly two feet, so we're talking about tree trunks at least 20 feet long and 3 feet in diameter. And then the Torah tells us that there will be a total of 48 planks. And that's just the wood for the outer structure! So imagine them pulling over 50 of these massive trees behind them as they flee Egypt, cross the Red Sea, and gather around Mount Sinai – all because they had a tradition, passed down from Jacob, that one day they were going to need this!

Now, if you think that sounds just a little too far-fetched to be plausible, you're in good company. The great **Ibn Ezra**, our second go-to medieval commentator, takes issue with the tradition Rashi is recording. Along with the unbelievable effort it would have required, the Ibn Ezra sees another problem with this epic hauling project:

Look, the Egyptians thought that they were just going to sacrifice to their God, and would then return. That is why they lent them supplies. But how would they take out huge planks, each one 10 cubits long, along with poles, and then pass through Egypt, the place of their rulers? What would their answer be to those who asked, 'Why are you bringing those acacia trees?' when they were only supposed to be going to worship for three days?

הנה המצרים חושבים כי לזבוח הם הולכים ואחר כך ישובו ועל כן השאילום ואיך יוציאו קרשים רבים אורך כל א' מהם עשר אמות גם בריחים והם עברו על מצרים מקום המלוכה ומה היתה תשובה לשואליהם למה יוליכו עצי שטים והם הולכים לזבוח דרך שלשת ימים.

Ibn Ezra is raising a narrative discrepancy. When the Israelites were leaving Egypt, the last thing they had told the Egyptians was that they were only going for three days, to worship their God *(Exod. 8:23)*. Then presumably, they would return. But if they were really only going on a short, three-day trip, well, then what did they need all this lumber for? That would have looked awfully suspicious.

So Ibn Ezra doesn't like that answer. But he isn't overly quick to throw it out. This idea of Jacob foreseeing the enslavement and the Exodus, and preparing for the journey in advance – this is a story recorded in the tradition, by Rashi and by Rabbi Tanchuma before him. And the very existence of this story in Jewish lore, is itself worthy of consideration.

So while Ibn Ezra ultimately prefers a different explanation, he prefaces it with a caveat:

And really, we do not know. If there was a '*kabbalah,*' a received tradition, carried down from our forefathers, that they took [these trees] out from Egypt, then we, too, must defer to that interpretation. But if this was a '*svara,*' an attempt to make sense of the text through reasoning, then we may seek an alternative understanding. And then we would say that right near Mount Sinai, there must have been a forest of acacia trees.

והנה לא ידענו אם קבלה היתה היא ביד אבותינו שממצרים הוציאום גם אנחנו נסור אל משמעתם. ואם סברא היא יש לבקש דרך אחרת. ונאמר כי היה סמוך אל הר סיני יער עצי שטים.

In this short reflection, we get an incredible insight into the Ibn Ezra's theory of *parshanut*. When we look at these stories in the Bible, do we read them as they have been traditionally understood, or do we look at them fresh, and try to make sense of them ourselves? Well, that depends. The tradition is always a starting point, and if it seems to be very well-established, perhaps even an unbroken link to the original tellers of the story, then we accept it. But if we believe that the tradition we have been handed down is, in itself, a record of our ancestors struggling to figure out how to make sense of the story, then we, too, are entitled to engage in that struggle, and to come up with our own – perhaps unique – understanding.

This is a tension that exists in religion generally. We are always weighing the authority of tradition against the need for innovation and creativity. We expect religion to preserve the wisdom of the past, the sacred stories and rituals we have inherited from ancient times. But we also know that a religion that cannot evolve to meet the needs and insights of the future will lose its vitality and relevance. Religion must always be looking backwards and forwards for answers.

Remarkably, that is just where Rashi and Ibn Ezra, respectively, have found their answers to the question at hand. Where did the Children of Israel get the wood for the Tabernacle? Rashi says they brought it with them from Egypt, and before that from their homeland. They carried it with them because they had a tradition that linked them back to their forefather Jacob. The Ibn Ezra says that they discovered a new forest in the midst of their journey forward. They found what they needed along the way. Indeed, these trees awaited them at the foot of Mount Sinai, the place of new revelation.

And of course – though it cannot logically be so – both Rashi and Ibn Ezra are right. For this wood will be used to construct the Tabernacle, the structure which dares to contain the presence of God. How is such a thing possible? How do we encounter the intangible, ineffable, mysterious God here in this physical time and space? Do we rely on the wisdom of our sacred traditions, or do we seek out new forms of revelation and discovery?

We must have both. We will need the strength of the past and the resilience of the future if this structure is to hold. This wood must bend, but it cannot break.

CHAPTER 20
THE EYE OF THE BEHOLDER – Parshat Tetzaveh

Do Jews value beauty?

Wisdom, we love. Justice, certainly. Holiness, for sure. But what about beauty?

"Beauty is emptiness," said King Solomon, in the Book of Proverbs *(31:30)*.

Emptiness! Pretty harsh words there, from the wisest of all men. But they do reflect a certain Jewish uneasiness with the kind of aesthetic beauty that is celebrated in so many other cultures.

Now, maybe that's not so surprising. This is, after all, the religion whose second commandment warns against making, *"an image of anything in the heavens above, or on the earth below." (Exod. 20:4)*. So maybe that prohibition against religious iconography filters down into a general mistrust of artistic expression. And likewise, maybe the worship of a God with no physical form tends to produce a devaluing of physical beauty.

There is, however, one place in the Torah where beauty takes center stage. And that is in this week's Torah portion, *Tetzaveh*. The entire first chapter of the reading is devoted to describing, in great detail, the garments of the High Priest. And the Torah makes it very clear that these clothes are to be beautiful:

"Make holy garments for your brother Aaron," says one of the opening verses, "for honor and for beauty." That phrase is then repeated, at the end of the chapter, as if for emphasis: "for honor and for beauty."

And these clothes are beautiful indeed. The kind of clothes fit for royalty. A golden robe. A turban on the Priest's head and a sash around his waist. He wears a jewel-studded breastplate. There are even little bells and pomegranates stitched all around the hem. This is the section of the Torah written for fashion designers.

Here, in the service of God, beauty is okay. Not just okay – required! And not just plain beauty – but ornate, lavish, radiant beauty! This is supposed to be the most awe-inspiring beauty imaginable.

On Yom Kippur, there is a song in our prayers called *"Mareh Kohen,"* – literally, "The Sight of the Priest" – that describes just how awesome it was to see the High Priest come out of the Temple on Yom Kippur:

Like the canopy of the heavens, stretched out on high…

like a rainbow that appears in the clouds…

like a rose planted in a garden of delight… was the appearance of the Priest.

Truly, how radiant was the High Priest, when he emerged from the Holy of Holies.

כאהל הנמתח בדרי מעלה...
כדמות הקשת בתוך הענן ...
כורד הנתון בתוך גינת חמד – מראה כהן
אמת מה נהדר היה כהן גדול בצאתו מבית קדשי הקדשים

Now *that* is a tribute to beauty! To rich, extravagant, *physical* beauty. So we *do* have a place for this value in Jewish tradition.

But it is contained.

All of this ornate beauty is reserved for one man, performing one job, in one place. And the song that celebrates the sight of this man is referring to a rare glimpse that is possible only once a year. Beauty is bound to the Temple, used only in the service of God, and generally hidden from the eyes of the world. In fact, the Talmud rules explicitly *(in Yoma 69a)* that it was forbidden for the High Priest to leave the Temple with the priestly garments on. He never took this beauty outside.

Except once.

That same section of the Talmud continues with a story of one exception, a day when the Samaritans were petitioning Alexander the Great for permission to destroy the Temple in Jerusalem. He eventually agreed, and so the Jews went and informed Shimon the Righteous, the High Priest at the time. And then Shimon did something quite dramatic:

He put on his priestly garments, wrapped himself in all the ornaments of the High Priest. Some of the noblemen of Israel went with him, carrying fiery torches in their hands. They walked all night, some on one side of him, some on the other, until the dawn rose.

When the dawn rose [and Alexander saw them], he asked, "Who are they?" They answered, "These are the Jews who have rebelled against

you." He went out to the City of Antipatris, and he met them, just as the sun began to shine.

When he saw Shimon the Righteous, he got down from his chariot and bowed before him. They said to him, "Does a great king like yourself bow down before this Jew?"

He said to them, "It is his image that wins all my battles for me."

לבש בגדי כהונה ונתעטף בבגדי כהונה ומיקירי ישראל עמו ואבוקות של אור בידיהן וכל הלילה הללו הולכים מצד זה והללו הולכים מצד זה עד שעלה עמוד השחר כיון שעלה עמוד השחר אמר להם מי הללו אמרו לו יהודים שמרדו בך כיון שהגיע לאנטיפטרס זרחה חמה ופגעו זה בזה כיון שראה לשמעון הצדיק ירד ממרכבתו והשתחוה לפניו אמרו לו מלך גדול כמותך ישתחוה ליהודי זה אמר להם דמות דיוקנו של זה מנצחת לפני בבית מלחמתי

And so the Jews were saved. Hooray! The beauty of the High Priest won the day.

But what exactly happened here? Why was Alexander so impressed with the vision of the High Priest, and what did he mean that this image won his battles for him?

The story seems to suggest that supernatural forces were at play. Perhaps God planted this image in Alexander's head, a kind of mysterious sign, for just this occasion. And Shimon the Righteous somehow knew this, and knew exactly what to do to save the Jews. Read this way, the story is about God's direct intervention to save God's chosen people – a triumph of Judaism over its enemies.

But if we think of the image of the High Priest as the ultimate Jewish symbol of beauty, and remember that ancient Greece was famous for its celebration of beauty, perhaps this story can be read differently. For Alexander, after all, was the great representative of the Greeks. Did he see, in the beauty of Shimon the Righteous, something that reminded him of a value from his own world, something that symbolized the glory of Greece?

And perhaps it was even more than just beauty. We know that, in his youth, Alexander was tutored by the philosopher Aristotle. And Aristotle famously saw a relationship between beauty and virtue, suggesting that ethical behavior was a way of striving toward true beauty. So if Alexander had that connection in his mind, perhaps what he bowed before was not merely Shimon's beautiful image, but also his Righteousness, and the harmony between the two.

If that is true, then this moment was not the triumph of one culture over another, but a real meeting of two cultures, one in which there was a moment of reflection and recognition.

To reach this moment, each side had to make a concession. Each one defies the standards of their own traditions. Alexander, the mighty king, prostrates himself before Shimon the Righteous. Shimon, meanwhile, violates the law against taking the priestly clothing out of the Temple in order to go meet Alexander where he was.

The Talmud remains quite puzzled by Shimon's decision. How could he have done such a thing?! How did he justify taking the law into his own hands, and making this exception?

But actually, this is not the only place in the Talmud where an exception is made for an encounter with something Greek. The Talmud (*Megilah 9a*) rules that the only language other than Hebrew that the Torah can be written in is Greek. And why does Greek merit this special exception?

The proof comes from a seemingly random verse in the story of Noah, in which he blessed two of his sons saying that, *"Yefet will dwell in the tents of Shem."* Yefet is understood to be a progenitor of Greece, and Shem is understood to be the ancient ancestor of Israel. So, says Rabbi Yochanan, this means that the words of Greece are allowed into the tents (or, study halls) of Israel.

But the name, *Yefet*, also means, "beauty." So Rabbi Chiya bar Abba adds this final thought to the discussion:

***"He will dwell in the tents of Shem,"* meaning that the beauty of Yefet will be in the tents of Shem. (*Talmud, Megilah 9b*)**

יפת אלהים ליפת יפיותו של יפת יהא באהלי שם

In other words, the beauty of Greece will be – *should* be – brought into the heart of Israel.

If Alexander could see and respect what was virtuous in Jewish culture, we likewise recognized and admired the quality of beauty so magnificently perfected in Greek culture. And just as Shimon the Righteous would make an exception to bring our beauty outside, to be seen by Alexander, so do we seek to bring the beauty of Greece inside – into our holiest tents, into our Torah itself.

So do Jews value beauty? Yes, indeed. We may be suspicious of it – worried that it can be superficial or fleeting. We may insist that it be bound up in righteousness. But when do we see this kind of true beauty, we admire it. And perhaps we even want to *be* admired for it. And that requires an encounter.

So Solomon may have questioned beauty in the Book of Proverbs. But that same Solomon is also credited with the Song of Songs, which has in it this interchange between two lovers:

Ah, you are beautiful, my love. Ah, you are beautiful, with your eyes like doves.

הִנָּךְ יָפָה רַעְיָתִי הִנָּךְ יָפָה עֵינַיִךְ יוֹנִים.

Ah, but *you* are beautiful, my beloved, and pleasant. And the soft grass is our bed. *(1:16)*

עַרְשֵׂנוּ רַעֲנָנָה. הִנְּךָ יָפֶה דוֹדִי אַף נָעִים אַף

To be beautiful, one must be seen. To be seen, we need the eyes of the other.

CHAPTER 21

BREAKING THE LAW – Parshat Ki Tisa

Every so often, roaming through the world of *parshanut*, we come across a piece of commentary so startling, so profound, and so complex, that it demands our full attention for the week. This is such a week, and the piece in question comes from one of the great works of Torah commentary of the 20th century, the **Meshekh Chokhmah**, by Rabbi Meir Simcha of Dvinsk, Latvia.

This collection of novellae on the Torah, published posthumously by one of Rabbi Meir Simcha's students, is known for its long discursions into legal or philosophical matters. But the author of the Meshekh Chokhmah is also distinguished by his willingness to offer entirely novel interpretations of classic scenes from the Torah. Occasionally, he is able to reread just one verse in such a way that it completely shifts our understanding of a whole chapter.

That is the case with his commentary on the following verse from this week's parsha:

As soon as Moses came near the camp and saw the calf and the dancing, he became enraged, and he hurled the tablets from his hands and shattered them at the foot of the mountain. ***(Exod. 32:19)***

וַיְהִי כַּאֲשֶׁר קָרַב אֶל הַמַּחֲנֶה וַיַּרְא אֶת הָעֵגֶל וּמְחֹלֹת וַיִּחַר אַף מֹשֶׁה וַיַּשְׁלֵךְ מִיָּדָיו אֶת הַלֻּחֹת וַיְשַׁבֵּר אֹתָם תַּחַת הָהָר.

This famous image of the breaking of the tablets takes place as Moses descends from Mount Sinai after a forty-day communion with God, only to find that the people have built a golden calf – transgressing the very commandment against idolatry now inscribed by God upon those tablets. Moses was warned by God that this was happening, but the sight of it is just too much for him; he flies into a rage and smashes the tablets to the ground.

But how could Moses have done such a thing?

The sin of the people was great, to be sure, but here he was not merely punishing them – he was destroying a sacred object, the work of God's own hands. How dare Moses presume the authority to shatter this precious testament to God's commandments? Or perhaps he simply lost his temper, and wasn't thinking clearly. But then, what does that say about the character of our greatest leader?

The commentators do their best to explain these difficulties away. Some say that Moses received approval from God to destroy the tablets, while others suggest that he was simply so startled by what he saw that he simply dropped them.

But the Meshekh Chokhmah has a very different answer. He begins with what appears to be a tangential theological point:

The idea here is that Torah and Faith are the essential principles of the nation of Israel, and all the holiness of the Land of Israel, and of Jerusalem, etc. For these are all just particulars and extensions of the Torah, and are made holy only through the holiness of the Torah. Because of this, in matters of Torah, there are no differences based on time or place – it is the same whether one is in Israel or outside of the Land. Nor does it matter whether one is the most exalted person, like Moses, the Man of God, or the lowest of the low – for anyone who transgresses the commandments of God, there is one law for all, even down to the lowliest.

הענין, כי התורה והאמונה המה עיקרי האומה הישראלית וכל הקדושות א"י וירושלים כו' המה פרטי וסניפי התורה ונתקדשו בקדושת התורה, ולכך אין חילוק לכל עניני התורה בין במקום בין בזמן והיא שוה בא"י ובחו"ל. וכן הוא שוה בין לאדם הגבוה שבגבוהים, משה איש האלהים להשפל שבשפלים.

This is a lovely statement of equality under the law. It almost reads like a description of modern democracy. The main takeaway here, however, seems to be that Moses is no greater than any other Israelite, and the Meshekh Chokhmah builds on this point as he pivots into our story in Exodus. He writes:

Moses was only the middleman for the Torah, but the Torah was not essentially connected to his being… But when they saw that Moses was taking so long to come down, they lost their faith and so they sought to make the calf, in order to bring a spirit from above down upon this sculpture…

ומשה לא קראו התורה רק סרסור, אבל אין התיחסות התורה לו... והמה כאשר ראו כי בושש משה נפלו מאמונתם ובקשו לעשות להם עגל ולהוריד על הצורה ההיא רוח ממעל...

The people, the Meshekh Chokhmah is implying, believed Moses to be endowed with a unique holiness, such that the word of God could only come from him. So when Moses delayed in returning, they panicked, fearing their only connection to God had been lost. They built the Golden Calf, according to this logic, not as a thing to be worshipped in itself, but as an object of holiness that might summon the Divine down upon it. Their crime did not begin with the Golden Calf, then, but was already present in their distorted understanding of Moses. And once Moses understood this, writes the Meshekh Chokhmah, he cried out:

"Did you think that I had any holiness without God's command, so that when my presence was gone, you made this calf?! God forbid! I am just a man like you! The Torah is not dependent on me, and even if I had never come, the Torah would have its own existence, without any change, God forbid... So do not think that the Sanctuary or the Tabernacle themselves are holy things, God forbid. Through them the Holy Blessed One dwells among His children, but if they transgressed the covenant, all holiness would be removed from them. These things are mere vessels... And even more so, the tablets, with the writing of God – these too have no holiness in themselves, but only for your sake.

האם תדמו כי אני ענין ואיזו קדושה בלתי מצות ד', עד כי בהעדר כבודי עשיתם לכם עגל, חלילה גם אני איש כמוכם, והתורה אינה תלויה בי, ואף אם לא באתי היתה התורה במציאותה בלי שנוי חלילה... ואל תדמו כי המקדש והמשכן המה ענינים קדושים בעצמם, חלילה, השי"ת שורה בתוך בניו, ואם המה כאדם עברו ברית, הוסר מהם כל הקדושה והמה ככלי חול... ויותר מזה הלוחות מכתב אלהים, גם המה אינם קדושים בעצם רק בשבילכם.

Here we begin to get an understanding of what might have prompted the breaking of the tablets. Moses realized that if his absence created a religious crisis, and if the people tried to fill that void with a golden statue, then they were likely to attribute divinity to any physical representation of God – including the Tabernacle, the Land of Israel, and especially... the tablets.

And that is why, *as soon as Moses came near the camp and saw the calf and the dancing*, he understood their error, and *he became enraged*; and he hurled the tablets from his hands, in order to declare that there was no holiness or divinity at all apart from the being of the Creator, of Blessed Name. And if he were to bring them the tablets, they would have simply exchanged the calf for the tablet, and would not have corrected their error.

וזהו ויהי כאשר קרב אל המחנה וירא את העגל ומחולות הבין טעותן ויחר אף משה וישלך מידיו את הלוחות, ר"ל כי אין שום קדושה וענין אלקי כלל בלעדי מציאות הבורא ית"ש, ואם הביא הלוחות היו כמחלפים עגל בלוח ולא סרו מטעותן.

As soon as Moses handed over these rocks, which had been touched by the hand of the Lord, they would become the new idols. The people would place the tablets in the Ark and then come to worship at the Tabernacle – not just God, but the tablets themselves. For what they really wanted was a representation of God they could touch and see.

It is an understandable impulse, perfectly human, to seek a physical manifestation of one's spiritual beliefs. Yet that is precisely the impulse that the Torah intends to counteract, argues the Meshekh Chokhmah. The message of the Torah is that no object has inherent holiness, for the only true holiness comes from God, and God is beyond all physicality or representation.

And so Moses *had* to break the tablets, in order to show the people, "Look, these are just rocks! They have no meaning other than the one God gives to them. If you do not understand that, you are not ready for them." Moses did not break the tablets out of mere rage, but in order to teach the people a profound spiritual lesson – that religion itself can become an object of idolatry.

The implications of the Meshekh Chokhmah's interpretation are potentially quite devastating for many of our traditional assumptions. They directly undermine the sanctity of any material aspect of Judaism: *places* – like Israel, or Jerusalem, or the Cave of the Patriarchs; *people* – like Moses, or the Arizal, or the Ba'al Shem Tov; or *objects* – like the tablets, or a *lulav,* or a *mezuzah.* All of these things are, in the language of the Meshekh Chokhmah, mere vessels, with no holiness of their own.

*

One wonders, however, just how accurate this theory of Torah is. The Meshekh Chokhmah wrote earlier, for example, that the principles of the Torah operate irrespective of time and place – *"it is the same whether one is in Israel or outside of the Land."* Yet that seems to belie the many agricultural laws in the Torah that are specifically designed for settlement in Israel. And in fact, the Meshekh Chokhmah later adds a rather significant amendment, in brackets:

[except for those commandments which are tied to the land]

[לבד מצות התלוים בארץ]

Well, yes. Except for those.

Israel is, after all, described by the prophet Zechariah as, *"the holy land." (2:16)*

And there are holy people mentioned in the Torah as well. Israel is to be *"a holy nation." (Exod. 19:6)* The High Priest wears a golden sign on his forehead designating him as *"holy to the Lord." (Exod. 29:1)* Later in the Hebrew Bible, Elisha is described as *"a holy man of God." (II Kings 4:9)*

As for holy objects, we need look no further than our own *parsha* for vessels that seem to be imbued with holiness. Just two chapters earlier, we read:

You shall anoint the Tent of Meeting, the Ark of the Covenant, the table and all its utensils, the lampstand and all its fittings, the altar of incense, the altar of burnt offering and all its utensils, and the laver and its stand. You shall sanctify them and they will be most holy; whatever touches them will also become holy. ***(Exod. 30:26-29)***

וּמָשַׁחְתָּ בוֹ אֶת אֹהֶל מוֹעֵד וְאֵת אֲרוֹן הָעֵדֻת. וְאֶת הַשֻּׁלְחָן וְאֶת כָּל כֵּלָיו וְאֶת הַמְּנֹרָה וְאֶת כֵּלֶיהָ וְאֵת מִזְבַּח הַקְּטֹרֶת. וְאֶת מִזְבַּח הָעֹלָה וְאֶת כָּל כֵּלָיו וְאֶת הַכִּיֹּר וְאֶת כַּנּוֹ. וְקִדַּשְׁתָּ אֹתָם וְהָיוּ קֹדֶשׁ קָדָשִׁים כָּל הַנֹּגֵעַ בָּהֶם יִקְדָּשׁ.

Not only are these items holy, but whatever touches them becomes holy as well! Now that certainly sounds like the holiness has become attached to the object itself.

Of course, the Meshekh Chokhmah would likely respond: it is simply because God deemed these things holy that they are so, and if they can transmit that holiness, then that, too, is simply by the command of God. There is, again, no holiness that exists independently of God.

It is a powerful position, and certainly has a great deal of truth to it. Yet one cannot help but feel that the Meshekh Chokhmah is sometimes reaching a bit too far, sometimes willfully ignoring things that are right in front of him.

In other words, this theory of Torah, in its most extreme formulation, doesn't always fit the words of the Torah itself. Rather, the Torah has to be to be selectively quoted, and intentionally interpreted, in such a way as to fit the true message of the Torah – at least as the Meshekh Chokhmah understands it.

In that way, the Meshekh Chokhmah is not so different from his own vision of Moses. He is breaking the actual Torah apart, in order to make a higher point about the *purpose* of Torah. He wants us to be able to receive the Torah in its purest form, and to do that, he will have to shatter some of our basic understandings of the actual Torah we have before us.

You can't make a Torah, it seems, without breaking some tablets.

CHAPTER 22

AN INVISIBLE PALACE - Parshat Vayakhel

There is something hidden in the Tabernacle.

Nechama Leibowitz, the great 20th century compiler of Torah commentary, in her essay, "A sanctuary for Me to dwell in," calls our attention to a group of modern scholars who sensitized us to the use of repetition as a rhetorical device in the description of the building of the Tabernacle. She cites a list of some of the greats: "Buber, Rosenzweig, Benno Jacob, Cassuto, Meir Weiss and others," who all highlight the way key phrases in our text echo an earlier story in the Torah – the earliest, in fact.

It is the famous Jewish philosopher **Martin Buber** – also a fine Biblical scholar – who is credited with "discovering" the striking parallels between the language of the Tabernacle instructions and the story of Creation. He lays it out magnificently for us and, though it requires some rearranging, the resemblance is undeniable. Listen:

Creation:

And God saw all that God had made, and behold, it was very good. And it was morning, and it was evening, one day. And the heavens and the earth **were finished**, and all their array. On the **seventh day**, **God finished God's work,** which God had made, and God rested on the seventh day. **And God blessed** the seventh day, and **sanctified** it. *(Gen. 1:31-2:3)*

וַיַּרְא אֱלֹהִים אֶת כָּל אֲשֶׁר עָשָׂה, וְהִנֵּה טוֹב מְאֹד. וַיְהִי עֶרֶב וַיְהִי בֹקֶר יוֹם הַשִּׁשִּׁי. **וַיְכֻלּוּ** הַשָּׁמַיִם וְהָאָרֶץ, וְכָל-צְבָאָם. **וַיְכַל אֱלֹהִים בַּיּוֹם הַשְּׁבִיעִי מְלַאכְתּוֹ** אֲשֶׁר עָשָׂה. וַיִּשְׁבֹּת בַּיּוֹם הַשְּׁבִיעִי מִכָּל מְלַאכְתּוֹ אֲשֶׁר עָשָׂה. **וַיְבָרֶךְ אֱלֹהִים** אֶת יוֹם הַשְּׁבִיעִי **וַיְקַדֵּשׁ** אֹתוֹ.

Tabernacle:

And Moses saw all of the work, and behold, they had **made** it just as the Lord had commanded... *(Exod. 39:43)* And all the labor of the Tabernacle **was finished**... *(39:32)* And on the **seventh day**, God called out to Moses from within the cloud... *(24:16)* **And Moses finished the work...** *(40:33)* **And Moses blessed** them... *(39:43)* Make me a **sanctuary**, and I will dwell among you. *(25:8)*

וַיַּרְא מֹשֶׁה אֶת **כָּל הַמְּלָאכָה וְהִנֵּה** עָשׂוּ אֹתָהּ כַּאֲשֶׁר צִוָּה ה' כֵּן עָשׂוּ... **וַתֵּכֶל** כָּל עֲבֹדַת מִשְׁכַּן... וַיִּקְרָא אֶל מֹשֶׁה **בַּיּוֹם הַשְּׁבִיעִי** מִתּוֹךְ הֶעָנָן... **וַיְכַל מֹשֶׁה אֶת הַמְּלָאכָה... וַיְבָרֶךְ אֹתָם מֹשֶׁה**... וְעָשׂוּ לִי **מִקְדָּשׁ** וְשָׁכַנְתִּי בְּתוֹכָם.

The reverberation is stunning, and the message of this parallelism seems easy enough to extrapolate. As Nechama Leibowitz puts it:

The Lord created heaven and earth and all therein for man to dwell in, and created them in six days and rested on the seventh day. Similarly, Moses was summoned on the seventh day to the cloud to see the pattern of the Tabernacle that it was his duty to erect, in order to provide a place on earth for the Divine Presence. *(Leibowitz, Studies in Shemot, Terumah 2)*

God made a home for us on earth, so now we make a home for God on earth. Buber's excavation of the symmetry embedded in the text through modern literary technique appears to us like a revelation.

But if Ecclesiastes is right that there is "nothing new under the sun," then we should not be surprised to find that the rabbis of the midrashic period had already spotted much of this pattern, many centuries earlier. Here is a version we find in the *Midrash Tanchuma* on *Parshat Pekudei*:

Rabbi Yaakov said in the name of Rabbi Asi, why does it say *(in Psalms 26:8), "Lord, I loved your House and abode, the dwelling place of your glory"?* Because it is being equated with the creation of the world. How so...? On the seventh day, *"the heavens and the earth were finished."* And with the Tabernacle it is written, *"And all the labor was finished."* With the creation of the world, it is written, *"And God Blessed."* And with the Tabernacle, it is written, *"And Moses blessed them." (Tanchuma, Pikudei 11:2)*

אמר רבי יעקב ברבי אסי, למה הוא אומר, ה' אהבתי מעון ביתך ומקום משכן כבודך (תהלים כו ח), בשביל ששקול כנגד בריאת עולם. כיצד....בשביעי, ויכולו השמים והארץ. ובמשכן כתיב, ותכל כל עבודת. בבריאת העולם כתיב, ויברך אלהים. ובמשכן כתיב, ויברך אותם משה.

There you have it – the very same references, suggesting the very same comparison, picked up hundreds of years earlier by the ancient rabbis, whose keen literary eyes were never sleeping.

And they didn't stop there. For there was one other primary link between Creation and Construction that they wanted to establish. That is, they noticed that, over the course of the chapters that detail the building of the Tabernacle, the observance of the Sabbath day is mentioned twice: once back in *Parshat Ki Tisa* (Ch. 31), and again this week in *Parshat Vayakhel*. Here is how our *parsha* begins:

Moses gathered together the whole community of the Children of Israel and said to them, "These are the things that the Lord has commanded you to do: On six days you shall do all your work, and on the seventh day you shall have a sabbath of complete rest, holy to the Lord; whoever does work on it shall be put to death." ***(Exod. 35:1-2)***

וַיַּקְהֵל מֹשֶׁה, אֶת כָּל עֲדַת בְּנֵי יִשְׂרָאֵל וַיֹּאמֶר אֲלֵהֶם. אֵלֶּה הַדְּבָרִים אֲשֶׁר צִוָּה ה', לַעֲשֹׂת אֹתָם. שֵׁשֶׁת יָמִים תֵּעָשֶׂה מְלָאכָה וּבַיּוֹם הַשְּׁבִיעִי יִהְיֶה לָכֶם קֹדֶשׁ שַׁבַּת שַׁבָּתוֹן לַה'. כָּל הָעֹשֶׂה בוֹ מְלָאכָה יוּמָת.

What did the rabbis make of this abrupt insertion of the commandment to keep the Sabbath, just before the final description of the Tabernacle? Surely this can be fit into the framework of the other creation parallels we have seen so far. The Sabbath is the culmination of Creation, after all – the time to stop and reflect on the work that has been done, and to refresh.

But the rabbis went further than just observing these thematic parallels. In their discussion of laws of the Sabbath in the Talmud, this passage above, from *Parshat Vayakhel*, contains the very phrase they use as the source for the 39 categories of prohibited work. The derivation is based on an intricate bit of play with the words, *"These are the things..."*:

It was taught, Rebbe [Yehudah HaNasi] said *"things"* counts for 2, *"the things"* makes it 3, and [the letters in the Hebrew word for] "these" has the numerical value of 36 – so *"these are the things"* is a hint for the 39 forbidden labors that Moses was told on Mount Sinai. ***(Babylonian Talmud, Shabbat 97b)***

והתניא רבי אומר דברים הדברים אלה הדברים אלו ל״ט מלאכות שנאמרו למשה בסיני

The interpretive method here is rather extreme. The rabbis see the phrase, *"These are the things that the Lord has commanded you to do,"* and in order to figure out what and how many of those things there are (or to confirm the number they already have), they give themselves permission to count up the words in the sentence, and then even the numerical value of the Hebrew letters in the word for "these," following the numerological tradition of *'gematria.'* With all those rules in place, they arrive at the number 39 – so 39 forbidden labors.

Add to that the use of the word *melakha* (מלאכה), 'work,' as both the term for that which is forbidden on the Sabbath, and for that which is required to build the Tabernacle, and we soon come to the conclusion that the work that is to be forbidden on the Sabbath is precisely those 39 categories of work which were required in the Tabernacle. That is, after all, precisely what God rested from on that first seventh day: all the work that God had done (כָּל מְלַאכְתּוֹ אֲשֶׁר עָשָׂה).

The parallel between the Sabbath and the Sanctuary slowly becomes clear. We engage in work to build the Tabernacle, and then we refrain from just that work when it is completed – and then, as promised, God dwells among us. This mirrors the way that God engaged in work to build the world and then refrained from that work when it was completed. And the name for that completion was "Shabbat" – the Sabbath day. And so, it turns out that this Tabernacle, the thing we have been building now for five weeks of *parshot*, is in fact the Sabbath herself. It is she who will be the Eternal Sanctuary, in which both God and Israel shall dwell.

The Tabernacle was to be temporary, after all, only lasting through the desert journey. And even the Temple turned out to be temporary – for physical buildings can always be destroyed. But the Sabbath is to carry us through time.

These links forged with the words of the Torah – first, broadly, between the creation of the world and the building of the Tabernacle, and then, specifically, between the Sabbath and the completion of the Tabernacle – lend new force to Abraham Joshua Heschel's famous phrasing in his book, *'The Sabbath'*:

The seventh day is a *palace in time* which we build. *(p. 15)*

He may have meant that poetically, but now we are able to understand it literally. We actually *build* ourselves a Sabbath; at least, we did so once. For it was not enough to create a sanctuary in space for God to dwell in, as God had once done for us. We then had to finish all the work we had done, to step back and see it completed, and then to rest and be refreshed on the seventh day – as God also once did.

And so we build and complete this palace in time again, anew, every week. We bless it with the light of our candles, and sanctify it with wine. And though our structure is invisible to the naked eye, we who sit within it know that God dwells there among us.

CHAPTER 23

ROOM FOR ONE MORE – Parshat Pikudei

God has entered the building.

We are at the end of the Book of Exodus, and we've spent the last five weeks – nearly half the book – reading about the construction of the Tabernacle. The purpose of building this portable sanctuary, God said at the outset, was *"so that I may dwell among them." (Exod. 25:8)* But now that it's all done, and God finally comes and "dwells," there doesn't seem to be any room for any of "them."

When Moses had finished the work, the cloud covered the Tent of Meeting and the Glory of God filled the Tabernacle. And Moses could not enter the Tent of Meeting, because the cloud was dwelling upon it, and the Glory of God filled the Tabernacle. *(Exod. 40:34-35)*

וַיְכַס הֶעָנָן אֶת אֹהֶל מוֹעֵד וּכְבוֹד ה׳ מָלֵא אֶת הַמִּשְׁכָּן. וְלֹא יָכֹל מֹשֶׁה לָבוֹא אֶל אֹהֶל מוֹעֵד כִּי שָׁכַן עָלָיו הֶעָנָן וּכְבוֹד ה׳ מָלֵא אֶת הַמִּשְׁכָּן.

This scene feels somehow climactic and anti-climactic, all at once. On the one hand – there's God! We did the impossible – we brought the very presence of God down to earth, and contained it in a physical space. Nothing could be more amazing.

But on the other hand... Moses is stuck outside. The presence of God is so overwhelming, so filling, that there's no room for anyone else in there. What was the point of inviting God down among us, if there is no way to actually encounter God?

And yet, we know, from many other places in the Torah, that Moses does encounter God, and seems to exist in the same space. In fact, he even manages to squeeze his way into this very Tent of Meeting that at the moment seems so bursting full. **Rashi** quickly points this out:

Moses could not come into the Tent...* – But another verse (in Numbers Ch. 7) says *"When Moses would come into the Tent of Meeting."

ולא יכל משה לבוא אל אהל מועד — וכתוב אחד אומר ובבא משה אל אהל מועד (במדבר ז').

So what does it mean here when we read that the Presence of God filled the Tabernacle? And if that is what God's presence does, then how does Moses eventually find a way in?

The commentators give many answers to these questions, but there is one approach in particular that ends up laying the ground for a whole new form of Jewish theology: The Doctrine of Tzimtzum.

The Hebrew word *tzimtzum* (צמצום) means "contraction," and that motion – contracting – will eventually become very important for answering some gigantic theological questions. But first, let's see how the term appears in one answer to the question of how God gets into the Tabernacle, from Rashi's grandson, Rabbi Samuel ben Meir (or, the '**Rashbam**'). He notes that this same problem, of God's presence making it impossible for anyone else to enter into a space, reappears once the great Temple is built in Jerusalem, centuries later:

And so we find in the permanent Temple: "And the priests were not able to remain and perform their service because of the cloud, for the glory of God filled the House of God." (I Kings 8:11). For at the completion of the Temple, God would sanctify it with a cloud, and then God would contract His presence upon the Ark between the poles.

וכן אתה מוצא בבית עולמים: ולא יכלו הכהנים לעמוד לשרת מפני הענן כי מלא כבוד ה' את בית ה' בשעת השלמת הבית היה הקב"ה מקדשו בענן ואחר כך היה מצמצם שכינתו על הארון בין הבדים.

In fact, the Rashbam is drawing from an earlier expression of this idea in the *Midrash Tanchuma*, where (I believe) it first appears:

Even though the verse is written, *"the glory of God filled the tabernacle,"* even so, praise Him upon the Earth and in the Heavens. And do not say only that God *tzimtzem* (contracted) His divine presence into the Tabernacle. But even into the ark that Bezalel made did He contract His presence, as it says *(Joshua 3:11)*, *"Here is the Ark of the Covenant, the Master of all the Earth."* This is God, who was in it. *(Tanchuma, Vayakhel 7)*

אף על פי שכתוב וכבוד ה' מלא את המשכן (**שמות מ, לד**), אף על פי כן, הודו על ארץ ושמים (**תהלים קמח, יג**). ולא תאמר, שצמצם הקדוש ברוך הוא שכינתו בתוך

המשכן, אלא אף בתוך הארון שעשה בצלאל, צמצם שכינתו, שנאמר: הנה ארון הברית אדון כל הארץ (יהושע ג, יא), זה הקדוש ברוך הוא שהיה בתוכו.

So how does the infinite and intangible and God enter into physical space? God contracts Godself, somehow concentrating imperceptible godliness into a perceptible presence. I won't pretend to know what that means, or how physical a phenomenon it is meant to suggest. But the point is that this idea of a godly contraction begins, in Jewish literature, here with the Tabernacle.

But then the concept is repurposed, about a thousand years later, by the towering giant of Jewish mysticism, Rabbi Yitzchak Luria – or, the 'Arizal' – in order to address a difficult theological problem. The question is, if God is infinite, and then God created the world, where exactly did this happen? That is, once there was nothing but God. Then, there was something else. So where did that something else go? How was there any space that wasn't God?

This may sound like a ridiculous line of inquiry, an example of the kind of absurd, hair-splitting theoretical logic that gives theologians a bad reputation. But at its core is an important basic question: are we a part of God, or is God a separate being? Jewish theology seems to suggest both, in different ways. On the one hand, God is Infinite – the supreme force that controls everything, and from which everything comes forth. But on the other hand, God is the Wholly Other, the exalted and transcendent Being that we call out to from afar. So which is it? Did God create a world that was separate from God, or is our sense of separateness just an illusion, and is everything we know just a part of God?

Here is the Arizal's attempt to answer the question, as written down by his chief student, Rabbi Chayim Vital. And I'm going to quote it in full, even though it is dense and confusing, because it represents such a watershed moment in Jewish theology:

Know that before emanations were produced and creatures were created, there was a simple supernal light that filled all existence; and there was no empty space, like a vacuum, but all of existence was filled with a simple, infinite light. It had no aspect of beginning or end; rather all was one simple light equally distributed, and this is called the light of the *Ayn Sof*, The Infinite One. Then, when it arose in God's simple will to create worlds and produce emanations, to bring to light the completion of acts, names, and designations – which is the cause of the creation of the worlds – the *Ayn Sof* then concentrated Itself in the central point, and there in the actual center of that light, God concentrated the light

and removed it on all sides from around the central point. Then there was an empty space, a complete vacuum, from that actual central point. Now, this contraction (*tzimtzum*) was equal all around that central, empty point, in such a manner that that empty space was a circle completely equidistant all around. Now, after this contraction, there remained a completely empty vacuum in the middle of the actual light of the *Ayn Sof*, and there was now a space in which the things to be emanated, created, formed, and made could exist. *(Etz Chayim 1:1)*

דע, כי טרם שנאצלו הנאצלים ונבראו הנבראים, היה אור עליון פשוט ממלא את כל המציאות. ולא היה שום מקום פנוי בבחינת אויר ריקני וחלל, אלא הכל היה מלא אור האין סוף הפשוט ההוא. ולא היה לו לא בחינת ראש ולא בחינת סוף, אלא הכל היה אור אחד פשוט שוה בהשואה אחת, והוא הנקרא "אור אין סוף".וכאשר עלה ברצונו הפשוט לברוא את העולמות ולהאציל את הנאצלים, להוציא לאור שלמות פעולותיו, שמותיו וכינוייו, שהיתה זאת סבת בריאת העולמות. הנה אז צמצם את עצמו אין סוף בנקודה האמצעית, אשר בו באמצע ממש, וצמצם את האור ההוא, והתרחק אל סביבות צדדי הנקודה האמצעית. ואז נשאר מקום פנוי, אויר וחלל ריקני מהנקודה האמצעית ממש. והנה הצמצום הזה היה בהשואה אחת בסביבות הנקודה האמצעית הריקנית ההיא. באופן שמקום החלל ההוא היה עגול מכל סביבותיו בהשואה גמורה. והנה אחר הצמצום, אשר אז נשאר מקום החלל והאויר פנוי וריקני באמצע אור האין סוף ממש, הנה כבר היה מקום, שיוכלו שם להיות הנאצלים, והנבראים, והיצורים, והנעשים.

In that space, said the Arizal, the world we know was created. The process he is describing takes place before creation story that begins the Torah, and indeed allows for it to happen. If not for the empty space in the "middle of God," so to speak, there would have been no place for the world to exist.

Note that this dilemma is the same one we were struggling with above on a smaller scale. When God enters the Tabernacle, there is no space for anyone else to enter. Moses cannot "exist" in the Tent, because the presence of God fills it so completely.

In the cosmology of the Arizal, this problem is solved by God contracting Godself, hollowing out a place in the middle to make room for something else. He uses that same language of *tzimtzum* – contraction – that we saw above. But here there is a significant difference: God is contracting outward, in order to vacate space, rather than contracting inward (as we saw in the Rashbam and the Midrash), in order to enter the space of the Tabernacle. In the Arizal's *tzimtzum*, God becomes more absent, rather than more present.

Now this image took powerful hold in Jewish thought, and eventually became the dominant theology in rabbinic Judaism. But it also soon produced a debate so fierce that the two sides actually began to regard one another as heretics. The debate revolved around the question of how literally to take the picture of God's contraction, and the removing of God from the world. And again, the importance of this comes down to the question of whether or not our world is separate from God, or a part of God.

On one side, there were those that took the Arizal to mean that God was completely transcendent, unfathomably apart from us. God had contracted Godself outward, after all. In order for the world to exist, God had to leave this space, and now was truly gone – unreachable and unknowable.

The only contact we could have with God was through some attempt on God's part to bridge the great chasm of separation, temporarily, such as at the Revelation at Mount Sinai or – perhaps now – through the Tabernacle. But aside from these brief encounters with God, which were themselves really only pale traces of God's true existence, we were, by our very nature, forever disconnected from God.

On the other side of this debate, however, were those who held that we could not take the image of God's contraction literally – including any spatial language. God had not been removed from any real "place" in existence – such a thing was impossible, for God cannot be described in terms of physical space.

Instead, the idea of the *tzimtzum* was a metaphor for the concealment of God that must take place in order for us to perceive ourselves as separate beings. God had not actually contracted Godself away; rather, the contraction represented a kind of hiding of the true reality, which can never change – that all is really God.

This second school of thought, then, claimed that those who misunderstood the metaphorical nature of the *tzimtzum* had made two serious theological mistakes: 1.) They had taken the contraction to be a physical phenomenon, and thereby ascribed physicality to God. 2.) They were implying there could be a limit to God's Infinity.

Here is the foremost representative of the metaphorical doctrine of the *tzimtzum*, Rabbi Schneur Zalman of Lyadi (or, the '*Ba'al HaTanya*'), the founder of the Chabad Hassidic movement:

We must understand the error of some, scholars in their own eyes, may God forgive them, who erred and misinterpreted in their study of the writings of the Arizal, and understood the doctrine of Tzimtzum literally – that the Holy Blessed One, removed Himself and His Essence, God

forbid, from this world, and only guides from above with individual Providence all the created beings which are in the heavens above and on the earth below. Now it is altogether impossible to interpret the doctrine of Tzimtzum literally, for then it is a phenomenon of corporeality... *(Shaar HaYichud ve-HaEmunah Chapter 7)*

והנה מכאן יש להבין שגגת מקצת חכמים בעיניהם, ה' יכפר בעדם ששגו וטעו בעיונם בכתבי האריז"ל, והבינו ענין הצמצום המוזכר שם כפשוטו שהקב"ה סילק עצמו ומהותו חס ושלום מעולם הזה רק שמשגיח מלמעלה בהשגחה פרטית על כל היצורים כולם אשר בשמים ממעל ועל הארץ מתחת והנה מלבד שאי אפשר כלל לומר ענין הצמצום כפשוטו, שהוא ממקרי הגוף...

If we take the idea of *tzimtzum* literally, in other words, we are treating God as if God had a body – the very definition of heresy in Jewish theology. God does not actually move, neither outward nor inward, in physical space.

And yet, Rabbi Schneur Zalman also accepts the Arizal's description of *tzimtzum* as authoritative. So how do we understand the contraction that allowed our world to come into being? Here he explains:

The fact that every creation and act appears to us to exist and have substance is only because we are unable to perceive and to see with our eyes of flesh the power of God and the breath of His mouth. But were we able to see and perceive the life force and spirituality that is in each creation which is sustained from the mouth of God and the breath of His mouth, there would be no physicality to creation or substance or reality apparent to our eyes at all. It is nullified in actuality when compared to the life and spirituality which it contains, since without this spirituality it would literally be nothing and naught like before the six days of creation...Hence, there is truly nothing besides God. *(Shaar HaYichud ve-HaEmunah Chapter 3)*

ומה שכל נברא ונפעל נראה לנו ליש וממשות זהו מחמת שאין אנו משיגים ורואים בעיני בשר את כח ה' ורוח פיו שבנברא אבל אילו ניתנה רשות לעין לראות ולהשיג את החיות ורוחניות שבכל נברא השופע בו ממוצא פי ה' ורוח פיו לא היה גשמיות הנברא וחומרו וממשו נראה כלל לעינינו כי הוא בטל במציאות ממש לגבי החיות והרוחניות שבו מאחר שמבלעדי הרוחניות, היה אין ואפס ממש כמו קודם ששת ימי בראשית ממש... אם כן אפס בלעדו באמת.

The contraction the Arizal is describing, in this formulation, was not a real contraction that took place in space and time. It is a phenomenon of consciousness, a description of the perception of separateness that must be created in order for us, as independent beings, to recognize the being of God. But in truth, there is no separation, no independence, no recognition. There is only God. And we are a part of that.

*

Now, to return back to where we started, if we read this theology back into our final scene in Exodus, we have an answer to the question of how Moses is able to eventually enter the Tabernacle which, at the moment, seems so overwhelmingly full of God. What does it mean, after all, that God has "contracted" Itself into the Tabernacle? It appears that God is especially present here, that God has taken on a physical form, and leaves no room for any other being to exist alongside it.

But contraction is just a metaphor. God cannot be "more present" here than elsewhere. For God is not absent from anywhere. God is not absent, and then present – rather, God is hidden, and then revealed. And none of this describes a physical reality, for our God is not physical. Instead, when we speak of God, we are speaking of *"the life force and spirituality that is in each creation."* And that includes us.

In this theology, we are one with God. Our separateness is just an illusion. Moses stands outside of the Tabernacle because he senses the presence of God and assumes that he is other than that presence. But in truth, Moses is a part of God – as we all are, as everything is.

All it takes, then, for Moses to enter the Tabernacle, is to awaken to the Ultimate Reality, and to realize that he is not at all separate from It. And then he can just walk right in.

III

Leviticus

CHAPTER 24
THE CALLING - Parshat Vayikra

What did Moses hear when God called out to him?

The great Jewish philosophers try to answer this question literally, some insisting that God spoke actual words and Moses heard them with his ears, while others suggest that God's "speech" was communicated silently to Moses' intellect, and only uttered in sound by Moses himself. **Maimonides**, even as he affirmed the communication between God and Moses as a fundamental Jewish belief, ultimately conceded the mysteriousness of that process:

The entire Torah reached Moses from God in a manner that is figuratively described as "speech." But no one has ever known how that took place except Moses himself, whom that speech reached. ***(Commentary on the Mishnah, Sanhedrin, Ch.10)***

שהגיעה אליו כולה מאת ה' יתברך בענין שנקרא על דרך השאלה דבור ואין ידוע היאך הגיע אלא הוא משה ע"ה שהגיע לו

The rabbis of the Midrash, however, have a different approach to the question, probing the language of the Torah itself for clues that might give us some sense of Moses' inner experience of God's voice. They are especially curious about the moment that forms the grand opening of the Book of Leviticus:

The Lord called out to Moses and spoke to him from the Tent of Meeting, saying... ***(Lev. 1:1)***

וַיִּקְרָא אֶל מֹשֶׁה וַיְדַבֵּר ה׳ אֵלָיו מֵאֹהֶל מוֹעֵד לֵאמֹר.

'Called,' 'Spoke,' 'Saying' – three words for God's voice come at us, here in this first sentence, almost all at once. But it is the 'calling' that

leads the charge, and it is from this word that Leviticus takes its Hebrew name: *vayikra* (ויקרא). And so, the rabbis wonder, what was the nature of this special call? What did Moses hear – and what should we be hearing – in it? They offer various answers, all playing on linguistic connections in order to form narrative associations.

Perhaps, suggests *Vayikra Rabbah*, this call reminded Moses of the *first* time God called out to him:

It says here, *"And the Lord called out to Moses and spoke,"* and elsewhere Iit says, "And the Lord saw that [Moses] turned to see, and God called to him from the bush, and said, 'Moses, Moses!'" *(Vayikra Rabbah 1:15)*

שנאמר (ויקרא א, א): ויקרא אל משה וידבר, להלן הוא אומר (שמות ג, ד): וירא ה' כי סר לראות וגו'.

Moses had never heard the voice of God until that day at the burning bush. He was tending a flock of sheep, out in the wilderness, when something caught his eye. He turned, *"to look at this marvelous sight"* – and suddenly, God called out to him. And what was the first word God spoke to him? His own name: Moses, Moses. As if to say, "I already know you. I've been waiting for you."

That was the day his life changed forever, the day he came to know God. And now, when God calls out to him again, by name, he remembers that first encounter. Then from the bush, now from the tent – but it is the same God, the same recognition. Everything that has happened, everything that he now is, started in that moment.

Or did it start even earlier?

The *Midrash Tanchuma* imagines that this 'calling' in Leviticus echoed back even further, not just to the first time God called Moses, but to the first time God called anything at all:

Moses was a great man. For see how it is written, "God *called* the light, 'Day.'" *(Gen. 1:5)* And here it says, "The Lord *called* out to Moses." This was a calling, and that was a calling. *(Tanchuma, Vayikra 3:1:4)*

גדול היה משה, ראה מה כתיב, ויקרא אלהים לאור יום (ברא' א ה). וכאן, ויקרא אל משה. זו קריאה וזו קריאה.

The very first creation, the light, was *called* something by God. For God does not just create. God relates to creation. When God sees something good, God names it. The light was called, 'Day,' the prophet was called 'Moses,' and when the prophet heard God calling his name, in that sound he could hear a vibration from the first calling. To hear God speak, then, is to hear the sound of the universe coming into being. And every naming contains an echo of the first naming.

But then again, as a point of narrative, God was not the one who actually named Moses. That action belongs to another character, as a final midrash points out:

The Holy Blessed One said to [Moses], "I swear by your life, that of all the names you have been called, I will only call you by the name that Bitya, the daughter of Pharaoh called you. *"She called him, 'Moses'"* *(Exod. 2:10)* [so] *"The Lord called to Moses."* *(Vayikra Rabbah 1:3)*

אמר לו הקדוש ברוך הוא למשה חייך מכל שמות שנקראו לך איני קורא אותך אלא בשם שקראתך בתיה בת פרעה (**שמות ב, י**): ותקרא שמו משה, ויקרא אל משה.

It is an astounding fact of Moses' life story that he received his name not from his own family, but from an Egyptian – and not just any Egyptian, but the daughter of the Pharaoh. And she did not just name him, she saved him from the Nile and raised him as her own. The child of the man who sought to kill Moses was to become his savior. Indeed, she became his second mother, not only in that she adopted him, but in the very real sense that she gave him life.

Bitya, the daughter of Pharaoh, like God, created a new light in a time of great darkness and – also like God – she then named what she had created. And so God, to honor her, would only call out to Moses using the name that Bitya gave him that day at the river.

So when Moses heard God calling out to him from the Tent of Meeting, somewhere deep in his consciousness he was transported back to his own first moment of being called. When he heard his name emerge from the mouth of the Almighty, he was suddenly back in his basket, drifting up amongst the reeds, by the bank of the Nile, his fate unknown.

And then, just as suddenly, he was being lifted – and held, and fed. And he was given a name. *"She called him, 'Moses,' for she said, 'I drew him up out of the water." (Exod. 2:10)* Up, out of the water, and into caring arms. He had been saved.

When God called out to Moses, it was a mother's voice he heard.

CHAPTER 25

UNDRESSED TO KILL – Parshat Tzav

It's time to get dressed.

We've been talking about the Tabernacle and the offerings for weeks now. The big inauguration ceremony is just around the corner, in next week's *parsha*. We have just finished detailing the various sacrifices that will be offered. Now that everything is in place, it's time to get the priests ready for work.

So Chapter Eight begins:

The Eternal Spoke to Moses, saying: Take Aaron, and his sons with him, and the priestly garments, the anointing oil… ***(Lev. 8:1-2)***

וַיְדַבֵּר ה' אֶל מֹשֶׁה לֵּאמֹר. קַח אֶת אַהֲרֹן וְאֶת בָּנָיו אִתּוֹ וְאֵת הַבְּגָדִים וְאֵת שֶׁמֶן הַמִּשְׁחָה...

Moses, the Master of Ceremonies, brings Aaron forward, and personally, step by step, he dresses his brother. First he washes him with water. Then he puts on the tunic, wraps the sash and ties it, overlays the robe, and ties that. He puts the breastplate on and fixes it in place. Then he begins to put his headdress on, slowly wrapping the turban, around, and around, and then setting the crown in place...

Now, at this point, the yearly reader of the Torah may be experiencing a sense of déjà vu. For there is something strangely familiar about this moment, as if we've seen it before. But no, something is different... backwards...

It isn't an earlier episode in the Torah that this passage evokes, but a later one. For this scene is the mirror image of Aaron's death.

Toward the end of the Book of Numbers, after a lot of wandering and a lot of drama, God suddenly commands Moses:

Take Aaron and his son Elazar and bring them up to Mount Hor. Strip Aaron of his garments and put them onto his son Elazar. There Aaron shall be gathered unto the dead. ***(Num. 20:25-26)***

קַח אֶת אַהֲרֹן וְאֶת אֶלְעָזָר בְּנוֹ וְהַעַל אֹתָם הֹר הָהָר. הַפְשֵׁט אֶת אַהֲרֹן אֶת בְּגָדָיו וְהִלְבַּשְׁתָּם אֶת אֶלְעָזָר בְּנוֹ וְאַהֲרֹן יֵאָסֵף וּמֵת שָׁם.

As usual, Moses does what he's told. They go up the mountain, again *"in the sight of the whole community,"* and Moses removes Aaron's priestly clothing, *"and Aaron died there on the summit of the mountain."*

What a devastating moment this must have been for Moses, not only to have to walk his brother to his death, but to be the one to physically strip him of his regal garments, leaving him to die as naked as he was born. How heavy those robes must have been, how agonizing every successive removal, as the two brothers said goodbye in silence.

But now we realize that the experience was weightier still. For Moses had done this all before, in reverse. In this final undressing, how could he not have been thinking of the day when he dressed Aaron in these same clothes, preparing him for holiness and glory? All of that honor, all of that beauty, all of the promise of that moment is over forever.

And we are invited to experience that haunting echo, together with Moses, through a linguistic connection there in the text:

In Leviticus: **Take Aaron, and his sons...** קַח אֶת אַהֲרֹן וְאֶת בָּנָיו אִתּוֹ

... and dress him up.

In Numbers: **Take Aaron, and his son...** קַח אֶת־אַהֲרֹן וְאֶת אֶלְעָזָר בְּנוֹ

...and strip him down.

The repetition of that verb, that command – *take Aaron* (קח את אהרן) – is striking. And then to follow it with the specific and unusual instruction that Moses be the one, first to robe, and then to unrobe, his brother.

The rabbis, rest assured, did not miss this connection.

In the *Sifra* – a work so classically associated with Leviticus that it's often referred to as *Torat Kohanim*, the 'Torah of the Priests,' we find this lovely reading:

And [Moses] placed the tunic upon him and tied the sash* – This teaches that Moses was Aaron's deputy. And just as he was to undress him, so he would be the one to dress him. For just as he was his deputy in life, so would he be his deputy in death, as it says, *"Take Aaron, and his son Elazar... and strip him of his vestments."

'ויתן עליו את הכתנת ויחגר אתו באבנט' – מלמד שנעשה משה סגן הכהנים לאהרן, והוא היה מפשיטו והוא היה מלבישו. וכשם שנעשה לו סגן בחייו כך נעשה לו סגן במותו שנאמר (במדבר כ, כה-כו) *'קח את אלעזר בנו...והפשט את אהרן את בגדיו'.*

Having thus sensed in this inauguration ceremony a premonition of Aaron's end, we can begin to detect other hints that, even in this moment of celebration, death was in the air. Look, for example, at the language used in the verse that describes Moses washing Aaron, just before clothing him:

Moses brought Aaron and his sons forward, and washed them in water. ***(8:6)***

וַיַּקְרֵב מֹשֶׁה אֶת אַהֲרֹן וְאֶת בָּנָיו, וַיִּרְחַץ אֹתָם בַּמָּיִם.

Brought them forward – *vayakreiv* (ויקרב) – is the same language we use for *bringing* forward offerings – *korbanot* (קרבנות) – onto the altar. Aaron then becomes, in a sense, the first offering in the Tabernacle. If that is true, then when Moses ties Aaron tight, first with one belt and then another, it is as if Aaron is being bound to the altar – just as Isaac once was. For as Aaron takes on this new role as High Priest, he is essentially offering up his life.

This is dangerous work, after all. In the very next *parsha*, we'll see two of Aaron's sons die for lighting the wrong fire in the Tabernacle. And every year on Yom Kippur, we sing about how, when the High Priest emerged from the Holy of Holies, we were elated – in large part because if anything had gone wrong, he would have died. Not to mention that the whole job is to oversee a constant stream of slaughter and sacrifice. Aaron will literally be surrounded by death.

So it is no wonder that the very moment he dons the priestly robe, it is glimmering with little flickers of ominous light, casting the foreshadows of his own death.

We, the careful readers, can pick up on these clues. But what about Aaron – did *he* sense, as he was being dressed that day, that he was beginning a march toward his own demise?

Perhaps, on some level. **Rashi** tells us that the command to *"Take Aaron"* meant:

pull him in with words – קחנו בדברים ומשכהו

In other words: convince him, talk him into it. Aaron had to be persuaded to accept the position – perhaps because some part of him knew that it was terminal.

And what about Moses? Did he know? Surely, when he led his brother up to the mountain to die, and undressed him there, he must have been reminded of that day when he dressed him up in those same clothes. But what about here, in our *parsha*? Did Moses, the greatest of prophets, already know that Aaron's death was coming?

Tradition tells us that Moses wrote the Torah, but there are various theories of how it was composed. One position, recorded in the Talmud (*Gittin 60a*) is that Moses wrote the Torah in many sittings, scroll by scroll, over the course of the story we read, transcribing his successive conversations with God, and the events of the journey. According to that theory, he can still be surprised by what happens.

But the other position is that Moses wrote the whole Torah down – or at least, heard what he was going to write – during his forty days and nights on Mount Sinai. What that would mean, strangely enough, is that when he came down from the mountain, he already knew everything that was going to happen for the rest of his life. So even as he was in the midst of wrapping Aaron up to be the High Priest, Moses knew exactly when he would eventually *un*wrap Aaron to die.

And what was it like for Moses, writing out the story of his own brother's death?

I bet he wrote it down exactly the way he dressed Aaron that Inauguration Day – with a lot of love, and a trembling hand.

CHAPTER 26

THE SOUND OF SILENCE – Parshat Shemini

It is the worst thing that can happen.

When a parent loses a child, it registers with us as the ultimate tragedy, because it contravenes the very nature of things. We all die sooner or later, of course – but it isn't supposed to happen this way. The older generation is to pass first, and leave the young to become old in their time. There is a cycle, an order to the world. And when sons and daughters die before their parents, that order is broken.

Aaron is the second major figure in the bible to lose not one, but two children. Adam and Eve lost Abel. Jacob *thought* he lost Joseph. Even Pharaoh only lost his firstborn. Only Judah also lost two sons.

But Aaron's loss feels even more harrowing, because he loses them both in one fiery instant:

Now Aaron's sons, Nadav and Avihu each took his fire pan, put fire in it, and laid incense on it; and they brought before the Lord a strange fire, which God had not commanded. And a fire came forth from before the Lord and consumed them, and they died before the Lord. ***(Lev. 10:1-2)***

וַיִּקְחוּ בְנֵי אַהֲרֹן נָדָב וַאֲבִיהוּא אִישׁ מַחְתָּתוֹ וַיִּתְּנוּ בָהֵן אֵשׁ וַיָּשִׂימוּ עָלֶיהָ קְטֹרֶת וַיַּקְרִבוּ
לִפְנֵי ה׳ אֵשׁ זָרָה אֲשֶׁר לֹא צִוָּה אֹתָם. וַתֵּצֵא אֵשׁ מִלִּפְנֵי ה׳ וַתֹּאכַל אוֹתָם וַיָּמֻתוּ לִפְנֵי ה׳.

Why this happened is not entirely clear. They were in the holy tabernacle, bringing an offering to God – which seems like a good thing. They came from the priestly family, so they presumably belonged there.

So what exactly did they do wrong? Why was their offering regarded as a "strange" fire? Some say they messed up the procedure. Some say they were drunk. Some say it is simply that they did it without God's explicit command.

Whatever the problem was, it was enough to provoke God to incinerate them instantly. They are gone so quickly, and we are left unsettled, confused. Did such a punishment really fit the crime, whatever it was? And regardless, didn't Aaron, the High Priest, deserve some special consideration?

Moses – perhaps a bit too soon – tries to explain it to Aaron, maybe even to justify it:

This is what God meant in saying, "Through those near me I show myself Holy, and gain glory before all the people." *(v. 3)*

הוּא אֲשֶׁר דִּבֶּר ה' לֵאמֹר בִּקְרֹבַי אֶקָּדֵשׁ וְעַל פְּנֵי כָל הָעָם אֶכָּבֵד...

But what is Aaron's reaction to all of this? Does he cry? No. Is he comforted? Or angry? We have no idea, because we read only this:

And Aaron was silent. *(v. 3)*

וַיִּדֹּם אַהֲרֹן.

That's all we get from Aaron. No emotional display. No response of any kind. Just silence. And then we move on from the scene.

So we are left to wonder: what was happening for Aaron in that moment? What was the nature of that silence? And what happens to a servant of God when that God takes his children away?

There are a wide range of opinions among the commentators. Some say Aaron remained every bit that servant of God, that his faith never wavered for a moment. His silence, in this reading, was a sign of total acceptance. Rabbi Ovadiah **Sforno** takes that position – and then pushes it even further:

***And Aaron was silent* – because he took comfort in the sanctification of God that they had achieved through their death.**

***וידום אהרן* – שהתנחם בקידוש ה' שנקדש במותם**

Aaron, says the Sforno, wasn't just dutifully accepting of their death. He actually saw their sacrifice itself as a kind of holy offering. Maybe Aaron understood Moses to mean exactly that: God has been glorified through this sacred immolation. Maybe he was even proud.

But this kind of interpretation is just too much for other commentators to accept. Don Isaac **Abarbanel**, for one, reads Aaron's silence not as acceptance, but catatonic despair:

It was as if his heart turned to lifeless stone, and so he did not raise his voice in tears and lament like a parent mourning his children. Nor did he accept Moses' consolation, for his breath left him and he was speechless...

והיה כאבן דומם ולא נשא קולו בבכי ובמספד כאבל אב על בנים. גם לא קבל תנחומים ממשה כי לא נותרה בו נשמה והדבור אין בו...

He could not be comforted, says Abarbanel. He could not feel anything at all. He was simply in total shock.

So which was it? A silence of faith or a silence of doubt? A silence of serenity or a silence of anguish?

Desperate to penetrate the mystery of Aaron's silence, I turn to a commentator with a more midrashic style, searching for echoes I cannot hear on my own. And I am not let down.

Rabbi Jacob ben Asher, the **Ba'al HaTurim**, famous for his savant-like mastery of the Bible, is always able to tell us exactly where else a phrase appears in the whole of the Hebrew canon. Look what he comes up with here:

***"was silent,"* in this form, is found twice in the tradition. Here: *"And Aaron was silent."* (וידם אהרן) And then: *"And the sun was silently [still]."* (וידם השמש)**

וידום ב' וידום אהרן וידום השמש

Now this brilliant connection takes us to the Book of Joshua, to the famous battle at Givon when, in order to have enough daylight to keep fighting, Joshua commanded the sun to stand still in the sky, and it "stopped" (using the same language as "silence," *va-yidom*). This event, along with the splitting of the Red Sea, is one of the paradigmatic miracles in the Bible: the day the sun stood still.

Now take that image and read it back into our moment with Aaron. What was happening to him in that silence? It was that sensation that often overtakes us in times of great trauma: time stands still.

Everything starts to move slowly, and then stops. And all the sounds around us become muffled as we sink into a chamber of stunned silence. The world recedes, and for an extended instant there is only that surreal state of shock that keeps the inevitable and overwhelming rush of pain temporarily at a strange distance.

Aaron was in that chamber of silence. He was reeling from the sudden loss – still confused, still putting together the impossible reality of what had just happened. Moses was trying to talk to him, but Aaron was far away...

As he looked out, the world around him had come to a halt. To Aaron, it was *we* who had gone silent, standing still, like the sun at Givon.

Meanwhile, what was taking place inside Aaron's reality?

Here I venture to suggest a connection of my own, for I am reminded of another great Biblical silence. It is in the Book of Kings, when Elijah has run off into the wilderness, to leave society and be alone with God. And God seems to pass by, first in a great wind, and then an earthquake. But we are told that "the Lord was not in the wind, nor the earthquake":

And after the earthquake – fire; and the Lord was not in the fire. And after the fire – a small, silent sound. ***(I Kings 19:12)***

וְאַחַר הָרַעַשׁ אֵשׁ, לֹא בָאֵשׁ ה'; וְאַחַר הָאֵשׁ, קוֹל דְּמָמָה דַקָּה.

This silence, like Aaron's, follows a display of fire. But here we are told that God was *not* in the fire, but in the silence.

The fire that killed Aaron's sons seemed to come from God, and to represent God's unmerciful will. But how does one find God in that? How can you possibly see God when your children lay dead before you? How dare Moses – how dare any of us – try to find some divine justification for such a tragedy?

No. Aaron would not hear it. Could not hear it. He was in his silence.

Yet maybe it was there, in the silence, that he found God again. Maybe, like Elijah, God spoke to Aaron through the sound of silence – and Aaron spoke back in silence.

For it is difficult to see God in all the terrible tragedies of this world. But we may discover God in our response to them.

Not in the fire, but in the silence.

CHAPTER 27

THE HAUNTED HOUSE – Parshat Tazria

We pass by this house every year.

It sits on a hill, somewhere out in the land of Canaan, rotting. There is something very wrong with this house. The walls are marked with streaks of green and red, corroding into the plaster... and spreading.

The door bursts open, and the owner of the house suddenly comes out, looking agitated. We see him run to the priest and say, in a string of uncertain words:

"Something like a plague has appeared before me in my house." ***(Lev. 14:35)***

כְּנֶגַע נִרְאָה לִי בַּבָּיִת.

What is it? He has no idea. Something. Something *like* a plague. **Rashi** tells us that:

Even if he is a scholar, who knows that certainly it is a plague, he does not render judgment with a definite statement.

שאפלו הוא חכם ויודע שהוא נגע ודאי, לא יפסק דבר ברור.

Because this doesn't seem real. It simply "appeared" before him, like some kind of phantom. So he can't exactly trust what he sees. Who's to say what this is?

But the Torah tells us explicitly – this is the plague of *tzara'at*. Leprosy. Or, at least, we often translate it as 'leprosy,' because it usually manifests as some kind of skin disease. But this can't be the leprosy we know about today, because we've seen it also attack clothing, infesting it with those same streaks of green and red. And now a house.

How can a house have a disease? And yet, that's exactly what it looks like. It looks like this house is dying.

The priest will tell him to put this house out of its misery. They will wait and watch for seven days, and then, if the plague continues to spread:

The priest will order the stones with the plague in them to be pulled out and cast outside the city, to a place of impurity. ***(Lev. 14:40)***

וְצִוָּה הַכֹּהֵן וְחִלְּצוּ אֶת הָאֲבָנִים אֲשֶׁר בָּהֵן הַנָּגַע וְהִשְׁלִיכוּ אֶתְהֶן אֶל מִחוּץ לָעִיר אֶל מָקוֹם טָמֵא.

Now the house is gone. It's just a pile of rocks, festering out on the edge of town.

What happened here? The old rabbis have their various theories. But one thing they all tend to agree on: this is no earthly force. The **Ramban** says it explicitly:

This is not in nature at all, and is not from this world... But when one of us sins, then some ugliness erupts on his skin, or his clothes, or his house – to show that God has turned away from him. ***(13:47)***

זה איננו בטבע כלל ולא הווה בעולם...וכאשר יקרה באחד מהם חטא ועון יתהוה כיעור בבשרו או בבגדו או בביתו להראות כי השם סר מעליו.

But if this was meant as a punishment, what did the owner of the house do to deserve it? There are surely sins that happen every day and cause no plague to erupt. What kind of crime has its sentence carried out on a piece of cloth, or a wall?

Rabbeinu Bachya has a theory:

This was someone who kept his house only for himself. He refused to lend his belongings out, and he never welcomed guests inside. And so the plagues came to attack his stinginess. ***(14:35)***

מי שמיוחד ביתו לו, כלומר שאינו רוצה להשאיל כלים או שאינו מכניס אורחים לביתו, שהנגעים באים על צרות העין.

He thought he could keep it all to himself, clutching his precious possessions, holed up inside his house. So God tore his house down, measure for measure. It is a lesson we see running through the Bible – in the freeing of the slave, or the sabbatical resting of the land – there is no real property. The earth belongs to the Lord. Try too hard to hoard things to yourself, and you will have them ripped away from you.

But Rashi tells a different version of this story, and manages to put a positive spin on the destruction of the house. He suggests that the miser was in the house long before we ever got there:

This is good news, when the plagues come! Because the Amorites hid gold treasures in the walls of their houses all forty years that Israel was in the desert. And as a result of the plague, the owner breaks down the house and finds them!

בשורה היא להם שהנגעים באים עליהם; לפי שהטמינו אמוריים מטמוניות של זהב בקירות בתיהם כל ארבעים שנה שהיו ישראל במדבר, ועל ידי הנגע נותץ הבית ומוצאן.

Hidden treasure! What we thought was a punishment turns out to be a reward. In an unexpected stroke of divine justice, the righteous man who lost his house is suddenly rich! This "plague" was actually a jackpot! It's all so exciting...

But this just feels too easy. Is this really the way God shows affection – by leading us to gold? Was the journey into the promised land really just some kind of treasure hunt?!

Even if we were willing to embrace this kind of shallow moral message, it still wouldn't make sense of the larger phenomenon of *tzara'at*. For what about the affliction of the clothes? Or the skin? Surely we won't be finding buried treasure under our own withering flesh! No, the legend of Amorite gold is a fun fantasy, but ultimately the Torah is pushing us to confront the fact that this plague is meant for us.

We turn, finally, to a powerful piece by the great **Kli Yakar**, who tries to come to terms with this responsibility by giving us a larger conceptual framework for understanding all of the *tzara'at* plagues:

You must know and understand, that these three types of tzara'at afflict three different things because these are the three "coverings" a person has. The first covering is the skin of his flesh. On top of that, are his clothes, which cover his skin. And then on top of them, is his house, which covers him completely, and protects him from the wind and rain. And one who has all these coverings removed from him is considered wild and exposed... Therefore, the plague of the skin is mentioned first, and then, the plague of the clothes, and finally the plague of the house, in order to remove all of his coverings, one by one, until he is completely wild and exposed.

ותדע ותשכיל כי ג' מיני צרעת באים על ג' דברים, שהם כסוי לאדם זה לפנים מזה מכסה ראשון הוא, עורו לבשרו. למעלה מעורו, בגדיו שהם כסוי לעורו. למעלה מהם, ביתו כי הוא מכסה לו להצילו ממטר ומזרם. ומי שהוסר מעליו כל מכסה נקרא פרוע ומגולה...ע"כ הזכיר תחילה נגעי עורו ואחר כך נגעי בגדיו ואח"כ נגעי בתים להסיר מכסהו אחת אחת עד שיהיה פרוע ומגולה מכל וכל.

These plagues are indeed devastating. But according to the Kli Yakar, they are not meant as a punishment, exactly. They are God's way of slowly, methodically breaking down all of the barriers we have that keep us at a distance from the world.

We move about in society, playing out a role, amassing possessions and accomplishments. We wear nice clothes, carefully selected to project an image of style or wealth, modesty or beauty – as if these were our essential traits. We try to present an impressive, invincible self to the world, and hope that we are convincing.

And then we run home, lock the door, and only there, behind the cover of the walls, are we left alone with our true selves.

But even then, we have our masks. You look in the mirror and see a face. Is that really you? Are you just your skin, your flesh? Or is there something more to you?

Where is the essential self? What are we, when everything is stripped away? If we took off all of our coverings, what would we find? It would not be hidden gold, that much is certain – not our money or our success. Not our intelligence, our charisma, or our beauty.

Forget about where you live, what you wear, or what you look like – none of that matters. When you are finally and completely exposed, what is waiting inside, at the core of your being?

Who are you, really?

That is the question that haunts us.

CHAPTER 28

LIKE A LEPER MESSIAH – Parshat Metzora

We Jews, who have been perennial outcasts, ought to read the Torah's account of the leper with particular care.

Throughout history, lepers have been demonized and feared, quarantined, and often even physically sent out of society to go and live in leper colonies. It's hard to fathom a more extreme version of the outcast. Surely, then, there is something in the leper's story that we need to know.

At the end of last week's parsha, *Tazria*, we begin to catalogue all manner of skin afflictions and finally came upon leprosy. Then, in *Parshat Metzora* – which literally translates into 'The Parsha of the Leper' – we move to the process for *curing* the leper.

This cure is effected through an intricate set of mysterious rituals. The priest orders two birds, one of which he slaughters and the other he sets free. He dips two kinds of wood into the bird's blood and sprinkles the blood seven times onto the leper. Then the leper washes his clothes, shaves off all his hair, and bathes in water. After seven days, he is pronounced clean.

Yet even before the leper is fully "cured," before the seven-day clock starts, as soon as he undergoes the ritual and bathes, we read:

...after that, he shall enter the camp. ***(Lev. 14:8)***

וְאַחַר יָבוֹא אֶל הַמַּחֲנֶה

This is rather surprising, since we were told earlier, when we first read about leprosy:

He shall be unclean as long as the disease is on him. Being unclean he shall sit alone; his dwelling shall be outside the camp. ***(Lev. 13:46)***

כָּל יְמֵי אֲשֶׁר הַנֶּגַע בּוֹ יִטְמָא טָמֵא הוּא בָּדָד יֵשֵׁב מִחוּץ לַמַּחֲנֶה מוֹשָׁבוֹ.

"He shall sit alone." It's very stark, very sad language. Yet his aloneness doesn't last long. The Torah launches right into the detailed procedure for treating him, and as soon as that begins, we bring him right back into the camp. No leper colony; not even a week of exile. There are still precautionary measures taken, but the leper comes back into the camp, among his people.

That's the paradigm. That's how the Torah wants us to deal with the leper. Help him. And bring him back in.

But that model doesn't last. We will read about the leper again, later in the Bible, and this time his situation is altogether different.

As we have seen before, every parsha is assigned a *haftarah,* a particular reading from the books of the prophets that is in some way thematically related to the parsha itself. *Parshat Metzora*'s *haftarah* is taken from the book of Kings, and it begins – as you might guess – with another story of lepers:

Four men, who were lepers, were outside the entrance to the gate. They said to one another, "Why should we sit here, waiting for death? If we decide to go into the town, we shall die there; and if we just sit here, we still die. So let us go down into the Aramean camp. If they let us live, we shall live; and if they put us to death, we would have died anyway." ***(II Kings 7:3-4)***

וְאַרְבָּעָה אֲנָשִׁים הָיוּ מְצֹרָעִים פֶּתַח הַשָּׁעַר וַיֹּאמְרוּ אִישׁ אֶל רֵעֵהוּ מָה אֲנַחְנוּ יֹשְׁבִים פֹּה עַד מָתְנוּ. אִם-אָמַרְנוּ נָבוֹא הָעִיר וְהָרָעָב בָּעִיר וָמַתְנוּ שָׁם וְאִם יָשַׁבְנוּ פֹה וָמָתְנוּ. וְעַתָּה לְכוּ וְנִפְּלָה אֶל מַחֲנֵה אֲרָם אִם יְחַיֻּנוּ נִחְיֶה וְאִם יְמִיתֻנוּ וָמָתְנוּ.

They end up going into the camp and finding it abandoned, and their report plays a pivotal role in the story. But leaving aside the context for a moment, let's just consider the opening image.

These lepers are sitting outside the gate, starving, abandoned, and totally desperate. Where is their healer? Where is their community? All they have is each other, the other lepers. It is eerily like a little leper colony.

The Book of Kings documents the chaotic years of wars and wicked monarchs. After Solomon's reign, things had begun to fall apart. So what we're seeing here is a society that has so completely devolved that it is no longer tending to its most needy. We went from a whole *parsha* devoted to bringing the leper in, to a story of lepers who are hopelessly outside, lingering pathetically at the gates.

Yet there is an even more harrowing account of the leper in Jewish tradition. It appears in the last chapter of Tractate Sanhedrin, one of the most fascinating sections in the Talmud. The rabbis here are dealing with all kinds of major theological issues, including theories of redemption.

One of the questions they ask (on page 98a) is: *'When will the Messiah come?'* There are lots of cryptic answers that read like riddles. There is even a radical opinion that there will be no messiah for Israel. But one of the most striking answers is given in a story that features our old friend the leper:

Rabbi Yehoshua ben Levi came upon Elijah (the prophet) standing by the entrance to the cave of Rabbi Shimon ben Yochai... He asked him, "When will the Messiah come?"

Elijah replied, "Go and ask him yourself."

"Where does he sit?"

"At the entrance to the city."

"And by what signs will I recognize him?"

"He is sitting among the poor lepers. They all untie their bandages all at once when they need to rebandage themselves. But he unties and re-bandages in parts, one by one, thinking, maybe I'll suddenly be needed, and I want to be ready at any minute."

ר' יהושע בן לוי אשכח לאליהו דהוי קיימי אפיתחא דמערתא דרבי שמעון בן יוחאי ... אמר ליה אימת אתי משיח אמר ליה זיל שייליה לדידיה והיכא יתיב אפיתחא דקרתא ומאי סימניה יתיב ביני עניי סובלי חלאים וכולן שרו ואסירי בחד זימנא איהו שרי חדואסיר חד אמר דילמא מבעינא דלא איעכב

Notice, by the way, how this story plays on the last two:

'Where does he sit?' (Talmud) / **'He sits alone.'** (Leviticus)

'The entrance to the city.' (Talmud) / **'The entrance to the gate.'** (Kings)

And the answer to the question of when the Messiah will come, in this version is: He's already here! But no one notices him. In fact, he's a total outcast – a leper.

That means, by all rights – in fact, by God's order – you should be doing everything you can to bring him in and heal him. But instead he sits there, with the other lepers, waiting for you.

Perhaps it is at this point that we ought to remember that none of these stories are really about leprosy – at least not as we know it today. There is some skin affliction going on, and we usually translate it as 'leprosy,' but most scholars now think that the Hebrew word, *'tzara'at'*

(צרעת) refers to some other kind of disease. In fact, the classical commentators generally agree that – though it had a physical manifestation – this was a spiritual malady.

If that is true, it lends an entirely different read to all of these stories. The one who sits alone outside the camp is suffering *spiritually*. When we go out to heal him, and to bring him in, we are tending not just to his body, but to his aching soul. Maybe that's why he's brought back in a week before he is fully cured. Because, in a sense, bringing him back into the camp *is* the cure.

But what happens? Time passes, society hardens, and we begin to forget to bring people in. We forget those who are suffering spiritually. They are left to sneak their way – or fight their way – back into the community.

And then, eventually, they give up. They sit outside, nursing their wounds, waiting. Waiting for something to change.

Meanwhile, there we are, just through the gate, also waiting. Waiting for the redemption. Waiting for the messiah to come save us, when he's right there behind the wall. We wait for him on one side while he waits for us on the other.

That's why the book of Lamentations, which we read on the day we mourn the destruction of Jerusalem and beg, in agony, for our redemption, begins as follows – with "leper language":

Alas! The city, once great with people, *sits alone… (Lam. 1:1)*

אֵיכָה יָשְׁבָה בָדָד הָעִיר רַבָּתִי עָם...

Back in the Talmud, the story ends with Rabbi Yehoshua ben Levi going up to the leper Messiah and asking him:

"When will you come, Master?"

"Today," he answered.

א"ל לאימת אתי מר א"ל היום

The rabbi is confused. Today?! He goes back to Elijah and says, "He lied to me! He said he would come today, but he has not." Elijah explains that, no, it's true, but what he meant was "today" as it appears in line from the Psalms:

"Today, *if* you will hear God's voice." *(Psalms 95:7)*

הַיּוֹם אִם בְּקֹלוֹ תִשְׁמָעוּ.

Redemption could come today, any day, any moment. But first, we have to "hear God's voice." And what does God say? We've long forgotten, but it was right there in our *parsha*, in the beginning of the procedure for curing the leper:

The priest shall go outside the camp. ***(Lev. 14:3)***

וְיָצָא הַכֹּהֵן אֶל מִחוּץ לַמַּחֲנֶה

The redeemer doesn't come to us. We go out to find the redeemer. We go out to the sick, the suffering, the outcasts of all kinds. We comfort them, cleanse them, heal them. And we bring them back into the camp, in through the gates, back into the community.

When we remember how to do that, our redemption is at hand. In fact, maybe that is our redemption.

The leper, it turns out, is the one who can save us all.

CHAPTER 29

THE MEANING OF LIFE – Parshat Acharei Mot

What is the meaning of life?

I am not asking the ultimate philosophical question. Not yet, anyway. For now, I am simply asking for some semantic help. Tell me – what exactly does "life" mean in the following verse:

You shall keep my rules and my laws. A person shall do them and live by them – I am the Eternal. ***(Lev. 18:5)***

וּשְׁמַרְתֶּם אֶת חֻקֹּתַי וְאֶת מִשְׁפָּטַי אֲשֶׁר יַעֲשֶׂה אֹתָם הָאָדָם וָחַי בָּהֶם אֲנִי ה'.

That phrase: *"and live by them"* – in Hebrew, "וחי בהם," just two words, just six letters long – has generated a mountain of commentary. What does "living by" (or 'through,' or 'with') the laws mean? Does keeping the commandments ensure a long life? Or an especially fulfilling life? Or is it just that following the laws is the right *way* to live? Every rabbi who put his quill to ink, it seems, has some novel interpretation of what "life" means here.

But two of these interpretations, in particular, are the best known. The first forms the classic Jewish legal principle of *pikuach nefesh*, the idea that (almost) any commandment can be violated in order to save a life. Here is the source of that derivation in the Talmud:

From where do we learn that one can break the Sabbath in order to save a life? Rabbi Yehuda said in the name of Shmuel... "*and he shall live by them*," and not die by them. ***(Yoma 85 a-b)***

מניין לפקוח נפש שדוחה את השבת... א"ר יהודה אמר שמואל... (ויקרא יח, ה) וחי בהם ולא שימות בהם

Life is the ultimate overriding principle. These laws are meant to ensure life, not endanger it, so they become immediately invalidated if one's life is in danger. An observant Jew may see himself as forbidden from using a car on the Sabbath; but if there is suddenly a life-threatening emergency and he needs to go to the hospital, then not only *can* he get into the car and drive – he must! There is no tolerance for religious martyrdom here.

It is from this very pragmatic approach to the maintenance of physical health and well-being that Judaism has earned a reputation as a *worldly* religion, one concerned mostly with righteous conduct in *this* life, rather than some far-off spiritual reward in the afterlife.

And yet, the other most classic rabbinic interpretation of this verse, cited by **Rashi** from the *Sifra*, takes us in exactly the opposite direction:

"And live by them" **– in the World to Come. For if you thought it was referring to life in this world – well, a person always eventually dies!** ***(Sifra, Acharei Mot 8:10)***

"וחי בהם" – לעולם הבא. ואם תאמר בעולם הזה, והלא סופו מת הוא!

The rabbinic voice in this midrash arrives at this metaphysical interpretation by assuming that the phrase, *"and live by them,"* means to tell us that someone who keeps the commandments will never die! Yet, it is quite clear that this is not what happens: experience tells us that just about everyone in history who has kept the commandments has eventually died. The practice of these laws does not at all seem to grant eternal life – at least, not here in this world. The only way to maintain this reading of the verse, then, is to assume that the commandments *do* grant eternal life – not here, but in the World to Come.

Now these two interpretations clearly represent very different theological orientations. In the first model, the Torah's highest concern is the preservation of life in this world. Religious observance does not trump basic human survival. In the second model, however, the whole point of observing the commandments is to attain a share in the World to Come. This earthly life is just a prelude to some eternal existence in the Great Beyond.

So which of these is the "authentic" Jewish message? Does the Torah present us with a theology of immanence or transcendence – of material realism or spiritual idealism?

The **Ramban** manages to read both possibilities – and even some nuanced positions in between – into the Torah's phrasing, *"A person shall do them and live by them."* He writes:

Know that a person's life in the commandments is determined by his own orientation to them. If someone does them not for their own sake,

but only to receive a reward, then that person will simply live a long life in this world – with wealth, property and honor…

Then there are those who perform the commandments in order to merit the World to Come. They are driven by fear, and so they receive just what they have intended, which is just to be saved from the punishment of the wicked. Their good life is held over [until the World to Come]...

And then there are those who labor in the commandments out of love, exactly as they should be performed… They will first have a good life in this world, and then their merit will be completed in the World to Come...

That is why the verses always speak of the reward for the commandments in the second person: *"In order that your life is lengthened," (Exod 20:12)*, or, *"In order that you live," (Deut. 16:20)* or, *"You will lengthen your days," (Deut. 22:7)* – because the language is meant to include all the possible "lives" – each one set in accordance with the person it fits.

ודע כי חיי האדם במצות כפי הכנתו להם כי העושה המצות שלא לשמן על מנת לקבל פרס יחיה בהן בעולם הזה ימים רבים בעושר ובנכסים וכבוד...

וכן אותם אשר הם מתעסקין במצות על מנת לזכות בהן לעולם הבא שהם העובדים מיראה זוכים בכוונתם להנצל ממשפטי הרשעים ונפשם בטוב תלין.

והעוסקין במצות מאהבה כדין וכראוי... יזכו בעולם הזה לחיים טובים כמנהג העולם ולחיי העולם הבא זכותם שלמה שם...

ולכך יאמרו הכתובים בשכר המצות למען יאריכון ימיך (**שמות כ יב**) למען תחיה (**דברים טז כ**) והארכת ימים (שם כב ז) כי הלשון יכלול מיני החיים כולם כפי הראוי לכל אחד

What the Ramban has done, in this feat of interpretive prowess, is to suggest that the answer to the question of what "life" means in our verse is determined by the belief system of the reader. If you are primarily concerned with living well in the here and now, then your reward for the commandments will be in this world. If you are fearfully fixated on the afterlife, then your good life will be waiting for you there, in the World to Come. And if you truly love these commandments, because you recognize in them both possibilities, then you will find her life enriched first in this world, and then even more so in the next one. The verses about life speak in the language of "you," because *you* are the one who decides what that life means.

In other words, all the commentators, with all their various interpretations of the phrase, "and live by them – וחי בהם," over the centuries – they have all been right. For they have each found in the verse the meaning of life they wanted to find, according to the kind of life they could believe in.

The language of the Torah, the Ramban dizzyingly suggests, is meant to include *all* these possibilities. This verse that speaks of "living" in the commandments is deliberately vague, because it remains to be seen what kind of life, you, dear reader, will find therein.

CHAPTER 30

THE MYSTERY OF MOLEKH – Parshat Kedoshim

Who is this Molekh, and what is he doing in my Torah?

The Book of Leviticus mentions him twice, and both times in reference to the same frightful idolatrous practice: child sacrifice.

We heard a brief mention of him in last week's parsha, but now, in *Parshat Kedoshim*, we get a more extensive treatment:

Anyone among the Children of Israel, or among the strangers residing in Israel, who gives any of his offspring to Molekh, shall be put to death; the people of the land shall pelt him with stones. And I will set My face against that man, and will cut him off from his people, because he gave his offspring to Molekh and so defiled My sanctuary and profaned My holy name. And if the people of the land shut their eyes to that man when he gives of his offspring to Molekh, and do not put him to death, then I Myself will set My face against that man and his family, and will cut off from their people him and all who follow him in going astray after Molekh. ***(Lev. 20:2-5)***

וְאֶל בְּנֵי יִשְׂרָאֵל תֹּאמַר אִישׁ אִישׁ מִבְּנֵי יִשְׂרָאֵל וּמִן הַגֵּר הַגָּר בְּיִשְׂרָאֵל אֲשֶׁר יִתֵּן מִזַּרְעוֹ לַמֹּלֶךְ מוֹת יוּמָת עַם הָאָרֶץ יִרְגְּמֻהוּ בָאָבֶן. וַאֲנִי אֶתֵּן אֶת־פָּנַי בָּאִישׁ הַהוּא וְהִכְרַתִּי אֹתוֹ מִקֶּרֶב עַמּוֹ כִּי מִזַּרְעוֹ נָתַן לַמֹּלֶךְ לְמַעַן טַמֵּא אֶת מִקְדָּשִׁי וּלְחַלֵּל אֶת שֵׁם קָדְשִׁי. וְאִם הַעְלֵם יַעְלִימוּ עַם הָאָרֶץ אֶת עֵינֵיהֶם מִן הָאִישׁ הַהוּא בְּתִתּוֹ מִזַּרְעוֹ לַמֹּלֶךְ לְבִלְתִּי הָמִית אֹתוֹ. וְשַׂמְתִּי אֲנִי אֶת פָּנַי בָּאִישׁ הַהוּא וּבְמִשְׁפַּחְתּוֹ וְהִכְרַתִּי אֹתוֹ וְאֵת כָּל הַזֹּנִים אַחֲרָיו לִזְנוֹת אַחֲרֵי הַמֹּלֶךְ מִקֶּרֶב עַמָּם.

This is serious business. Molekh is mentioned four times – once in each of these verses – as if the Torah were bitterly spitting out the name of its arch enemy. And the punishment for the crime of worshipping this deity is doubled: death *and* excommunication – as if death alone were not enough. Now certainly the Torah is always railing against the worship of foreign gods, but this seems different. This seems personal.

The obvious explanation for this hyper-severity is that this is not just any idolatry – this is the murder of innocent children! There are many ways to transgress the commandment against idolatry, and the Torah mentions several of them: bowing down to statues, ritually shaving the sides of your head, planting trees in the name of a god. That kind of thing. But Molekh isn't satisfied with those silly offerings. Molekh wants your kids.

So when idolatry crosses over into child homicide – that's when our God gets really angry.

But it's a bit more complicated than that. Because if you've been reading the Torah since Genesis you know... our God asked for a child sacrifice as well.

It's a classic scene – one of the most disturbing and incomprehensible moments in all of Jewish literature: The *Akeidah*, the Binding of Isaac:

After these things, God tested Abraham. God said to him, "Abraham," and he answered, "Here I am." And God said, "Take your son, your only son, whom you love, and go to the land of Moriah, and offer him there as a burnt offering on one of the mountains that I will point out to you." ***(Gen. 22:1-2)***

וַיְהִי אַחַר הַדְּבָרִים הָאֵלֶּה וְהָאֱלֹהִים נִסָּה אֶת אַבְרָהָם וַיֹּאמֶר אֵלָיו אַבְרָהָם וַיֹּאמֶר הִנֵּנִי. וַיֹּאמֶר קַח נָא אֶת בִּנְךָ אֶת יְחִידְךָ אֲשֶׁר אָהַבְתָּ אֶת יִצְחָק וְלֶךְ לְךָ אֶל אֶרֶץ הַמֹּרִיָּה וְהַעֲלֵהוּ שָׁם לְעֹלָה עַל אַחַד הֶהָרִים אֲשֶׁר אֹמַר אֵלֶיךָ.

And Abraham did just that, seemingly without hesitation. He went, he built an altar, he laid his son on top of the wood and tied him there. He went so far as to raise the knife to slaughter the boy... when suddenly an angel of the Lord stopped him, satisfied that he had been willing to give up his child. And Abraham was given a blessing for his faith in God.

What do we make of this? How can we accept this horrifying story as a part of our sacred literature? Are we supposed to celebrate what Abraham did? And what kind of mad God would ask him to do it?

Those difficult questions have busied and perplexed the commentators for centuries. Many have asserted that God never intended for Abraham to go through with it, that it was only a test. Some have even suggested that Abraham never believed that God would allow such a thing to happen, and was just going through the motions, waiting for an inevitable salvation.

We will not be able to answer such questions here. We could spend a lifetime trying. But whatever we might propose, we could never wash away the stain of uneasiness that remains on the fabric of this harrowing tale. We wince when we read it. We wish, sometimes, that the Torah could just take it back.

And that, perhaps, is precisely what the Torah is doing here, in these invectives against Molekh. Perhaps they are a subtle way of pushing back against the *Akeidah* story, lest you learn the wrong lesson from it. This is the Torah's way of making sure that no one is inspired to imitate the great faith of Abraham. Whatever happened back there, that was then, it never ended up happening anyway, and it certainly was never meant to happen again. So we point to the Molekh-worshippers, and we castigate them – but really we are talking to ourselves, to our history, and to our fear that we will repeat it.

But then, why make such a big deal of the deity Molekh himself? Why not just ban the practice? As we said before, the Torah prohibits all kinds of idolatrous practices. But rarely does it mention one of these foreign gods by name – and never does it repeat that name again and again the way it does with Molekh.

Who is this dark figure that looms so large in the background of our holiest book?

There are some classic answers. **Rashi** describes Molekh (in his commentary on the book of Jeremiah, 7:31), as a gigantic metal statue, around which the killing ritual took place:

Molekh was made of brass; and they heated him from his lower parts; and his hands stretched out, and were made hot. They put the child between his hands, and it was burnt. And the child would cry out; but the priests beat a drum, so that the father would not hear the voice of his son and feel pity for him.

הוא המולך שהיה של נחשת ומסיקין אותו מתחתיו וידיו פשוטות וניסקות ונותנין את הילד על ידיו והוא נכוה ונוהם והכומרים היו מקישין בתופים שלא ישמע האב קול הבן ויכמרו רחמיו.

The **Ibn Ezra** and the **Ramban**, meanwhile, are convinced that Molekh is the same god that the Ammonites are said to worship, in the Book of Kings – though there the name is 'Milkom' (מלכום).

Either way, the standard assumption is that Molekh was the name of some Canaanite deity.

But I have never been able to shake the feeling that the word, *Molekh* (מולך), is meant to be more than just the name of a foreign god. For as the word reads in the Hebrew, it is strikingly close to our word for 'king,' *melekh* (מלך). It is spelled almost exactly the same, except that its vowelization is slightly changed, which changes the noun form so that it implies something broader, like "the act of being a king." So I went looking around and – to my great delight – I found just such an interpretation in the commentary of Rabbi **Samson Raphael Hirsch** (who is a tremendous resource in the book of Leviticus). He says:

If we ask for the meaning of the word, *Molekh,* מלך, the form tells us that it does not convey the idea of a person as melekh, but is an abstract conception, like holiness קדש (*kodesh*), greatness גדל *(godel)*, so it does not designate the king, the ruler, but reigning, ruling, governing. We think we find in it the heathen idea of irrevocable fate, luck, which "rules" the world, on which even the gods have no power to change, to whose decisions they themselves cannot but submit. *(Hirsch on Lev. 18:21)*

Molekh, according to Hirsch, is not a separate god, but a concept – the idea of pure, driving power that cannot be pushed back or contained. Molekh may appear capricious, like luck or fate, but it must be obeyed – not because it is respected, but simply because it is inevitably crashing toward its destination, and will destroy anything that stands in its way. You cannot negotiate with a force like this; you *"cannot but submit."*

Is this not the god that Abraham was reckoning with at the *Akeidah*? The God he thought he knew was suddenly unpredictable and enigmatic. The God who once consulted with him before taking action (*"can I hide from Abraham what I do?"*) now demands and leaves no room for dialogue or debate. This god has nothing to do with justice or mercy; it is simply an all-powerful, absolute Ruler of the Universe. When this god asks for your child, you hand him over. You simply have no choice.

Now can this god be reconciled with the God who hears our cries and delivers us from bondage, a God who makes contact and reveals a plan for the good of humankind? Can the god who asks our forefather to slaughter his son be the same God who spoke the words "Thou shalt not kill"? Can the Merciful One suddenly appear in the form of Molekh?

Rabbi Hirsch says yes. In fact, that's just the problem:

Paying tribute to Molekh is not renouncing God for idolatry, but the erroneous idea that there is a force of fate, inimical to Man, which is to be feared and placated, a force which is side by side with God, or even within the conception of God... the Molekh illusion concedes the power of Molekh a place at the side of God and His Law, and makes its influence to be feared as something that is beyond the power of God Himself and His Laws to annul. *(Hirsch on Lev. 20:3)*

And so our laws against Molekh in this week's *parsha* come to do just that: to annul. But *what* do they annul? The killing of children and worship of foreign gods, yes. But those things we knew were forbidden. The problem is that we don't know what we would do if God asked for our children. Does the sudden word of our God override everything else we know to be true? Are all of our ethics suspended in the name of our faith? Do we follow our father Abraham's example?

These laws, then, come to annul the *Akeidah*. They are there to tell us that, whether God intended Abraham to offer up his child or not back then, that chapter of our story is now closed. We can debate the meaning of that incident throughout the ages; surely there is some profound message in it for us. But we are not to take from it any call to action, any model of practice.

And we are not to worship the god of the *Akeidah*. That god no longer exists. Perhaps that god never existed. We were in error, Abraham was in error, in placing a god of terror side by side – or even within – the God of mercy.

CHAPTER 31

THE CURSE - Parshat Emor

This is the saddest story I know.

It is a story that gets told in fragments, mostly through the commentary of **Rashi**. But it begins, abruptly – and ends savagely – in the text of the Torah, here in this week's parsha.

Parshat Emor is, like much of Leviticus, mostly full of laws, one after the other. Notably, it contains the first major treatment of the Jewish calendar, laying out all the festivals in order. In fact, that's just where we are in the reading, when, out of nowhere, appears this strange little piece of narrative:

The son of an Israelite woman – and he was the son of an Egyptian man – went out among the Children of Israel. And this son of the Israelite woman and another Israelite man fought in the camp. The son of the Israelite woman pronounced The Name, and cursed it. And they brought him to Moses. The name of his mother was Shlomit bat Divri of the Tribe of Dan. They placed him under guard to clarify the matter.

God spoke to Moses, and said, "Take the blasphemer out of the camp, and everyone who heard him should place their hands upon his head, and the entire congregation shall stone him." ***(Lev. 24:10-14)***

וַיֵּצֵא בֶּן אִשָּׁה יִשְׂרְאֵלִית וְהוּא בֶּן אִישׁ מִצְרִי בְּתוֹךְ בְּנֵי יִשְׂרָאֵל וַיִּנָּצוּ בַּמַּחֲנֶה בֶּן הַיִּשְׂרְאֵלִית וְאִישׁ הַיִּשְׂרְאֵלִי. וַיִּקֹּב בֶּן הָאִשָּׁה הַיִּשְׂרְאֵלִית אֶת הַשֵּׁם וַיְקַלֵּל וַיָּבִיאוּ אֹתוֹ אֶל מֹשֶׁה וְשֵׁם אִמּוֹ שְׁלֹמִית בַּת דִּבְרִי לְמַטֵּה דָן. וַיַּנִּיחֻהוּ בַּמִּשְׁמָר לִפְרֹשׁ לָהֶם עַל פִּי ה'.

וַיְדַבֵּר ה' אֶל מֹשֶׁה לֵּאמֹר. הוֹצֵא אֶת הַמְקַלֵּל אֶל מִחוּץ לַמַּחֲנֶה וְסָמְכוּ כָל הַשֹּׁמְעִים אֶת יְדֵיהֶם עַל רֹאשׁוֹ וְרָגְמוּ אֹתוֹ כָּל הָעֵדָה.

Brutal.

Now, *any* mention of stoning in the Torah is hard to read. It is a punishment whose violence is so stark as to feel primitive, totally out of step with the sensibilities of modern civilization.

But this stoning in particular seems personal, even vindictive. What's going on here? Why are we introduced to this nameless man before we see his crime? What is he so angry about? And why does God make such a point of having him killed in this public ceremony? The whole thing is hauntingly mysterious.

So let's turn to Rashi, who will give us some of the backstory, bit by bit. And I warn you ahead of time: each step we take with Rashi will bring us deeper and deeper into dark places...

Step 1, then: Why were these men fighting to begin with? Rashi gives us an answer:

He went out **– From where did he 'go out'...? He went out of Moses' court, with a losing verdict. He had tried to plant his tent in the camp of the Tribe of Dan. They said to him, "What is your claim to this place?" He said to them, "I come from the children of Dan." They said to him, "It is written: 'Each man dwells under his banner, assigned by the house of his *father*.'" So he went into the Court of Moses [to protest], but he lost his case. So he got up and cursed!**

ויצא בן אשה ישראלית – מהיכן יצא...? מבית דינו של משה יצא מחוייב. בא ליטע אהלו בתוך מחנה דן, אמרו לו מה טיבך לכאן, אמר להם מבני דן אני. אמרו לו (במדבר ב) איש על דגלו באותות לבית אבותם כתיב. נכנס לבית דינו של משה ויצא מחוייב, עמד וגדף.

Heartbreaking.

This man was just looking for a place to pitch his tent, a place to rest in the desert encampment. So he came, naturally, to his closest relatives – the tribe of his mother. But they turned him away. Because although membership in the *nation* could be had through maternal lineage, belonging to one of the twelve tribes was a status that came from one's father.

But this man's father was Egyptian. In other words, he *had* no tribal connection. And so he had nowhere to be. He had left Egypt, with his people, in the dark night of the tenth plague, crossed through the walls of the Red Sea in their midst, and stood at their side at Sinai to receive God's revelation. And now, suddenly, no one would have him; having come this far to be with his people, he was all alone.

Imagine him, wandering around, from camp to camp, seeking entry, and being turned away from every group. And for what reason? A consequence of his birth. A situation he had no control over. He was an outcast by virtue of nothing he had done, but simply because of who he was.

So he tried to protest, tried to seek justice. Only to find rejection from the highest authority in this new nation. One certainly begins to understand where his curse came from.

Oh, but it gets worse.

Step 2: Who was this Egyptian father of his, Rashi?

The son of an Egyptian man – **This was the Egyptian that Moses killed.**

בן איש מצרי – הוא המצרי שהרגו משה

Devastating.

Back in Exodus, Chapter Two, we saw Moses go out to see the conditions of slavery in Egypt and:

He saw an Egyptian beating a Hebrew, one of his kinsmen. He looked this way and that and, seeing there was no one around, he struck down the Egyptian and buried him in the sand. *(2:11-12)*

וַיַּרְא אִישׁ מִצְרִי מַכֶּה אִישׁ עִבְרִי מֵאֶחָיו. וַיִּפֶן כֹּה וָכֹה וַיַּרְא כִּי אֵין אִישׁ וַיַּךְ אֶת הַמִּצְרִי וַיִּטְמְנֵהוּ בַּחוֹל.

So now, Rashi, picking up on the specific reference to "The Egyptian" here and there, makes a connection and tells us that the Egyptian who was beating the slave in Exodus must be the same nameless Egyptian who fathered our poor tribeless fellow in Leviticus.

But what does that mean? It means that when this man went into court, seeking his place amongst the Children of Israel – seeking, essentially, a family – the man who ruled that he could have none of that... was the same man who had killed his father.

This is beyond trauma. This borders on psychological torture. He must have been out of his mind, trembling with bitterness and rage. So yes, I see how the curse could form in his heart. I see how it could erupt from his lips. Rejected by all, finally condemned by his father's killer – how could anyone endure this fate? Could this story be any more tragic?

Oh, but it can.

Step 3: So how did this Egyptian come to father an Israelite boy, anyway?

One more Rashi, this one from back in the Exodus story where Moses saw:

An Egyptian man beating a Hebrew – ... **This Hebrew was the husband of Shlomit bat Divri. The Egyptian took a liking to her, and one night, he**

came and woke up the Hebrew and dragged him out of his house. Then the Egyptian came back to the house and had sex with [Shlomit], while [in the darkness] she thought it was her husband. The Hebrew returned and understood what had happened. And when the Egyptian realized that the Hebrew knew, he began to beat him and torture him all day long.

מכה איש עברי – ...בעלה של שלומית בת דברי היה, ונתן בה עיניו, ובלילה העמידו והוציאו מביתו, והוא חזר ונכנס לבית ובא על אשתו, כסבורה שהוא בעלה, וחזר האיש לביתו והרגיש בדבר, וכשראה אותו מצרי שהרגיש בדבר, היה מכהו ורודהו כל היום.

Oh, dear God.

So it turns out our homeless, fatherless, tribeless wanderer was actually the product of a rape. His own ambiguous status was not only a fact of his existence, beyond his control – it was also the consequence of a terrible, terrible crime.

Here, then, stands before you a man whose mother was raped, whose adoptive father was humiliated, whose biological father was killed, who had no tribe, no place to lay his head, no recourse in court and, seemingly, no mercy from his God – the God for whom he had left everything and followed out into the desert.

So yes, yes, I understand how he could have come to curse God! I get it. I daresay I might have done so myself.

But my sympathy is no help. My understanding cannot save him. His fate is sealed. He is to die. For God will tolerate no desecration of God's Holy Name. Take him out of the camp – the very place in which he sought to dwell – and stone him.

I am at a loss. I cannot bear this. It is too much.

I searched in vain for some commentary that would redeem this story, some great insight that would make sense of it all. I found no consolation. There is, it seems, only sadness in this tale.

There is one final glimmer of meaning, however, that may point us toward a way out of the darkness. It is a curious detail back in the text of the Torah itself. Remember that when God has the blasphemer taken out to be stoned, God specifically required that:

...everyone who heard him should place their hands upon his head...

וְסָמְכוּ כָל הַשֹּׁמְעִים אֶת יְדֵיהֶם עַל רֹאשׁוֹ

This is unusual. Certainly it is not required of every capital punishment. And standing where we are in the Torah, in the midst of Leviticus, the laying of hands cannot help but make us think of a scene from two *parshot* ago, in the Yom Kippur ceremony. Remember:

Aaron shall lay both his hands upon the head of the live goat and confess over it all the sins and crimes of the Children of Israel, whatever their transgressions...Thus shall the goat carry on it all of their sins to an inaccessible region, and the goat shall be sent out into the wilderness. ***(Lev. 16:21-22)***

וְסָמַךְ אַהֲרֹן אֶת שְׁתֵּי יָדָו עַל רֹאשׁ הַשָּׂעִיר הַחַי וְהִתְוַדָּה עָלָיו אֶת כָּל עֲוֹנֹת בְּנֵי יִשְׂרָאֵל וְאֶת כָּל פִּשְׁעֵיהֶם לְכָל חַטֹּאתָם... וְנָשָׂא הַשָּׂעִיר עָלָיו אֶת כָּל עֲוֹנֹתָם אֶל אֶרֶץ גְּזֵרָה וְשִׁלַּח אֶת הַשָּׂעִיר בַּמִּדְבָּר.

Back there, the symbolism of the priests laying his hands upon the goat is a transference of the sins of the community onto this "scapegoat."

Could it be, then, that here, when God asks *"everyone who heard him"* to lay their hands upon this cursing sinner before he is put to death, God is forcing them to acknowledge their own sins, their own part in his damnation?

For it is true that by the strict letter of the law, he is guilty of a crime that merits the death penalty. Just as by the strict letter of the law, no tribe had to allow him to camp with them.

But why didn't they?

How could they have turned him away? The law was on their side – but where was their compassion?

And where were we when his mother was raped? Did we do everything we could to support him and his family in the aftermath of that tragedy?

And where were we that day when he wandered from camp to camp, weary, seeking refuge? Did we open our tents and offer him some shade and a meal?

And where were we when he received the ruling from Moses' court? Did we rush to console him and offer him alternatives?

No.

"Everyone heard him" – but no one listened.

If he had no home, it is because we gave him none. If he cursed, it is because we allowed him to feel cursed. If he is guilty, then we are guilty.

Perhaps, then, despite the bleak final judgment that ends this man's tale, somewhere in it lies an injunction for us as well. When we see someone go this far astray, so that he is ready to curse everything we believe in and to destroy himself in the process, then our responsibility is not simply to condemn him, but also to turn and painfully ask of ourselves:

How did we fail him? How did we fail him?

CHAPTER 32
SLAVE TO FREEDOM – Parshat Behar

See, now, this is the problem.

We rabbis, from Maimonides on, spend all our time trying to show people that the Jewish conception of God is sophisticated. God is an abstract and mysterious concept, beyond representation or comprehension, and all of those concrete descriptions in the Torah – of God's hand, or God's anger, or God's kingship – those are just metaphors, you see? The true God, we say, is not so physical as to reach out a hand, nor so petty as to lose a temper, nor so power-hungry as to desire human subservience. We work so hard defending God's pristine image.

And then we come across a line like this:

For the Children of Israel are slaves to Me, they are My slaves, whom I have taken out of the Land of Egypt – I am the Lord your God. ***(Lev. 25:55)***

כִּי לִי בְנֵי יִשְׂרָאֵל עֲבָדִים עֲבָדַי הֵם אֲשֶׁר הוֹצֵאתִי אוֹתָם מֵאֶרֶץ מִצְרָיִם אֲנִי ה׳ אֱלֹהֵיכֶם.

Oh dear. Well now, that doesn't sound very appealing. We are supposed to be God's... slaves?! The verse is pretty stark; even repeats the phrase – *"they are My slaves"* – in case we didn't think it was serious the first time. Now, it's one thing to suggest that descriptions of *God* are meant as metaphor. But when the Torah describes *us*... well, that's hard to explain away.

You might translate the word *avadim* (עבדים) as "servants," to soften it a little. But the gist is the same. You used to serve Pharaoh; now serve God. We were slaves in Egypt, and we're slaves again.

What was the point of the Exodus, really? Just to get a better master?

Well, some strains of Jewish theology have gone in exactly that direction. Look, for example, the commentary of the medieval Rabbi Yosef ben Yizchak of Orleans – (or, the **'Bekhor Shor'**) – back in Exodus, on what seems like a very lovely, inspiring verse:

And I will take you to be My people, and I will be your God. And you shall know that I, the Lord, am your God who freed you from the labors of the Egyptians. ***(Exod. 6:7)***

וְלָקַחְתִּי אֶתְכֶם לִי לְעָם וְהָיִיתִי לָכֶם לֵאלֹהִים וִידַעְתֶּם כִּי אֲנִי ה' אֱלֹהֵיכֶם הַמּוֹצִיא אֶתְכֶם מִתַּחַת סִבְלוֹת מִצְרָיִם.

Now that's nice! We're God's people, we're free from bondage. *This* is the message of the Exodus that we like to hear. But look at how the Bekhor Shor interprets it:

And I will take you to be My people **– And you will be slaves to Me, because it is better for you to be My slaves than to be the slaves of Pharaoh.** ***And I will be your God*** **– I will be your master and not Pharaoh.** ***And you shall know that I, the Lord, am your God*** **– And you will serve Me willingly, because you will say, it is better to serve the Greatest of Kings, than to serve someone arbitrary, like Pharaoh.**

ולקחתי אתכם לי לעם **– והייתם עבדים לי כי טוב לכם להיות עבדי מהיות עבדי פרעה.** ***והייתי לכם לאלהים*** **– אני אהיה אדון לכם ולא פרעה.** ***וידעתם כי אני ה' אלהיכם המוציא אתכם*** **– ועבדתם אותי ברצון כי תאמרו מוטב לעבוד המלך הגדול מלעבוד אותו הדיוט פרעה.**

Hmm. It may well be better to serve the Greatest of Kings than someone arbitrary. But this is not a theology that will appeal to most people born after the great modern revolutions, when the values of freedom and democracy have become widely accepted as essential for human flourishing. The very notion of servitude is repellant to the contemporary ear, and all the more so when it is God who seems to desire human subjugation.

And yet, there it is, in black and white, right here in our *parsha*: *"The Children of Israel are slaves to Me. They are My slaves."* It hardly gets more subjugated than that.

*

Rashi, however, uses this same verse in a way that takes it in a very different direction. He cites it, not here, but back in the Book of Exodus, in *Parshat Mishpatim*. Just after the giving of the Ten Commandments, we dive into a long catalogue of laws, mostly civil and criminal ordinances, though some religious ritual as well. And the very first one is the Law of the Hebrew Slave. Slave isn't the right word, really – it's more like, 'indentured servant,' because the whole point of the law is that the servant can only work for six years, and must then be freed in the seventh.

That seems to be the strong recommendation of the Torah, anyway. However, there is an alternate option. If that servant does not wish to go free, if he says, "I love my master!" then he may remain a slave. But first, a strange ritual must be performed:

His master shall bring him to the court, and then bring him to the door or the doorpost, and his master shall pierce through his ear with an awl, and then he shall serve forever. ***(Exod. 21:6)***

וְהִגִּישׁוֹ אֲדֹנָיו אֶל הָאֱלֹהִים וְהִגִּישׁוֹ אֶל הַדֶּלֶת אוֹ אֶל הַמְּזוּזָה וְרָצַע אֲדֹנָיו אֶת אָזְנוֹ בַּמַּרְצֵעַ וַעֲבָדוֹ לְעֹלָם.

Strange enough that the Torah mandates the freeing of slaves, and then allows the slave himself to take it back. But then this ear-piercing is really odd. What does pinning this man's ear to the door have to do with his choiceful submission. Is it just a humiliation ritual? Or perhaps a form of branding?

Rashi has a different answer:

Now, why was the ear chosen to be pierced through, of all the organs of the body…? [Because] the very ear that heard on Mount Sinai, *"For the children of Israel are slaves to Me," (Lev. 25:55)* and then went and acquired a master for itself – this ear shall be pierced!

ומה ראה אזן לרצע מכל שאר אברים שבגוף? ...אזן ששמעה על הר סיני *כי לי בני ישראל עבדים*, והלך וקנה אדון לעצמו, תרצע.

Rashi imagines that our verse, here in *Parshat Behar*, was said to all of the Children of Israel during the Revelation at Mount Sinai. (The word *'Behar,'* (בהר) after all, does mean "On the Mountain.") So this servant heard God say "you are to serve Me," and then he turns around and chooses some lowly *person* to serve instead?! How dare he! How disgraceful, that he would pick a human master over – as the Bekhor Shor said it – the "Greatest of Kings"? And so, he too, must be disgraced.

But if the primary purpose of the verse is to keep people from submitting to human authority, then we might say that the whole relational dynamic of 'God as Master and we as slaves' is fundamentally a mechanism for preventing slavery. It is less about God's desire to rule over people and more about how divine rulership undermines all earthly power structures. I become a slave to God so that I will bow before no human being.

The Torah, after all, does seem rather fixated on freedom. Our people's founding narrative is a liberation from bondage. Think of that. Our most sacred text is not a utopian tale of our mighty and magnificent origins as powerful beings in a perfect society, but a story of how we were brought down to the lowest form of human existence, endured it for centuries, and then found God – who was to us, first and foremost, a Force of Liberation.

And then the first mandate we receive, after we have been liberated from slavery, and elevated to the status of potential masters ourselves, is to never hold one another in captivity. And the regulations continue: *"Do not subjugate your servant with harsh labor." (Lev. 25:45) "When you do send him away from you free, do not send him away empty-handed. Reward him generously, from your flocks, from your threshing floor and from your wine cellar." (Deut. 15:14)* And why, says the next verse? Because, as the Torah repeats, again and again, *"You shall remember that you were a slave in the Land of Egypt, and the Eternal your God redeemed you; therefore, I command you in this regard today."* To obey God's commandments *is* to insist on freedom.

As a matter of fact, nowhere is freedom more vociferously proclaimed than in this week's parsha, which spends most of its time detailing the laws of the Jubilee year. Every fifty years, all servants and prisoners would be freed, all debts would be released – even the land would be left to grow freely, undisturbed by human hands. And the hallmark phrase announcing this regime of freedom (the very one that appears on the side of the Liberty Bell in Philadelphia), is taken from right here in our parsha:

Proclaim Liberty throughout the land, for all its inhabitants. (*Lev. 25:10*)

וּקְרָאתֶם דְּרוֹר בָּאָרֶץ לְכָל יֹשְׁבֶיהָ.

The word for "liberty" here is unusual: *dror* (דרור). It seems to be a special kind of freedom. And for whom do we "proclaim" this *dror*? Who is the "all"? Most of the land's inhabitants are already free. So Rashi tells us who, and among them is a character we've met before:

Proclaim liberty **– To the slaves, whether they be "pierced," or have not yet finished their six years of service.**

וקראתם דרור – לעבדים, בין נרצע בין שלא כלו לו שש שנים משנמכר.

Now this is interesting. We are taking the laws we had that limited slavery and pushing them further. First of all, we had already seen that no one could work for more than 6 years, but now, if the Jubilee rolls around, they can go out early. Lucky for them – good timing.

And then there is the "pierced" slave, the one who wanted to remain a slave his whole life. Surely he who rejected freedom once, will not deserve it this time around. But no – he goes free, too. In fact, this is not a question of what he "deserves," for it is not meant as a "kindness" to him, per se. He *must* go free. He has no choice. He thought he could stay a slave forever, and it seemed for a time that he could.

But every fifty years, we are reminded that no one stays a slave forever. Freedom comes to everyone, whether they want it or not.

But why now? What has changed? Why was this man allowed to opt for more servitude then, but now must face release – even against his will?

Perhaps it is a question of time. That earlier permission to stay was first given not long after the Exodus. Freedom was still a new thing for these people, and though God wanted them to embrace it, perhaps there was an understanding that not everyone could.

This lingering "slave mentality" is what the **Ibn Ezra** (in his comments on Exodus 14:13) describes when he wonders why the Israelites never fought back against the Egyptians:

Why didn't they fight for their lives, and for their children's lives? The answer is, that the Egyptians had been their masters, and this generation that left Egypt had learned from their youth to endure the yoke of Egypt, and its spirit was debased. How could they now fight against their masters?

ולמה לא ילחמו על נפשם ועל בניהם. התשובה כי המצרים היו אדונים לישראל וזה הדור היוצא ממצרים למד מנעוריו לסבול עול מצרים ונפשו שפלה. ואיך יוכל עתה להלחם עם אדוניו?

They had learned to "endure the yolk." It had become natural for them to serve; this was the only existence they knew. For slavery does not only hold the body captive; it also subjugates the mind. These people were finally free, but they did not know how to live out that freedom. It would take them another generation or two before they understood what their liberation meant and how to own it. It would take, suggests the Torah, approximately fifty years.

But there may be something more at work here than just "time served." For the declaration of the Jubilee is also accompanied by a particular *sound*. The great proclamation of liberty is preceded by this verse:

You shall sound the blast of the shofar [the ram's horn] on the seventh month, on the tenth of the month, on the Day of Atonement you shall sound the shofar throughout your land. ***(Lev. 25:9)***

וְהַעֲבַרְתָּ שׁוֹפַר תְּרוּעָה בַּחֹדֶשׁ הַשְּׁבִעִי בֶּעָשׂוֹר לַחֹדֶשׁ בְּיוֹם הַכִּפֻּרִים תַּעֲבִירוּ שׁוֹפָר בְּכָל אַרְצְכֶם.

The shofar. The shofar sounding throughout the land. Where had they all heard the shofar before? On Rosh Hashanah, yes. But the echo goes back further. Where had they heard this sound first?

At Mount Sinai, of course:

On the third day, when it was morning, there was thunder and lighting, and a heavy cloud was on the mountain, and the sound of the shofar was very powerful, and all the people in the camp trembled. ***(Exod. 19:16)***

יְהִי בַּיּוֹם הַשְּׁלִישִׁי בִּהְיֹת הַבֹּקֶר וַיְהִי קֹלֹת וּבְרָקִים וְעָנָן כָּבֵד עַל הָהָר וְקֹל שֹׁפָר חָזָק מְאֹד וַיֶּחֱרַד כָּל הָעָם אֲשֶׁר בַּמַּחֲנֶה.

And then God came down on the mountain. They could not see God, but they heard words. First, *"I am the Lord your God."* Then the rest of the Ten Commandments. And then, at some point, said Rashi above, they also heard:

The Children of Israel are slaves to Me, they are My slaves...

But some of them could not hear it. Or maybe they heard it, but they didn't hear it right. All they could hear, all that they knew, was that they were to be slaves. They didn't understand that *this* service was meant to liberate them from slavery forever. They couldn't understand it then.

But now, fifty years later, the shofar blast sounds again, and they are suddenly back at the mountain. They see the lighting, hear the thunder. But now, this time, they can also hear the words. Now they can understand the real meaning of those words.

They are finally, finally free.

CHAPTER 33

THE SECRET OF THE WORLD – Parshat Bechukotai

Leviticus just never lets up.

From the start, this book seems to be going out of its way to make for difficult reading. We open immediately with an oppressively detail-heavy overview of the Temple sacrifices – blood and guts and all. Then, the second parsha, already trying our patience, is mainly just a more intricate repetition of the first. When we finally finish with animal slaughter, we move straight into the laws of purities and impurities – complete with vivid descriptions of bodily discharges and skin diseases. Eventually we branch out into various other areas of law, casting about from topic to topic, with no clear ordering principle, and very little narrative backdrop. Nothing but details, details, details.

And how does our book end? What is the very last thing Leviticus has to say?

All tithes from the land, whether seed from the ground or fruit from the tree, are for the Eternal; they are holy to the Eternal. If anyone wishes to redeem any of his tithes, he must add one-fifth to them. All tithes of the herd or flock – of all that passes under the shepherd's staff, every tenth one – shall be holy to the Eternal. ***(Lev. 27:30-32)***

וְכָל מַעְשַׂר הָאָרֶץ מִזֶּרַע הָאָרֶץ מִפְּרִי הָעֵץ לַה׳ הוּא קֹדֶשׁ לַה׳. וְאִם גָּאֹל יִגְאַל אִישׁ מִמַּעַשְׂרוֹ חֲמִשִׁיתוֹ יֹסֵף עָלָיו. וְכָל מַעְשַׂר בָּקָר וָצֹאן כֹּל אֲשֶׁר יַעֲבֹר תַּחַת הַשָּׁבֶט הָעֲשִׂירִי יִהְיֶה קֹּדֶשׁ לַה׳.

Tithing. A simple statement of the commandment to give one-tenth of all one's produce or livestock to God (indeed the word 'tithe' is related to 'tenth'). That, of all things, is what forms the less-than-thrilling conclusion to this less-than-thrilling book.

Now, I'm not saying there is anything wrong with tithes. The principle of marking off a portion of one's wealth as a contribution is surely a noble one – indeed, it helps form our modern practice of *tzedakah* (charity). But it seems a rather arbitrary note on which to end an entire book of the Torah – yet another way in which Leviticus refuses to entertain.

The classical medieval commentators mostly go about their duty of explaining what kind of tithe this is, and how it is to be performed. They let Leviticus come to its prosaic end.

But the **Ibn Ezra** leaves us off with a particularly enigmatic final thought:

Whoever has the heart to understand the secret of the world, will know the secret of the firstborn and the tenth. For, see, Abraham gave the tithe, as did Jacob, peace be upon him.

ומי שיש לו לב להבין סוד העולם אז ידע סוד הבכור והעשירי. והנה אברהם נתן מעשר גם כן יעקב אבינו עליו השלום.

The "secret of the world"?! Well, that's some pretty strong language! What, in our short passage on tithing, could possibly deliver the promise of such profound mysteries?

It is true, as the Ibn Ezra suggests, that Abraham once gave away a tenth of the possessions he had won in a great battle, to the King Malkitzedek:

He gave him a tithe of everything he had. ***(Gen. 14:20)***

וַיִּתֶּן לוֹ מַעֲשֵׂר מִכֹּל.

Malkitzedek is also said to be a kind of priest, which helps us make a connection to the later tithes, many of which will also be given to the Temple priests.

And Jacob, also, just after his famous dream of the ladder, vows a tithe to God:

From all that You give me, I will give a tenth as a tithe to You. ***(Gen 28:22)***

וְכֹל אֲשֶׁר תִּתֶּן לִי עַשֵּׂר אֲעַשְּׂרֶנּוּ לָךְ.

Okay, so we can thank the Ibn Ezra for making some interesting connections for us. This tradition of tithing goes far back, it seems. The patriarchs performed some version of it, and so our later institution may, in part, be meant to emulate their practice.

That, however, hardly qualifies as the "secret of the world."

And anyway, what was that reference to the "firstborn and the tenth"??

Now, it is not unlike the Ibn Ezra to speak in coded language. We have discussed some of his "secrets" before (see *Parshat Lech-Lecha*). But whereas those clues tipped us off to the Ibn Ezra's historical sensibility, and his willingness to question the dating of the Torah's composition – that is, his rational, critical side – in order to understand *this* secret we will have to take a dive into his numerological system, and get to know Ibn Ezra the Mystic.

We find a long discussion of his theory of numbers back in his comments on Exodus *(3:15)* and there, we notice immediately that the Ibn Ezra sees some strong relationship between the numbers one and ten – the "first" and the "tenth."

Know that The One is the secret of all the numbers, and its foundation... For all the numbers are nine, from one perspective, and ten from another.

ודע כי האחד סוד כל המספר ויסודו... והנה כל המספרי' הם תשעה מדרך אחת והם עשרה מדרך אחרת.

By this, the Ibn Ezra seems to mean simply that we count through nine numerals to form all of our single digits – 1, 2, 3 ... on to 9 – and then move to a new order of counting with the number ten. Then we could begin counting through the same nine places, but in multiples of ten: 10, 20, 30 ... on to 90. So every grouping of ten contains all the numerals together as one unit. Fair enough. That's just an explanation of the decimal system. But then he goes on and adds an opaque line:

And from another perspective, these are the ten countings without anything. For you cannot begin one, if you will not have ten. For ten is just like one.

ומדרך אחרת הם עשר ספירות בלי מה. כי לא תוכל להחל אחד אם לא יהיו עשרה.

What?! We moved from mathematics to mysticism in an instant, and now seem to have lost all sense of the meaning of the words we are reading.

Except that the Ibn Ezra has given the knowing reader a clue. For this phrase, "ten countings without anything" is nearly a direct quote from the Sefer Yetzirah, or "The Book of Formation," the oldest work of Jewish esoterica (traditionally attributed to Abraham). Except that there, we usually translate the word for "countings" differently, as follows:

Ten *sefirot* without anything. Ten and not nine. Ten and not eleven. ***(1:3)***

עשר ספירות בלימה עשר ולא תשע, עשר ולא אחת עשרה.

This is the first record we have of the Ten *Sefirot*, a central concept in Jewish Mysticism. It is not yet clear, here in the *Sefer Yetzirah*, what exactly they are, but by the time we reach the medieval period, they are understood to be the ten emanations through which God both creates the world and manifests within it. We interface with God, the kabbalists understand, through the ten *sefirot*.

This system of ten divine forces, however, was seen by some rationalist Jewish philosophers as highly problematic, for it seemed to contradict the pure monotheism which had become the defining feature of Jewish theology. So defenders of the mystical tradition often took great pains to clarify that these ten were really just different aspects of The One – like a spectrum of colors refracted through a prism, all of which emanate from the same, singular light (see, for example, Rabbi Moses Cordovero, in *Pardes Rimonim*).

This, then, seems to be the polemic that the Ibn Ezra is hinting at with the "secret of the first and the tenth." And his numerology makes the case nearly explicitly, if rather obliquely. *"The One"* – that is, the one God, *"is the secret of all the numbers"* – that is, all the manifestations of God. *"For ten is just like one."* Though God manifests in various qualities, understand that underlying that multiplicity is a great Unity.

*

Now what does that have to do with tithing? Well, think for a moment about how the act of tithing is performed. For every ten, we take one. That is, symbolically, we extract the principle of The One, from every multiple set of Ten. And what do we do with that one? We dedicate it to God. For every appearance of abundance in our lives, we must remember to acknowledge The One from whom it all comes forth.

This is, in a sense, the foundational Jewish act: recognizing the one divine source of all of creation. And every tithe is a miniature version of that – both in the numerical symbolism, and in the act of dedication. And so, of course, Jacob, the father of the Children of Israel, performed the tithe. And Abraham, the alleged author of the *Sefer Yetzirah*, also performed the tithe.

And that is why, the Ibn Ezra is hinting to us, the tithe is actually the perfect conclusion to the Book of Leviticus. Because we have been, for twenty-seven chapters now, bombarded with precise rituals, graphic depictions, arcane laws. Details, details, details. The reader can easily become, at a certain point, so overwhelmed with the minutiae that they forget the point of it all.

And the point of it all – the sacrifices, the purity laws, the holiness codes, all of it – is to come close to God. We are being trained, throughout Leviticus, to see the ultimate Oneness that underlies the dizzyingly manifold nature of our existence.

That is the secret of the world: God is in the details.

IV

Numbers

CHAPTER 34
FLAGS OF LOVE AND WAR – Parshat Bamidbar

What's the big deal with burning a flag? A flag is just a symbol of the state, after all. It isn't the state itself. Who cares if someone wants to set a colored piece of cloth on fire?

A lot of people, it turns out. Most modern nations have some sort of law against flag desecration, some of them imposing punishments of imprisonment, or even death. The United States Supreme Court, an exception, has ruled that it is unconstitutional to prohibit the destruction of a flag for the purposes of political protest; but many – including several U.S. presidential candidates – have called for that ruling to be overturned.

We sure do love our flags. But can we love them a bit too much?

Flags were important in the ancient nation of Israel as well, as we learn this week in the first reading from the Book of Numbers. The book begins with a census (hence the name 'Numbers'), and then moves on to describe the official placement of the tribal camps. These placements were formed whenever the Children of Israel would stop during their journey through the desert. So we read:

The Children of Israel shall camp, each with his flag, as a sign of their ancestral house; they shall camp around the Tent of Meeting at a distance. ***(Numbers 2:2)***

אִישׁ עַל דִּגְלוֹ בְאֹתֹת לְבֵית אֲבֹתָם יַחֲנוּ בְּנֵי יִשְׂרָאֵל מִנֶּגֶד סָבִיב לְאֹהֶל מוֹעֵד יַחֲנוּ.

The tribes were arranged in a square around the Tabernacle, with three tribes positioned on each side. And each tribe had its own special flag, with – according to a midrash on our verse above – a specific color and emblem. That midrash is worth reading through, to see just how much thought the rabbis put into these flags, and how vividly they were described:

Reuben's was red, and had a picture of mandrakes.

Shimon's was green, and had a picture of the city of Shechem.

Levi's was green, black, and red, and had a picture of the Urim and Tumim.

Judah's was sky blue and had a picture of a lion.

Issachar's was bluish-black and had a picture of a sun and moon.

Zevulun's was white and had a picture of a ship.

Dan's was sapphire and had a picture of a snake.

Gad's was grey and had a picture of an encampment.

Naftali's was wine-red and had a picture of a deer.

Asher's was pearl and had a picture of an olive tree.

Joseph's was deep black and had a picture of two princes.

Benjamin's was multicolored and had a picture of a wolf. ***(Bamidbar Rabbah 2:7)***

ראובן אבנו אדם ומפה שלו צבוע אדם ומצייר עליו דודאים. שמעון פטדה ומפה שלו צבוע ירק ומצייר עליו שכם. לוי ברקת ומפה שלו צבוע שליש לבן ושליש שחר ושליש אדם ומצייר עליו אורים ותומים. יהודה נפך וצבע מפה שלו דמותו כמין שמים ומצייר עליו אריה. יששכר ספיר ומפה שלו צבוע שחר דומה לכחל ומצייר עליו שמש וירח... זבולון יהלם וצבע מפה שלו לבנה ומצייר עליו ספינה... דן לשם וצבע מפה שלו דומה לספיר ומצייר עליו נחש... גד שבו וצבע מפה שלו לא לבן ולא שחר אלא מערב שחר ולבן ומצייר עליו מחנה... נפתלי אחלמה וצבע מפה שלו דומה ליין צלול שאין אדמותו עזה ומצייר עליו אילה... אשר תרשיש וצבע מפה שלו דומה לאבן יקרה שמתקשטות בו הנשים, ומצייר עליו אילן זית... יוסף שהם וצבע מפה שלו שחר עד מאד ומצייר לשני נשיאים... בנימין ישפה וצבע מפה שלו דומה לכל הצבעים לשנים עשר הצבעים ומצייר עליו זאב...

These flags were regal, artfully crafted, and each one displayed an image drawn from the particular story of the son of Jacob who founded that tribe. They were clearly symbols of great pride.

But even as these flags were being so exuberantly waved about, the same midrash imagines Moses beginning to worry about all the pomp and ceremony surrounding tribal identification:

When the Holy Blessed One told Moses to make these flags as they desired, Moses began to feel distressed. He said, "Now there will be future conflicts between the tribes. If I say to the Tribe of Judah to camp on the east side, they will say they can only camp in the north, and the same with Reuben, and with Ephraim, and with every single tribe. What shall I do??"

בשעה שאמר הקדוש ברוך הוא למשה עשה אותם דגלים כמו שנתאוו, התחיל משה מצר, אמר עכשו עתידה המחלקת להנתן בין השבטים, אם אני אומר לשבטו של יהודה שישרה במזרח והוא אומר אי אפשי אלא בדרום, וכן ראובן וכן אפרים וכן כל שבט ושבט, מה אני עושה?

We see in Moses' anxiety a keen intuition about the perils of nationalistic fervor. It is true, the more a group becomes attached to their tribal, ethnic identity, the more they tend to be insistent in their claim to a particular plot of land – and willing to fight for it. Moses is worried for good reason: flag-waving has often enough been a prelude to violence.

But then the midrash continues with God answering Moses back, arguing the other side:

The Holy Blessed One said, what does it matter to you? They won't need you. They know their own dwelling places. They have a diagram passed down from their father Jacob telling them exactly how to dwell under their flags, and I am not changing that. They already have a traditional ordering from their father Jacob. Just as they arranged themselves as they surrounded him on his deathbed, so will they surround the Tabernacle.

אמר לו הקדוש ברוך הוא משה מה אכפת לך אין צריכין לך, מעצמן הן מכירין דירתן, אלא דיתיקי יש בידן מיעקב אביהם היאך לשרות בדגלים, איני מחדש עליהם, כבר יש להן טכסיס מיעקב אביהם כמו שטענו אותו והקיפו את מטתו כך יקיפו את המשכן.

The flags, God assures, will not only help the tribes locate themselves in an orderly fashion out on the desert plain, but will also provide them with a deep and meaningful sense of belonging in the world. As they raise their banners, they remind themselves of where they come from, and connect themselves to their ancestors. Remember that the Torah called the flags "a sign of their father's house." As the midrash imagines it, that is literally the house of their father Jacob, who first mapped out his sons' positioning by summoning them to his bed in a certain arrangement, to receive the final blessings – many of which contain the symbols that will one day appear on their flags.

And there are other little clues in our parsha's layout of the tribal encampment that link us back to the story of Jacob. The north, east, south, west placements may remind us of a verse back in Genesis, early in Jacob's life, when God blesses him in a dream, saying:

Your descendants shall be like the dust of the earth, you shall spread out to the west and to the east, to the north and to the south. ***(Gen. 28:14)***

וְהָיָה זַרְעֲךָ כַּעֲפַר הָאָרֶץ וּפָרַצְתָּ יָמָּה וָקֵדְמָה וְצָפֹנָה וָנֶגְבָּה...

A careful reader will also note the mention of the camp of Ephraim, and then, just afterwards, the camp of Menashe, and remember a similar ordering in the story of Jacob giving blessings to his grandsons, Menashe and Ephraim. For though Menashe was the elder, and therefore in line for the first blessing, Jacob insisted on blessing Ephraim first. And so, says the Torah:

Thus he placed Ephraim before Menashe. ***(Gen. 48:20)***

וַיָּשֶׂם אֶת אֶפְרַיִם לִפְנֵי מְנַשֶּׁה.

The flag procession replicates the blessings of Jacob – both 'to' and 'from' – because these tribal identities descend from a family tree whose roots can be traced back to a beloved father. This is not just a matter of territory or pride; these flags also represent a profound connection to home, and tradition, and even love.

Our midrash, then, in the dialogue between Moses and God, astutely lays out the tension inherent in any form of nationalism. On the one hand, when masses of people are mobilized together through shared ethnic identity, there is always a great danger of their coming to violence. But on the other hand, through these tribe-like national affiliations we are able to experience a sense of belonging to our society, as if it were our own family.

Nations can breed hatred; but they can also cultivate love. Flags can be symbols of aggression, or of affection.

*

With that dichotomy in mind, it is worth remarking that after the Book of Numbers, the word for 'flag,' (*degel* – דגל) appears in only two other books in the Hebrew Bible – and their contexts offer a striking parallel to the binary we have seen so far.

The next time we find the word used comes in the book of Psalms, in the following verse:

Let us sing for joy in your salvation, flagged (*nidgol*) by the name of our God. May the Eternal fulfill all that you ask for. *(Psalms 20:6)*

נְרַנְּנָה בִּישׁוּעָתֶךָ וּבְשֵׁם אֱלֹהֵינוּ נִדְגֹּל יְמַלֵּא ה׳ כָּל מִשְׁאֲלוֹתֶיךָ.

This is the flag-waving of victory, of the satisfaction of desires. One senses behind these words a battle recently won, the glorious triumph over an enemy. Rashi even alludes to such imagery when he comments:

***flagged* – meaning, gathered together and made strong**

נדגול נתאסף ונעשה חיל.

The word he uses for 'strong' (*chayil* – חיל), is one usually reserved for soldiers. And why not? For who else carries a flag just after a victory?

The other book which mentions flags, however, gives them a very different connotation – for it is a very different book: Song of Songs, the sensuous poetic account of two lovers in pursuit of one another. And here is the first mention of our word:

He brought me into the wine-house, and his flag *(diglo)* **of love was draped over me. *(Song of Songs 2:4)***

הֱבִיאַנִי אֶל בֵּית הַיָּיִן וְדִגְלוֹ עָלַי אַהֲבָה.

Now a flag is a tender sign of love – even intimacy. And the Song of Songs persists in using this image, again and again asking us to imagine the flag as symbol of love:

My beloved is pure and flushed, and flagged (*dagul*) **among the multitudes. *(Song of Songs 5:10)***

דּוֹדִי צַח וְאָדוֹם דָּגוּל מֵרְבָבָה.

So a flag can be a marker of love, or the banner of war. Which is it, then, in our parsha, when the Children of Israel first set up camp under their flags? As they form this one nation made up of many tribes, are they bonding together as a family, or defensively marking out separate, tribal territory?

All of that potential is within them. They might go either way. In fact, the rest of the Book of Numbers will continue to play out this tension. There will be episodes of mutiny, civil war and assassination in the chapters ahead. But the people will also gather together for national ceremonies, communal blessings, and collective mourning. Through their long desert journey, they will be learning what it means to be a nation – the good, the bad, and the sometimes very ugly. And when the Book of Numbers draws to a close, they will find themselves standing at the Jordan, ready to cross over into the promised land, where all of these lessons of nationhood will be put to the test.

It is a test that continues, even today, for every nation standing under a flag.

CHAPTER 35
THE GARDEN OF EARTHLY DELIGHTS - Parshat Naso

Asceticism – the idea that physical pleasure stands in the way of spiritual enlightenment – has a long and storied history in the annals of religious thought. All the great religious traditions have some expression of it, including such practices as: fasting, celibacy, sleep deprivation, wearing simple clothing, poverty, and even – in the most extreme cases – the active pursuit of pain.

But Judaism has always had an uncomfortable relationship with the uncomfortable life. While it is always impossible to define a single, official Jewish theology, it seems fair to say that most modern Jews have inherited a basic assumption that Jewish tradition – from the Garden of Eden on – regards the physical world as a fundamentally good place, full of things that are meant to be enjoyed by human beings.

In rabbinic literature, perhaps the most explicit celebration of physical pleasure is this statement from the Jerusalem Talmud:

Rabbi Chizkiah HaKohen, in the name of Rav, said, "A person will have to give a justification and accounting for any delight he saw but did not consume." ***(Kiddushin 4:12)***

רבי חזקיה הכהן בשם רב עתיד אדם ליתן דין וחשבון על כל שראת עינו ולא אכל.

But then, on the other end of the spectrum, we can find more ascetic rabbinic voices, like this one from *Pirkei Avot*:

This is the Way of Torah: eat bread with salt, drink small amounts of water, and sleep on the ground; live a life of deprivation and toil in the Torah. ***(Avot 6:4)***

כך היא דרכה של תורה, פת במלח תאכל, ומים במשורה תשתה, ועל הארץ תישן,
וחיי צער תחיה, ובתורה אתה עמל.

So which is it? What is the Jewish ideal – pain or pleasure? Well, these rabbis can debate it all they want, but what does it say in the Torah itself?

Many have claimed that the ascetic tradition in Judaism finds its roots in this week's parsha, with the laws of the "Nazir." We have already come across the institution of vows (*nedarim* – נדרים), whereby someone can verbally pledge something they own to God. But the Nazirite vow is a particularly intense version of this practice, in that the Nazir essentially pledges her*self* to God for a temporary period.

There are three prominent manifestations of this commitment:

1. No wine or any other grape product.

2. No cutting of hair.

3. No contact with the dead (even one's own parents).

The prohibition on haircutting may remind us of the most famous Nazir in the Bible – Samson (though he was a bit of an unusual case, because he had been pledged from birth). But it is the first rule – abstinence from wine – that most strongly suggests asceticism. Sobriety as a religious commitment is one of the classic forms of self-denial, and we find a prohibition on intoxicants in many spiritual traditions, from Islam to Buddhism.

Judaism does not ban wine, as a general rule. Quite the opposite – wine is used prominently for sacred purposes. So if this Nazirite practice is an authentic expression of Jewish asceticism, it seems to distinctly frame this kind of religious expression as the exception, rather than the rule. You *can* take on these extreme practices, but it is not expected, or even encouraged.

However, even this small a nod to the value of asceticism gets vehement pushback from a parade of Jewish thinkers throughout history:

First, in the Babylonian Talmud (*Taanit 11a*), Rabbi Eliezer Ha-Kappar, understands the Nazir not merely as an extremist, but in fact, a sinner:

His sin refers to his denying himself the enjoyment of wine. If then, the one who merely denied himself the enjoyment of wine is called a sinner, how much more so does that apply to the person who denies himself the enjoyment of the other pleasures of life!

וכי באיזה נפש חטא זה אלא שציער עצמו מן היין והלא דברים קל וחומר ומה זה שלא ציער עצמו אלא מן היין נקרא חוטא המצער עצמו מכל דבר ודבר על אחת כמה וכמה.

Then, in the medieval period, **Maimonides** – who famously revived Aristotle's concept of "the golden mean," or "middle path" – wrote the following about the Nazirite vow:

If a person should say... He will not eat meat or drink wine, or get married, or live in a nice house, or wear fine clothes, but only wool and sackcloth, like the heathen priests – this is an evil path, and it is forbidden to walk down it.

Therefore, the sages commanded that a person should not deny himself anything beyond what the Torah itself prohibits, and should not take on vows of abstinence on things permitted to him. ***(Mishneh Torah, Hilchot Deot, 3:1,3)***

שמא יאמר אדם... שלא יאכל בשר ולא ישתה יין ולא יישא אישה ולא יישב בדירה נאה ולא ילבוש מלבוש נאה אלא השק והצמר הקשה וכיוצא בהן, כגון כומרי אדום– גם זו דרך רעה היא, ואסור לילך בה.

לפיכך ציוו חכמים שלא ימנע אדם עצמו אלא מדברים שמנעה התורה בלבד, ולא יהיה אוסר עצמו בנדרים ובשבועות על דברים המותרים.

And finally, when we come to the modern Hassidic movement, we find that one of the key features of their theology was a strong affirmation of engagement with the physical world, not just as a form of pleasure, but as a means of unlocking spiritual potencies. So Rabbi Shalom Noach Berezovsky, the **Netivot Shalom**, writes this about the Nazirite vow:

The purpose of Creation and the purpose of divine service is for the Jew to immerse in all the physical things, and then to elevate them all in the name of God, for then he joins the lower with the upper. The path of separating from the things of this world is an easier path. But the higher level is to raise all the things of this world to God, May He Be Blessed. And that is the desired purpose.

תכלית הבריאה ותכלית עבודת ה' היא שיהודי יעסוק בכל הענינים הגשמיים וירים את הכל לשם ה', שאז הריהו מחבר תחתונים בעליונים. אמנם הדרך לפרוש להתנער מעניני עוה"ז היא דרך יותר קלה, אבל המדרגה היותר גבוהה היא להעלות את כל עניני עוה"ז להשי"ת שזוהי התכלית הנרצית.

Here the Nazirite path is not a problematic form of extremism. Just the opposite – it's total a cop-out! The real work of the world is to be immersed in its physicality, and then to lift it up, merging the material with the spiritual. The Nazir takes the "easier path," just letting go of the world entirely. Sure, he has found a more direct way to a spiritual experience. But he has also forsaken his true divine purpose.

But wait a minute. Before we allow these voices to write the Nazir out of the Torah altogether, we ought to wonder what he's doing there in the first place. Is it really plausible that the Torah would go out of its way to create this elaborate ritual if it were totally undesirable – even sinful – to carry it out?!

And after all, the Torah itself describes the Nazir with what seems to be quite lofty language:

All the days of his being a Nazir, he is holy unto the Eternal. ***(Numbers 6:8)***

כֹּל יְמֵי נִזְרוֹ קָדֹשׁ הוּא לַה'.

"Holy unto the Eternal" sounds pretty good! Surely, then, there is something deeply valuable in this practice.

In that spirit, one of the most celebratory approaches to the Nazir comes from the commentary of the **Ibn Ezra**, who – in his typical fashion – first focuses on linguistic nuances:

Some say that Nazir comes from the term *nezer*, meaning crown. Which is why it refers to the Nazirite hair "for God, upon his head." And this seems likely.

And know that all people are slaves to their worldly desires, and the true king, the one with the Nazirite crown upon his head, is the one who is free from these desires.

ויש אומרים כי מלת נזיר מנזרת נזר והעד כי נזר אלהיו על ראשו ואיננו רחוק ודע כי כל בני אדם עבדי תאות העולם והמלך באמת שיש לו נזר ועטרת מלכות בראשו כל מי שהוא חפשי מן התאות.

So back and forth, back and forth – the rabbis keep debating. Is it good to become a Nazir or not? Is it good to cut oneself off from the pleasures of the world, or is it contrary to the very purpose of creation?

But there is something that we have been ignoring all along, the great 19th century German commentator, Rabbi **Samson Raphael Hirsch**, points out. And that is – these Nazirite practices do not really constitute such a rigorous program of asceticism.

No wine, no haircuts, and no dead bodies? That's it?! What about fasting and sleeping on the ground? What about wearing sackcloth or going celibate?

In fact, the Nazir can still enjoy all kinds of physical pleasure. If the point of the Nazirite vow was to free the vower from all worldly desires, it really didn't take us too far down the list of desires.

Instead, Rabbi Hirsch understands the function of the Nazirite vow quite differently:

The basic meaning of *nezer* is quite definitely: to keep aloof, to keep separate.... So that just as *nezer* means a royal diadem which marks the person whose head it surrounds as being set apart and inaccessible, so here *nezer* designates a regime of living and striving that raises the person who vows of his own free will to undertake it, out of and about the midst of people amongst whom he lives and sets him the task to be completely "holy to God," to belong with the whole of his being and will exclusively to his God. He wishes to draw a circle round about himself in which only God is to be present.

The obstacle to spiritual enlightenment, according to this model, is not physical pleasure, but *social* pleasure. It is not temptations of the flesh that will keep me away from God, but the bonds of friendly and familial obligation. How can I cultivate a deep relationship to the Divine, if I am balancing it with all my other relationships? I need space to myself. I need time alone with my God.

And yet, Jewish life does not offer too much alone time. The laws that make up Jewish practice presume a community of practitioners. This is not a religion for individuals; it is the religion of a people. These people need me, and I need them. We cannot escape from one another.

But then, how does one ever find God, in the midst of all these people? How does one hear the still, small voice of God calling above the buzzing noise of human society? Religion takes place in the congregation, but sometimes God can only be found alone.

Rabbi Hirsch acknowledges this tension as he finishes his comments, and offers us a strange solution:

One who does so isolate himself [with and for God] is called a Nazir. But this is no hermit-like isolation, no shutting oneself up in the wilderness.

It is an isolation of one's mind and spirit with God in the midst of the most active ordinary life.

I will not run away – the Nazir is saying – far from the madding crowd. I will find a way to be alone with God right here, amongst you all. I will live in society, and I will give to it – but I will have a place of retreat, in my mind.

How will I do this? I will not drink wine, for then I will lose myself in the joy of celebrating, and drift away into the crowd of revelers. I will not cut my hair, so that I begin to appear strange, and others keep their distance from me. And for a time, I will not go to funerals, for in sorrow I am always bonded to my people.

For now, I must be alone. I am searching for something, and I have to find it by myself.

But this period of isolation will come to an end. And then I will return to you. For I belong here, in this world, with all its wonders and pleasures. And of all those earthly delights, you are chief among them.

CHAPTER 36
WHEN OPPOSITES ATTACK – Parshat Beha'alot'kha

The boy came running out of the camp, and he looked panicked. Moses and Joshua, standing near the Tent of Meeting, turned to him, wondering what was wrong. He caught his breath and blurted out:

"Eldad and Medad are prophesying in the camp!" *(Num. 11:27)*

אֶלְדָּד וּמֵידָד מִתְנַבְּאִים בַּמַּחֲנֶה.

Now, this was a very strange report, for a number of reasons:

- First: It is unusual to have two people receiving prophecy at once. All accounts of prophecy we have seen so far have been delivered directly to one prophet.

- Second: Who are these people? We've never heard of these characters before, and now suddenly they are channeling a divine message?!

- Third: We've already got a prophet! Moses, the greatest of all the prophets, has now been leading the people and delivering them God's message since the Book of Exodus. Why would we need two other people to come along and add something?

But the strangest thing about this episode is simply that we have no idea what these two men were saying. What was their prophecy? What were they telling the people that day in the camp?

The Talmud (*Sanhedrin 17a*) offers an intriguing suggestion:

Rav Nachman says: They were prophesying about the matter of Gog and Magog.

רב נחמן אמר על עסקי גוג ומגוג

And who are Gog and Magog? The names first appear together in the Book of Ezekiel, and there it seems that Gog is a person, and Magog is the name of his country. But by the time we arrive at rabbinic literature, these are taken to be the names of two kings who will do battle at the End of Days. Some descriptions have them fighting each other, while others depict them uniting to destroy the Kingdom of Israel, in a great final war that will precede the messianic era.

So the legend of the War of Gog and Magog becomes an important image in Jewish (as well as Christian and Muslim) eschatology, a prediction of future catastrophe. But why does Rav Nachman believe that future battle was first revealed to Eldad and Medad in the desert? He engages in some fancy wordplay to connect the verses in Ezekiel back to our parsha. But the real linguistic connection between the two stories seems glaringly obvious: both pairs of names rhyme, and in a similar scheme.

Gog and Ma-gog. Eldad and Me-dad. In both cases, the second name takes the last syllable of the first, and adds a *mem* (מ) sound to the beginning. That particular sound is significant because the letter *mem,* as a prefix in Hebrew, means "from." So '*Magog*' means 'From *Gog,*' and '*Medad*' is 'From *Dad.*' Of course, in the first formulation of Gog and Magog, this was literally true: the person Gog came from the place Magog. But once they have come to represent two warring factions, the names indicate that one side has come from the other, and so both are, in some essential way, the same.

The prophetic message of Eldad and Medad, then – hinted to us by their names – is that the ultimate battle, the war to end all wars, will be played out by two opposing violent forces that are actually drawn from the same source. What appear to be mortal enemies are, in fact, simply two sides of one larger phenomenon of destruction.

This motif of rhyming opposites is used again and again in Jewish literature at major crisis points in our national history. The ancient Kingdom of Israel is first broken apart after a rebellion against *Rechoboam* (רחבעם) by the troops of *Jeroboam* (ירבעם). And the ultimate destruction of Jerusalem, we are told in the Talmud, comes about through confusion over another pair of rhyming names:

The destruction of Jerusalem came about through Kamtza and Bar Kamtza.

A certain man had a friend, Kamtza, and an enemy, Bar Kamtza. He once made a party and said to his servant, "Go and bring Kamtza." But the man went and brought Bar Kamtza. *(Gittin 55b)*

אקמצא ובר קמצא חרוב ירושלים דההוא גברא דרחמיה קמצא ובעל דבביה בר קמצא עבד סעודתא אמר ליה לשמעיה זיל אייתי לי קמצא אזל אייתי ליה בר קמצא

The party host, who wanted to invite Kamtza, is outraged when Bar Kamtza shows up. And so Kamtza kicks Bar Kamtza out. Bar Kamtza is so humiliated that – even though he himself is Jewish – he takes revenge on his host by reporting a Jewish rebellion to the Roman authorities, who eventually send Nero to destroy Jerusalem.

In this story, Bar Kamtza might literally mean, the son of Kamtza. Or it might more symbolically mean, "from Kamtza," or "of Kamtza." In other words, the man arbitrarily loved one thing, but hated another thing that was really made up of exactly the same material as the first. Kamtza and Bar Kamtza are like matter and antimatter, thesis and synthesis, light and shadow. To hate one and love the other is to lose sight of the essential similarity between the two, and thereby to engage in a useless and all-consuming kind of violence. The War of Gog and Magog, and all struggles for total annihilation, emerge from the clash of two seemingly opposite extremes that are actually more alike than we realize.

Why does this matter? And why would the Torah spend time whimsically name-rhyming instead of just making its point directly?

It matters there, in the desert, because this journey will be filled with all sorts of terrible conflicts and, in most cases, both parties will descend from the same source. Just a chapter later, Moses will be accused of wrongdoing by his own siblings. The mutiny against Moses and Aaron will be led by Korach, their cousin and tribesman. Even the threat of curses from a foreign prophet are to come from a man who worships the same God as the Israelites – Bilaam is in many respects just like Moses, the Medad to his Eldad. In this landscape, we will soon see, enemies are often former friends, and twin siblings can produce warring tribes.

But it matters also out here, in the world beyond the desert, because we too go to war against people with whom we share a God. We denounce ideological extremists while proudly promoting the opposite extreme. We rage against one system of oppression by forcefully imposing our own value system on our oppressors.

Most of the time, however, we are blind to these ironies. We cannot see the similarities between our enemies and ourselves. Most of the time, we do not have the aid of a rhyme to call our attention to the ways we sound exactly like those whom we hate the most.

Eldad and Medad are sounding the echo of that rhyme out for us, to warn us of all the coming Gogs and Magogs of this world – those outside of our camp, and those within.

CHAPTER 37

DAY OF THE DEAD – Parshat Shelach

There were so many. How did they all die?

After the sin of the spies, God unleashes the most severe punishment in the whole of the Torah. The spies had come back from the land of Canaan in a state of panic, and they warned the people that God was sending them into dangerous territory:

Why is the Lord taking us to that land to fall by the sword? Our wives and children will be carried off! It would be better for us to go back to Egypt! ***(Num. 14:3)***

וְלָמָה ה' מֵבִיא אֹתָנוּ אֶל הָאָרֶץ הַזֹּאת לִנְפֹּל בַּחֶרֶב נָשֵׁינוּ וְטַפֵּנוּ יִהְיוּ לָבַז הֲלוֹא טוֹב לָנוּ שׁוּב מִצְרָיְמָה.

God is outraged at this critique and, measure for measure, decides that those with the gall to defame the promised land should not be allowed to enter it. Instead, says God:

In this very wilderness shall your carcasses drop. Of all of you who were recorded in the census lists, from the age of twenty years up, you who have muttered against Me, not one of you shall enter the land in which I swore to settle you...your children who you said, would be carried off – they will be allowed to enter, and they will know the land you have rejected. But your carcasses shall drop in the wilderness, while your children roam the desert for forty years, suffering for your faithlessness, until the last of your carcasses is down in the wilderness. ***(vv. 29-33)***

בַּמִּדְבָּר הַזֶּה יִפְּלוּ פִגְרֵיכֶם וְכָל פְּקֻדֵיכֶם לְכָל מִסְפַּרְכֶם, מִבֶּן עֶשְׂרִים שָׁנָה וָמָעְלָה. אֲשֶׁר הֲלִינֹתֶם עָלָי. אִם אַתֶּם תָּבֹאוּ אֶל הָאָרֶץ אֲשֶׁר נָשָׂאתִי אֶת יָדִי לְשַׁכֵּן אֶתְכֶם בָּהּ... וְטַפְּכֶם אֲשֶׁר אֲמַרְתֶּם לָבַז יִהְיֶה. וְהֵבֵיאתִי אֹתָם וְיָדְעוּ אֶת הָאָרֶץ אֲשֶׁר מְאַסְתֶּם בָּהּ. לבופִגְרֵיכֶם אַתֶּם יִפְּלוּ בַּמִּדְבָּר הַזֶּה. וּבְנֵיכֶם יִהְיוּ רֹעִים בַּמִּדְבָּר אַרְבָּעִים שָׁנָה וְנָשְׂאוּ אֶת זְנוּתֵיכֶם עַד תֹּם פִּגְרֵיכֶם בַּמִּדְבָּר.

So every man of fighting age is sentenced to death. Now that is over 600,000 people – an astonishing number. But they were not to perish all at once, in some plague or mass execution. Rather, the forty years of desert wandering was to serve as a force of attrition, slowly wearing the people down until a whole generation had fallen away.

How exactly did this work? We might imagine them staggering through the desert, a massive pack of bodies pushing forward in the sweltering heat – and then every so often, a body would drop. Someone had grown old and weak, and had used up all their strength. There would be shouts of alert, then the group would stop, the dead would be buried – with perhaps some tears and a word or two of prayer – and then they moved on.

But did this sad scene this really happen 600,000 times? Over forty years, that would be an average of around forty-one deaths a day! Attending to the fallen would have consumed every moment of their journey.

That calculus must have made little sense to the interpreters of the Torah, given all of the other events recorded in the narrative of the Book of Numbers. Perhaps they also simply found it difficult to bear the thought of such an unrelenting death march. So one of the rabbis of the midrash came up with an alternative system by which this massive punishment might have been meted out over time:

Rabbi Levi said: on the eve of the 9th of the month of Av, every year, Moses would send an announcement out through the camp, saying, "Go out and dig." And they would go out and dig graves, and then go to sleep in them. In the morning, he would send out another announcement, saying, "Arise, and separate the dead from the living!" They would get up and find 15,000 missing from the 600,000. In the final, fortieth year, they did this same thing, but when they got up, they found no one was gone. They said, "Maybe we miscounted." So they did the same thing on the 10th, the 11th, the 12th, the 13th, and the 14th of the month. But when the full moon appeared, they said, it seems that the Holy One has finished punishing us!

So they made [the 9th of Av] a holiday. But our sins caused it to become a day of mourning, with the destruction of the two temples. *(Eikha Rabbah, Petichta 33)*

אמר רבי לוי כל ערב תשעה באב היה משה מוציא כרוז בכל המחנה ואומר צאו לחפר, והיו יוצאין וחופרין קברות וישנין בהן, לשחרית היה מוציא כרוז ואומר קומו והפרישו המתים מן החיים, והיו עומדים ומוציאין עצמן, חמשה עשר אלף ופרוטרוט חסרו שש מאות אלף, ובשנת הארבעים האחרון עשו כן ומצאו עצמן שלמים, אמרו דומה שטעינו בחשבון, וכן בעשור ובאחד עשר ובשנים עשר ושלשה עשר וארבעה עשר, כיון דאתמלא סיהרא אמרו דומה שהקדוש ברוך הוא בטל אותה גזרה מעלינו וחזרו ועשאוהו יום טוב, וגרמו עוונותיהם ונעשה אבל בעולם הזה בחרבן הבית פעמים.

This is surely one of the most chilling images in all of rabbinic literature. Once a year, everyone digs their own grave, and then lies down in it, not knowing whether they will ever rise again. Most of them will wake up in the morning, look up at a rectangle of sky, and realize with a wave of relief that this was not their year. Then, in another wave of emotion, they will remember that 15,000 of their kinsmen have died.

So they will climb up out of the ground and begin to wander around the camp, peering anxiously into the holes in the ground, hoping to find them empty. But when they come upon someone who hadn't woken up that morning, they will sigh, fill the grave with dirt, take a moment to mourn the dead, and move on. This reaping ceremony will repeat itself every year, for forty years, until a whole generation is gone, and their children are finally free to leave their desert prison.

Beyond the haunting imagery itself, however, this midrash also offers an intriguing reframing of the origins of the primary day of mourning in the Jewish calendar year, the 9th of Av. As the midrash notes, this day is best known to us as the date on which both Temples in Jerusalem were destroyed, hundreds of years apart. The rabbis then build on the calendrical syncing of that double destruction and begin to conceive of the 9th of Av as a permanent day of doom, upon which, year after year, tragedies befall the people of Israel. So another rabbinic text, the Mishnah in Tractate *Ta'anit,* tells us:

Five tragedies befell our ancestors on the 9th of the Month of Av... It was decreed that our ancestors would not enter the Promised Land, the Temple was destroyed the first time, and the second time, the fortress of Beitar was entrapped, and the city of Jerusalem was plowed down. So, as we enter the Month of Av, we reduce our happiness. *(Mishnah Ta'anit 4:6)*

חמישה דברים אירעו את אבותינו..בתשעה באב...נגזר על אבותינו שלא ייכנסו לארץ, וחרב הבית בראשונה, ובשנייה, ונלכד הבית תור, ונחרשה העיר. משנכנס אב, ממעטין בשמחה.

This mishnah proposes that the 9th of Av is more than just a sad day of memorializing the Temples. There is a pattern of successive tragedies, throughout history, all occurring on this one day that seems to come from some unique metaphysical property embedded in this point in the calendar. The 9th of Av is like a fixed portal in time out of which, once a year, calamity threatens to emerge.

And the mishnah agrees that this cycle was set into motion here in *Parshat Shelach*, with the decree that barred the generation of the Exodus from entering into the Land of Canaan. But whereas this text jumps from that moment straight to the destruction of the Temple nearly a thousand years later, our midrash above envisioned the tragic repetition of this day in the calendar beginning immediately, and continuing for forty years straight. Throughout the long desert journey, every 9th of Av was a day of death.

But the midrash also did something rather surprising with the 9th of Av. For Rabbi Levi told us that the inherent danger of this day actually came to an end, and that it was even celebrated as a holiday. The cycle of tragedy, in other words, was once broken – so much so that we came to rejoice on the 9th of Av.

And then what happened? How did we get back to tragedy? Why were the two Temples destroyed on this same date, the 9th of Av? The midrash says that *"our sins caused it to become a day of mourning"* again. We somehow reactivated the latent destructive potential in this day that had never fully been expunged. If only we had been more righteous, more compassionate, and more faithful – the midrash suggests – perhaps we would still be celebrating a holiday instead of mourning all that we have lost.

Yet if the conclusion of the midrash is that our sins caused further tragedy, the structure of the midrash leaves us wondering if the opposite might also be true: that our tragedies caused us to sin. For what is the aftereffect of forty years of constant death? What happens to someone who wakes up every year on the 9th of Av having lost 15,000 friends and relatives? When all the killing suddenly ends, is the day so easily transformed into a holiday?

Or does the collective trauma linger? Are we anxious every year around this time because somewhere in our cultural DNA the recurring threat of death has been encoded? If we act irrationally, suspiciously, and defensively, is it because we sense some unknown harm looming on the horizon? If we lash out at one another or at the world around us, is it because we wonder if, any day now, we might wake up to another catastrophe?

We are carrying around with us all the horrors of the past. We have, always, some vague collective memory of loss buried in the back of our consciousness. We still wake up every morning, staring up at a rectangle of sky, and feel a wave of relief at having lived to see another day. And then the second wave hits, and we remember that we are only alive because others have died.

CHAPTER 38

WHAT WE TALK ABOUT WHEN WE TALK ABOUT GOD – Parshat Korach

You have to give it to Korach. He sounds so good.

The leader of the great mutiny against Moses and Aaron does not speak like a power-hungry rival, or a crazed terrorist, but a man of the people:

This whole congregation is holy, and the Eternal is among them. So why do you raise yourself above the congregation of the Eternal? ***(Numbers 16:3)***

כִּי כָל הָעֵדָה כֻּלָּם קְדֹשִׁים וּבְתוֹכָם ה' וּמַדּוּעַ תִּתְנַשְּׂאוּ עַל קְהַל ה'.

We are all holy, says Korach. No one of us is superior to any other. So be suspicious of leaders who claim a special role or a privileged access to God.

Sounds like a reasonable claim to me. Wise, even.

So what is the problem with Korach? Why is he seen as the greatest villain in the Torah to emerge from among the Israelites? Why is he punished so quickly, and so severely – famously swallowed up by the ground?

And why doesn't Moses respond to Korach? All we read, after Korach makes his great populist polemic, is that:

When Moses heard this, he fell on his face. (*Numbers 16:4)*

וַיִּשְׁמַע מֹשֶׁה וַיִּפֹּל עַל פָּנָיו

And then Moses proposes the test of competing offerings that will determine God's favor.

But Korach offers a fair critique of Moses and Aaron's hierarchical authority, doesn't he? Wasn't it at least worth a response?

The rabbis of the midrash, perhaps sensitive to the absence of any real dialogue here, imagine a very different kind of conversation between Korach and Moses.

In this version they are discussing, of all things, two very particular commandments: 1) *tzitzit* – the strings (one of which is blue) that the Torah requires on each corner of any four-cornered garment. 2) *mezuzah* – the parchment with a specific passage from the Torah that is affixed to the doorway of a house. So, in their version, the exchange between Korach and Moses went like this:

Korach arose and said to Moses, "If a garment is all blue is it exempt from the requirement of *tzitzit*?" Moses said, "No, it still requires *tzitzit*." Korach replied, "A garment which is all blue doesn't take care of itself, but four little strings take care of it?! What about a house, full of books? Is it exempt for the requirement of *mezuzah*?" Moses said, "No, it still requires a *mezuzah*." Korach replied, "The whole Torah, with all 275 sections doesn't take care of the house, but one little section of parchment in the *mezuzah* takes care of it?! No, these things were not commanded to us! You made them up on your own!!" ***(Bamidbar Rabbah 18:3)***

קפץ קרח ואמר למשה טלית שכלה תכלת מהו שתהא פטורה מן הציצית, אמר לו חייבת בציצית. אמר לו קרח טלית שכלה תכלת אין פוטרת עצמה, ארבעה חוטין פוטרות אותה. בית מלא ספרים מהו שיהא פטור מן המזוזה, אמר לו חיב במזוזה, אמר לו, כל התורה כלה מאתים ושבעים וחמש פרשיות אינה פוטרת את הבית, פרשה אחת שבמזוזה פוטרת את הבית, אמר לו דברים אלו לא נצטוית עליהן, ומלבך אתה בודאן.

Okay, now we have an actual conversation – but what a strange one it is! This story prompts more questions than it answers: Why would they suddenly care to be sifting through the minutiae of Jewish law, here in the midst of this desert journey? Why would Korach be concocting theoretical scenarios in order to highlight minor disagreements over legal technicalities? Where does this story come from anyhow, and what has it got to do with the Biblical story in front of us?

There is one fairly straightforward textual answer to the last question. The very section in the Torah that commands *tzitzit* was the last passage in last week's *parsha*. So when the rabbis see the Korach confrontation erupt at the beginning of this week's *parsha*, seemingly out of nowhere, they ask what prompted it and figure it must have something to do with the last thing we read. In a classic rabbinic interpretive move, they use the seemingly arbitrary juxtaposition of two passages to build them together into one larger story: Korach disagreed with Moses, but we don't know exactly why; it must be that he disagreed with Moses over *tzitzit*.

There is an elegance to this weaving together of two adjacent sections of the Torah, this assumption that every placement in this text has meaning and purpose. We might appreciate the dynamic style of the rabbis' method of interpretation as a thing of beauty in itself.

But that still doesn't answer so many of our other questions about this story. What was so important about this very arcane debate that it merited recording? And why does the midrash include also the question of the *mezuzah* commandment, which is conceptually similar, but is nowhere near the Korach story?

The great Spanish medieval commentator, **Rabbeinu Bachya**, has a brilliant answer which immediately exposes a direct parallel between this seemingly random story about an argument over two commandments and the original Korach story we encountered:

There is a hint in all of this. It is a metaphor for the people Israel, who are like an entirely blue garment, or a house full of books. He was saying that these things are like Israel, who are all holy, and all full of virtue. So why would they need others to rule over them and rise above them? And the rulers [Moses and Aaron] are being compared to the blue strings and the *mezuzah*.

ויש בכללם עוד רמז משל על ישראל כי המשילם לטלית שכלה תכלת ובית מלא ספרים, וכיון בזה לומר כי ישראל שכלם קדושים וכלם חשובים מלאים מן המעלות למה יצטרכו למשתררים ולמתנשאים עליהם, והמשיל המשתררים לחוט של תכלת ולמזוזה.

Once Rabbeinu Bachya says it, it's so obvious. These two legal cases are perfect metaphors for the exact claim we saw at the outset: *The whole congregation is holy*. They don't need any special leader to take care of them. They don't need a unique individual to bring them close to God. They don't need a blue string or a fragment of parchment to complete them. Like the garment that is already blue, and like the house that is full of Torah, they are already complete – God is already among them.

The brilliance of Rabbeinu Bachya's explanation is that it shows the brilliance of the rabbinic story itself. The midrash is operating on more than just the juxtaposition of two passages in the Torah; it is using the structure of the law in one to unpack the narrative claim in the other.

Still, the most basic question remains unanswered: Why do the rabbis believe that Korach – in this version – would have chosen to speak in the very particular language of legal debate instead of just making his moral case explicit? Why talk about strings and scrolls instead of just talking about the relationship between God and human beings?

But then, maybe that is all too often exactly the nature of internal religious debate. We fight fiercely over the codes and details of our traditions when in truth there are deeper human concerns that we have, but fail to articulate. We accuse one another of misinterpreting the law, when in fact we hold fundamentally different visions of religious life. We hide behind the particulars, instead of talking frankly about what we truly believe.

Because it is easier to talk about the law. It is discrete, applicable, linguistic. We can analyze it, categorize it, and render judgments. It is much harder to really talk about God, that infinite notion that matters so much to us, but is beyond all of our words.

Indeed, it is sometimes especially frightening for people of religion to speak openly to one another of God. For then they may be forced to admit that no one has all the answers.

CHAPTER 39
EIGHTEEN ANSWERS – Parshat Chukat

It's a big week in *parshanut.*

Now of course, the whole enterprise of *parshanut* – Torah commentary – is founded on asking questions about the Biblical text. But there are certain questions that are legendary in the genre – questions that have plagued scholars for centuries. This week we run into one of the classics:

"What did Moses do that was so wrong?"

The story goes like this: The people are – once again – complaining. They are hungry and thirsty and wishing they'd never left Egypt. In fact, they actually say they wish they'd *died* back there.

So Moses and Aaron nervously take the matter to God, who instructs them to raise their staff to convene the people, and then order a rock to produce water, which – God says – it will then miraculously do.

But when everyone had gathered together, Moses suddenly loses his temper and says, ***"Listen you rebels, shall we get water for you from this rock?!"*** and then strikes the rock with the staff, twice. And it works! Water starts flowing out of the rock, enough for all the people and their animals to drink.

But there seems to be a big problem. Because now God is angry, and proceeds to deliver Moses and Aaron a devastating punishment:

Because you did not believe in Me enough to sanctify Me in the eyes of the Children of Israel, therefore you shall not bring this congregation into the land that I have given them. *(Numbers 20:12)*

יַעַן לֹא הֶאֱמַנְתֶּם בִּי לְהַקְדִּישֵׁנִי לְעֵינֵי בְּנֵי יִשְׂרָאֵל לָכֵן לֹא תָבִיאוּ אֶת הַקָּהָל הַזֶּה אֶל הָאָרֶץ אֲשֶׁר נָתַתִּי לָהֶם:

You read that right. Moses – God's trusted servant, the greatest prophet who ever lived, the hero of the Torah, who led the people out of Egypt and watched over them for forty years in the desert, defending them tirelessly as they gave him nothing but grief – is now denied entry into the promised land. He will take the people all the way there, but never make it in himself. Instead, he will die on the border, and get left behind, all alone.

It seems so unfair. So cruel. And so wildly out of proportion to what Moses did.

But then, that's the question. What *did* Moses do, exactly? How did he not "sanctify" God?

What in the world is going on here?!

That is the question. And out of it springs a whole universe of *parshanut*. Now, most weeks, I bring you a selection of some of the major answers to whatever question we are looking at, and then focus in on one or two particularly rich commentaries. But this week, I want to do something different. Because I want you to see what can happen when the commentators come upon a real doozy of a question. I want you to get a sense of just how vast the catalog of attempts to reckon with one problem in the Torah can be.

So, without further ado, let's take a look at – as the saying goes – "how much ink has been spilled," trying to solve this problem. Here then, is a brief history – chronologically arranged – of (just some of) the answers to the question, "What did Moses do to deserve it?"

1. **Rashi** *(France, 1040-1105)*: We always start with Rashi, the Father of the Commentators. And his answer is simply that Moses hit the rock instead of speaking to it as God had commanded. So he disobeyed the order.

2. **Ibn Ezra** *(Spain, 1089-1167)*: The problem wasn't the striking of the rock per se, but the fact that Moses hit it twice. The first time, he hit it out of anger, and because of that, it did not produce water. So then he had to hit it again to fulfill God's wishes, and at that point, it worked. But that repetition made it look like God was less powerful, and could not produce the water in one try.

3. **Maimonides** *(Spain 1135 - Egypt 1204)*: The problem was not with the rock and the water at all, but in the fact that Moses lost his temper. That was a sin in and of itself, but especially so when he was acting as God's representative, because he made God look angry and unmerciful.

4. **Ramban** *(Spain, 1194-1270)*: Borrowing from the 10th century Rabbeinu Chananel, he says that Moses made the mistake of saying "Shall *we* get water for you from this rock," instead of "Shall *God* get water for

you," making it look like he was actually performing the miracle instead of God.

5. **Bekhor Shor** *(France, 12th century)*: Moses just didn't explain properly to the people what was happening.

6. **Rabbeinu Bachya** *(Spain, 1255-1340)*: Earlier (in Exodus 17), they had produced water from a rock by hitting it once. Now, by hitting it twice, Moses made it look like God's power had weakened since those days.

7. **Ba'al HaIkarim** *(Spain, 1380-1444)*: Moses should have believed enough in God that he didn't even have to ask, but simply called out for a miracle himself, and known that God would deliver.

8. **Abarbanel** *(Portugal, 1437-1508)*: They aren't actually being punished for this, but for previous sins (Moses for sending the spies, Aaron for making the golden calf). But God uses this event as a pretext to finally address those crimes without having to shame Moses and Aaron by bringing up the past.

9. **Sforno** *(Italy, 1475-1550)*: Moses and Aaron deliberately lessened the miracle from something totally supernatural (speech producing water) to something that seemed semi-natural (somehow they were able to strike the rock in such a way that it released water), because they didn't think the people were worthy of a full-blown miracle.

10. **Gur Aryeh** *(Prague, 1520-1609)*: The fact that they displayed anger simply showed that they lacked faith. If they had faith, they would have performed the miracle with joy.

11. **Or HaChayim** *(Morocco, 1696-1743)*: When they said "Shall we get water for you from *this* rock," they made it sound like water could only come from that particular rock, as if it were a magic rock, instead of making it clear that God could produce water from *any* rock.

12. **HaKtav v'HaKabbalah** *(Germany, 1785-1865)*: Their job was to teach the people theology. They should have explained carefully the nature of God's power to create something from nothing, instead of just performing the act itself.

13. **Kedushat Levi** *(Poland, 1740-1809)*: In calling the people "rebels," Moses humiliated them, and in doing so, missed the opportunity to bring them into a higher spiritual consciousness, a greater awareness of the kindness of God.

14. **Samson Raphael Hirsch** *(Germany, 1808-1888)*: When Moses heard God ask him to take his staff and raise it up, he assumed that he needed the staff as proof of his credibility (as he did 40 years before when he first led the people out of Egypt) and he was hurt because he assumed the people still did not trust him. So instead of just raising the staff, he bitterly smashed it against the rock.

15. **HaEmek Davar** *(Lithuania, 1816-1893)*: They should have led the people in prayer before they performed the miracle, to show that God was answering their prayers.

16. **Meshekh Chokhmah** *(Latvia, 1843-1926)*: Because Moses made it appear that he had performed the miracle himself, God was worried that the people would come to worship Moses in the land of Israel as a deity.

17. **Sfat Emet** *(Poland, 1847-1905)*: This was not a punishment at all, but a proof that the people were unable to deal with Moses' harsher style of leadership. Because Moses saw the divine vision clearly, he felt no need to explain it to people, to "speak" things out to them as he was supposed to speak to the rock. His hitting the rock instead represented his more rigid kind of leadership, which God now realized the people would not be able to handle in the land of Israel.

18. **ParshaNut** *(United States, 1976–present)*: To all of these answers, perhaps we can add one of our own. Maybe the sin had nothing to do with the incident at the rock at all. Maybe God was upset that when the people complained, Moses and Aaron had immediately come to God looking for a quick solution. Instead, they should have taken the opportunity to assure the people that God would take care of them somehow, as God had all these years. They should have encouraged faith, and thus "sanctified" God in the eyes of the people. Instead they went begging for a miracle.

*

Eighteen is a good Jewish number, so we'll stop here, though we could surely go on and on.

So how do we choose among them? Which is the right answer?

Well, maybe one of the above answers seems better to you than all the others. Or maybe you can come up with a different solution to the problem. But there is a more important point here about how we read *parshanut*. Whenever we are confronted with a case like this in the Torah, which seems to have prompted every commentator in history to come up with a new answer to an old question, one thing is clear: The question is better than the answers.

And in this case, the underlying question is one of the most difficult theological problems of all: Why do the righteous suffer?

Why do good people receive greater punishment than they seem to deserve? Why does God seem so merciless? Why is there no order to the world of pain and pleasure, reward and punishment?

Why is Moses left outside to die?

There are a million answers. But really, there are no good answers.

I like to think, however, that somehow Moses is comforted by all of our efforts to make sense of his death. Wherever he lies, perhaps the words of all the commentaries throughout the centuries have reached him, and wrapped around him, holding him like a shroud of woven letters.

I hope he knows that we have never forgotten him, and that we are still trying to figure this all out.

CHAPTER 40

THE PATH OF DESTRUCTION – Parshat Balak

What's so bad about Bilaam?

He seems like a nice enough guy. A holy man, even!

Now Balak, the king of Moab – for whom our parsha is named – *he's* a real villain. He's the one who wants to destroy the Israelites. True, it's Bilaam he tries to hire to put a curse on them. But that doesn't automatically make Bilaam a bad guy, does it?

In fact, when Balak's men come to Bilaam to make the request, Bilaam tells them he has to ask God what to do. And when God then tells him not to curse "that people," Bilaam immediately refuses and tells the men to leave.

When they come back a second time, promising riches, he tells them:

Even if Balak were to give me his whole house, full of gold and silver, I could not do anything, big or small, contrary to the command of the Eternal, my God. ***(Numbers 22:18)***

וַיַּעַן בִּלְעָם וַיֹּאמֶר אֶל עַבְדֵי בָלָק אִם יִתֶּן לִי בָלָק מְלֹא בֵיתוֹ כֶּסֶף וְזָהָב לֹא אוּכַל לַעֲבֹר אֶת פִּי ה' אֱלֹהָי לַעֲשׂוֹת קְטַנָּה אוֹ גְדוֹלָה.

Wow – so religious! Bilaam sounds like a perfect saint.

It turns out that God does let Bilaam go this time, but Bilaam makes it clear to Balak that he cannot promise a curse:

I can only utter the word that God puts into my mouth. ***(Num. 22:38)***

הֲיָכוֹל אוּכַל דַּבֵּר מְאוּמָה הַדָּבָר אֲשֶׁר יָשִׂים אֱלֹהִים בְּפִי אֹתוֹ אֲדַבֵּר.

And guess what! Bilaam ends up blessing the Israelites, much to Balak's dismay. In fact some of the words of this blessing are preserved in our daily liturgy:

How goodly are your tents, O Jacob; your dwelling places, O Israel! ***(Num 24:5)***

מַה טֹּבוּ אֹהָלֶיךָ יַעֲקֹב מִשְׁכְּנֹתֶיךָ יִשְׂרָאֵל.

So this is no enemy of Israel. This is the author of one of her greatest tributes!

And yet, the rabbis *hate* Bilaam. For them, he is the epitome of wickedness. They pile on him all the nastiest things they can think of. Including, even, the following unpleasant suggestion from the Talmud:

His donkey said to him…I've let you not only ride me during the day, but also to lay with me at night. ***(Avodah Zarah 4b)***

אמרה ליה.. אני עושה לך רכיבות ביום ואישות בלילה.

Well, as rabbinic insults go, it doesn't get much lower than, "You have sex with your donkey."

So why are the rabbis so virulently anti-Bilaam, when he seems from the plain text of the story to be such a righteous man? Most of the answers come down to the fact that he was willing to ask God again if he could go perform this curse for Balak, after he had already been told by God that this was a bad idea. Didn't he get it? God said no. So the rabbis suspect that deep down, he really *wanted* to hurt the Israelites. He was dying to curse them, chomping at the bit, looking for any opening.

But even so, what about the fact that God *allows* Bilaam to go? Surely Bilaam can't take the blame for that! It's pretty clear that he would never defy God openly. If God had said no, he'd never have left.

The rabbis of the Midrash respond to this difficulty with a startling theological statement:

[That night God came to Bilaam and said to him,] "If these men have come to call on you, you may go with them." (Num. 22:20) **From this, you learn that a person is taken down the path that he wishes to go. Because at first, he was told,** ***"Do not go!" (v. 12)*** **But since he stubbornly insisted on going – as it says** ***"God was angry that he went" (Num. 22:22)*** **– so the Holy Blessed One said to him, "Wicked One! Do you think I don't want the wicked to perish?! Since you want to go and perish from the world, then get up and go!"** ***(Bamidbar Rabbah 20:12)***

(**במדבר כב, כ**): אם לקרא לך באו האנשים קום לך אתם. מכן את למד שבדרך שאדם רוצה לילך בה מוליכין אותו, שמתחלה נאמר לו (**במדבר כב, יב**): לא תלך, כיון שהעז פניו להלך הלך, שכן כתיב (**במדבר כב, כב**): ויחר אף אלהים כי הולך הוא. אמר לו הקדוש ברוך הוא רשע איני חפץ באבודן של רשעים, הואיל ואת רוצה לילך לאבד מן העולם קום לך.

Well, this is bizarre! Is the suggestion really that God will tell you anything you want to hear? What kind of God is that, then, and what is the meaning of following God's will if it is really only an echo of your own deepest desires?

*

The moral significance of this radical claim may perhaps be discovered by sifting carefully through another rabbinic motif: their constant linking of Bilaam with Abraham.

Mishnah 5:19 in *Pirkei Avot,* for example, asks:

What is the difference between the students of our father Abraham and the students of the wicked Bilaam?

מה בין תלמידיו של אברהם אבינו לתלמידיו של בלעם הרשע?

...and then goes on at length to explain how different the two figures were – how one was humble and the other haughty, one was rewarded and the other one taken down to the pit of destruction.

The rabbis imagine Bilaam himself drawing this comparison, later, when he proposes to make an offering on:

seven altars – I will offer bull and a ram on each altar... *(Num. 23:4)*

אֶת־שִׁבְעַת הַמִּזְבְּחֹת עָרַכְתִּי וָאַעַל פָּר וָאַיִל בַּמִּזְבֵּחַ...

...whereas Abraham only offered a single ram! *(Rashi's comment on the verse, taken from Midrash Tanchuma)*

ואברהם לא העלה אלא איל אחד!

It is as if Bilaam is in competition with Abraham, knowing that he stands in Abraham's shadow and trying to outdo him.

But for all the rabbinic effort to distinguish between Abraham and Bilaam, the Torah itself offers some striking parallels between the two:

First of all, we are told *(in Deuteronomy 23:5)* that Bilaam is from *Aram-Naharayim.* This is a place we know from back in Genesis, when Abraham tells his servant to go back to the land of his birth to find a wife for his son, and then we read that the servant "made his way to *Aram-Naharayim.*" *(Genesis 24:10)* So Abraham and Bilaam come from the same homeland. They are, in a sense, kinsmen.

And, of course, the whole of the Bilaam story hinges on blessings and curses, which hearkens back to the opening scene in the Abraham narrative, where we read that:

I will bless those who bless you and curse him who curses you. *(Gen. 12:3)*

וַאֲבָרְכָה מְבָרְכֶיךָ וּמְקַלֶּלְךָ אָאֹר.

This is from the scene where Abraham is first told by God, "Go forth!" (לך לך) ... just as Bilaam is eventually told by God to "go" (לך).

In fact, it is the scene where Bilaam finally goes – the very part of the story for which he is most criticized – that has the most pronounced echoes of Abraham:

- **Bilaam arose in the morning and saddled his donkey.** *(Num. 22:21)*

  וַיָּקָם בִּלְעָם בַּבֹּקֶר וַיַּחֲבֹשׁ אֶת אֲתֹנוֹ.

  and

- **Abraham arose in the morning and saddled his donkey.** *(Gen. 22:3)*

  וַיַּשְׁכֵּם אַבְרָהָם בַּבֹּקֶר וַיַּחֲבֹשׁ אֶת חֲמֹרוֹ.

- **He was riding on his donkey, and his two young men were with him.** *(Num. 22:22)*

  וְהוּא רֹכֵב עַל־אֲתֹנוֹ וּשְׁנֵי נְעָרָיו עִמּוֹ.

  and

- **He saddled his donkey and took with him his two young men.** *(Gen. 22:3)*

  יַּחֲבֹשׁ אֶת־חֲמֹרוֹ וַיִּקַּח אֶת שְׁנֵי נְעָרָיו אִתּוֹ.

- **An Angel of the Eternal stood on the path to stop him.** *(Num. 22:22)*

  וַיִּתְיַצֵּב מַלְאַךְ ה' בַּדֶּרֶךְ לְשָׂטָן לוֹ.

  and

- **An Angel of the Eternal called to him from heaven ... and said, "Do not raise your hand against the boy, or do anything to him..."** *(Gen. 22:11-12)*

וַיִּקְרָא אֵלָיו מַלְאַךְ ה' מִן הַשָּׁמַיִם... וַיֹּאמֶר אַל תִּשְׁלַח יָדְךָ אֶל הַנַּעַר וְאַל תַּעַשׂ לוֹ מְאוּמָה...

So the incident for which the rabbis accuse Bilaam of wickedness, of pride, and of following his own murderous instincts under the cover of Divine command... turns out to be an eerie replay of that most difficult chapter in the Abraham story: the Binding of Isaac.

And the Binding of Isaac *also* begins with God's calling out of that same command: *lech lecha* (לך לך) – Go forth!

So of course the rabbis hurry in to show how Abraham was righteous and Bilaam was wicked: *that* command to go was from straight from God while *that* one was from Bilaam's own heart; *that* donkey should have been saddled while *that* one should have been left alone.

But there is another way that the critique of Bilaam can be read: as a subtle – almost subconscious – critique of Abraham.

Abraham, who like Bilaam, spoke in the language of faith. Abraham, who like Bilaam, had the power to deliver blessings or curses. Abraham, who, after all, was only following the voice of God.

We cannot condemn Abraham outright. For he is our father. And his unwavering faith was his greatest virtue, celebrated even by God.

Yet still... the story of the Binding of Isaac has never sat right with us. Was Abraham really supposed to obey that command? Didn't he jump up a little too quickly to carry it out? Shouldn't he have known that this wasn't really what God wanted? Shouldn't he have protested?

But maybe it wasn't just a matter of what God wanted. Maybe a part of Abraham didn't *want* to protest. Maybe he wanted to show what a great man of faith he was, and was willing to sacrifice his own son to do it.

A person is led down the path that he wishes to go.

God forbid, we could never say such a thing about Abraham.

So instead, we say terrible things about Bilaam. We accuse him of longing to curse us, even though he ultimately blessed us. And we condemn him for going, even though God told him to go.

Because he should have known better. Because sometimes, even when you think God is telling you to do something, you don't do it. Even though it sounds exactly like the call you've gotten before – *Go forth!* – this time, you just know it's wrong.

And if you don't, well then we have to wonder: just where is this voice of God coming from? Is it really out there, calling to you from somewhere up above? Or is it all in your head?

Be careful walking down this path of destruction – this path you thought God told you to take. For you may find an Angel of the Lord standing in your way, telling you to go no further.

Let's hope to God you see it in time.

CHAPTER 41
CRY FOR THE MOON – Parshat Pinchas

God has sinned.

I wouldn't dare say such a thing, you know. But what I can I do? **Rashi** told me so.

*

Here's how it all came out. In *Parshat Pinchas,* we get a long list of the sacrifices offered on each of the festival celebrations in the Jewish calendar. And on each of them, along with the various offerings of praise and thanksgiving, there is one goat sacrificed specifically to atone for our transgressions. And usually, that sacrifice is listed as:

One goat, as a sin offering, to atone for you.

וּשְׂעִיר חַטָּאת אֶחָד לְכַפֵּר עֲלֵיכֶם.

But on *Rosh Chodesh*, the celebration of the New Moon, the goat is mentioned slightly differently:

One goat, as a sin offering, for God *(Num. 28:15)*

וּשְׂעִיר עִזִּים אֶחָד לְחַטָּאת לַה'

Now that could be read as I've written it, with a comma, to mean: "This sin offering is for God. It is given over from me to God." But Rashi understands it as it would sound without the comma: "This is a sin offering for God." That is, this sin offering is offered on God's behalf.

That in itself is an astounding thing to say. But to add to the shock, the particular sin that he attributes to God is a rather strange one:

The Holy Blessed One said: Bring an atonement for Me, for having reduced the size of the Moon.

אמר הקב"ה הביאו כפרה עלי על שמעטתי את הירח.

Huh? When did God reduce the size of the Moon? And even if God did, what was so terribly wrong with that?

The Talmud, in Tractate *Chulin (60b)*, is where we find the backstory. And it develops out of a careful reading of one verse in Genesis, from the fourth day of the creation story:

And God made the two great lights, the big light to rule over the day and the small light to rule over the night… ***(Gen. 1:16)***

וַיַּעַשׂ אֱלֹהִים אֶת שְׁנֵי הַמְּאֹרֹת הַגְּדֹלִים אֶת הַמָּאוֹר הַגָּדֹל לְמֶמְשֶׁלֶת הַיּוֹם וְאֶת הַמָּאוֹר הַקָּטֹן לְמֶמְשֶׁלֶת הַלַּיְלָה...

So Rabbi Shimon ben Pazzi, one of the sages of the Talmud, has a question:

It is written, "God made the two great lights." But then it is written "the big light… and the small light."

כתיב (בראשית א, טז) ויעש אלהים את שני המאורות הגדולים וכתיב את המאור הגדול ואת המאור הקטן

There were two great lights! So how did two big lights become one big and one small? Ben Pazzi explains:

The Moon said before the Holy Blessed One, "Master of the World! Is it possible for two kings to share one crown?!"

So [the Holy Blessed One] said to her, "So then you go and make yourself smaller!"

אמרה ירח לפני הקב"ה רבש"ע אפשר לשני מלכים שישתמשו בכתר אחד

אמר לה לכי ומעטי את עצמך

The Moon didn't understand – how could she *and* the Sun both be "the great light"?! How could they both illuminate the sky at the same time? What would be the purpose of that?

God seems annoyed at the question – or perhaps reads in it a secret desire to bump out the Sun and take over. So God says, well since you asked, why don't you solve your own problem by being the smaller one! You'll now be relegated to the night, and your only light will come from the Sun. That'll teach you to question my decisions!

But then, the Talmud goes on to say, the Moon was devastated. She couldn't believe she had been so suddenly cast aside – and for what? A simple question? God saw her startle, and tried to make her feel better by telling her that people would count the months after her, reckon the calendar by her. But she was inconsolable.

So finally, God felt bad, and asked that a sin offering be brought to atone for the sin of humiliating the Moon.

*

Well, that is a tragic and touching story. But what is the point? Who cares if the Moon could have been bigger? Why does it matter to us that she is so very sad?

*

If we go back to the verse in Genesis about the two great lights, and take a look at the midrash on it, we find another version of the same story. It's pretty similar to the one in the Talmud: again the shrinking of the Moon, God's regret, and the sacrifice to atone for it all. But then, the midrash continues, and adds on another layer:

Rabbi Levi said in the name of Rabbi Yossi bar Ilai: It is the way of the world that the great ones count by the great ones, and the small ones count by the small. So Esau counts by the Sun, because it is great. And Jacob counts by the Moon, because she is small. ***(Bereishit Rabbah 6:3)***

רבי לוי בשם רבי יוסי בר אלעאי אמר, דרך ארץ הוא שיהא הגדול מונה לגדול, והקטן מונה לקטן. עשו מונה לחמה, שהיא גדולה, ויעקב מונה ללבנה, שהיא קטנה.

The Gregorian calendar follows the Sun. But our calendar, says Rabbi Levi, follows the Moon because we, the children of Jacob, are like the Moon.

We identify with her, because we, too, feel we are smaller than we should have been. We, the people of Israel, have always been few in number, and sometimes – for reasons unfair or unknown – we have been greatly reduced.

And if we tell the story of the Moon's tragedy, perhaps it is because we are too timid to openly blame God for our own tragedies. Yet we cannot help but wonder if it is God who allowed us to be reduced, diminished, and left alone in the long dark night of our history.

And perhaps we want God to ask for our forgiveness. Perhaps we want God to offer sacrifices and seek atonement, just as *we* have been commanded to do when *we* sin. For if God has truly authorized our suffering then God, too, has sinned.

So every month, when the new moon appears, it is as if God is coming before us to confess. Except that we must orchestrate the ritual. We bring the offering on God's behalf, and then we turn around and forgive God – as if, for a moment, we were God, forgiving us.

As if we were so big and powerful. As if we ruled the world.

CHAPTER 42

FACING THE ENEMY – Parshat Matot

It's time to kill the Midianites.

Actually, God already called for their destruction in last week's parsha, after they had attacked and seduced the Israelites. There had been many enemy attacks during the journey through the desert, but this one was particularly humiliating, for the Midianites had succeeded in drawing the Israelite men into idolatry and orgiastic debauchery.

And in this week's parsha comes the order to attack:

The Eternal spoke to Moses saying, "Avenge the Children of Israel on the Midianites! Then you shall be gathered unto your kin." *(Num. 31:1-2)*

וַיְדַבֵּר ה׳ אֶל מֹשֶׁה לֵּאמֹר. נְקֹם נִקְמַת בְּנֵי יִשְׂרָאֵל מֵאֵת הַמִּדְיָנִים אַחַר תֵּאָסֵף אֶל עַמֶּיךָ.

This war is so important, it seems, that it is marked as the last thing Moses will have to do before he dies. So he dispatches a thousand men from each tribe to "deliver the vengeance of the Eternal upon Midian!" Twelve thousand fighting men.

*

Well, twelve thousand and one.

Because we're specifically told that:

Moses sent them to battle, a thousand from each tribe – them, and Pinchas ben Elazar the Army Priest, with the sacred utensils and the battle trumpets in hand. *(Num. 31:6)*

וַיִּשְׁלַח אֹתָם מֹשֶׁה אֶלֶף לַמַּטֶּה לַצָּבָא אֹתָם וְאֶת פִּינְחָס בֶּן אֶלְעָזָר הַכֹּהֵן לַצָּבָא וּכְלֵי הַקֹּדֶשׁ וַחֲצֹצְרוֹת הַתְּרוּעָה בְּיָדוֹ.

Now we know about Pinchas from last week. That parsha was named after him, in recognition of his zealousness in defending God's honor – in what is one of the more horrifying moments in the Torah.

In the midst of the chaotic encounter with the Midianites, one of the Israelite men, Zimri, brought a Midianite woman, Kozbi bat Tzur, over to the Meeting Tent – where Moses and the Israelites were gathered together, weeping – and Zimri and Kozbi paraded their amorous connection in front of the people. We are left to imagine what the couple was doing.

And Pinchas couldn't take it. He exploded, grabbed a spear, and stabbed both Zimri and his Midianite mistress through the belly. They dropped dead immediately.

And then it seems God was pleased, because Pinchas received a special "Covenant of Peace." We can't help but detect a certain irony in the name of this tribute to a guy who's just stabbed two people. But there you have it. That's Pinchas.

*

But why does the Torah make special mention of him again, now that the Israelites are going out to battle against the Midianites? We know that he's a fighter, sure, and that he hates the Midianites. We also know that he is also from the priestly family, and is there serving as something like the chaplain. But what is so important about his role in this particular war that needs to be called out by name?

Rashi wonders this and gives us several answers. He begins with the obvious one:

For the Holy Blessed One said, "Let the one who started this commandment, when he killed Kozbi bat Tzur, be the one to finish it."

אמר הקב"ה מי שהתחיל במצוה, שהרג כזבי בת צור, יגמר.

Pinchas was the first to draw Midianite blood. He started this war, before it was even declared. We've already come to associate Pinchas with the Midianite conflict, so it's only right that he should be the one to lead the charge.

That answer alone might have been enough. We probably could have come up with it on our own, actually. But then Rashi goes on to give us another reason that Pinchas is mentioned here – and this one we wouldn't have seen coming:

Another interpretation is that he went to avenge Joseph, who was his mother's ancestor. For it says *(in Genesis 37:36)*, "The Midianites sold Joseph to Egypt..."

ד"א — שהלך לנקם נקמת יוסף אבי אמו, שנאמר (**בראשית ל"ז**) "והמדנים מכרו אתו"

Now, it is true that, way back in the Book of Genesis, after Joseph's brothers threw him in a pit, it was the Midianites who pulled him out and took him down to Egypt, where they sold him into slavery. So if Pinchas was from Joseph's family line, perhaps he held a special grudge against the Midianites that went beyond the conflict at hand.

But how do we know that Pinchas was descended from Joseph? The Torah never says that explicitly. Rashi tells us that the connection comes from a verse in Exodus:

And Aaron's son, Elazar, married one of Putiel's daughters, and she bore him Pinchas. *(Exod. 6:25)*

וְאֶלְעָזָר בֶּן אַהֲרֹן לָקַח לוֹ מִבְּנוֹת פּוּטִיאֵל לוֹ לְאִשָּׁה וַתֵּלֶד לוֹ אֶת פִּינְחָס

We know Aaron and Elazar are in the tribe of Levi, so this Putiel must be the link to Joseph, a direct descendant of either the tribe of Menashe or Ephraim, Joseph's two sons. Rashi confirms that, but then adds something:

[Putiel] was from the seed of Jethro, who fattened calves for idolatry, *and* from the seed of Joseph, who sublimated his desires.

מזרע יתרו שפטם עגלים לע"ז, ומזרע יוסף שפטפט ביצרו.

Putiel, Rashi claims, does descend from Joseph. So there's the connection from Joseph to Pinchas. But what is this business about descending from Jethro as well? Why do we need that information?

Well, what do we know about Jethro? He was Moses' father-in-law. He was not Jewish, though he appeared very supportive of the Israelite struggle. And as for fattening calves, indeed, rabbinic legend has it that Jethro was an idolater for many years, before he ever met Moses.

Oh, and one other thing: Jethro was a Priest of Midian.

In fact, that is the very first thing we ever hear about him:

Now the Priest of Midian had seven daughters… *(Exod. 2:16)*

וּלְכֹהֵן מִדְיָן שֶׁבַע בָּנוֹת...

So if Pinchas is the descendant of both Jethro *and* Joseph, then he is the heir to both Midian and Israel, the son of slave-traders and slaves, priests of the Lord and priests of Ba'al. The war that is going on outside, then, is raging also inside of him – in his blood, and in his psyche.

That is why, when Zimri brought the Midianite woman around, and exposed their forbidden union before the people, Pinchas could not contain himself. He suddenly *had* to kill them, because they represented the commingling of forces that were tearing him apart inside.

His ancestor had been ripped from his land and sold into slavery by the Midianites – who were also his ancestors. In a sense, one part of him had perpetrated a great injustice on another part of him. He had debased himself, unwillingly, before he had ever been born.

And so, now that Israel is going to war on the Midianites, Pinchas must lead the charge. He must avenge his grandfather Joseph. Only by fighting back against the Midianites can he atone for the sins of the Midianite within him. If he can destroy them all, he thinks, then perhaps he can purge himself of the blood of the enemy.

It's time, he says, to kill the Midianite in me.

CHAPTER 43

ALL SINNERS AND SAINTS – Parshat Masei

It's one of the strangest institutions in the Torah: The City of Refuge.

As the Children of Israel begin to prepare to cross over into Canaan, they receive a detailed description of the boundaries of the land and how it will be distributed among the tribes. Then there are specific instructions to set up six cities that will be separate from these tribal plots, in which the priestly tribe – the Levites – will live. And then comes an unexpected addition:

The cities you assign to the Levites shall also be the six Cities of Refuge that you shall designate for a killer to flee to... *(Num. 35:6)*

וְאֵת הֶעָרִים אֲשֶׁר תִּתְּנוּ לַלְוִיִּם אֵת שֵׁשׁ־עָרֵי הַמִּקְלָט אֲשֶׁר תִּתְּנוּ לָנֻס שָׁמָּה הָרֹצֵחַ...

That's right. Levites ... and killers. There will be six cities that will provide safe haven for killers seeking asylum.

What kind of bizarre and terrifying district is this?!

The Torah quickly clarifies. These cities are not for outright murderers, who have killed intentionally. They are for perpetrators of accidental killings, committed without malice or intent (what we now call "manslaughter"). These unfortunate criminals of happenstance are given places of refuge where they will be protected from the family members who, in their fury and anguish, would seek revenge for the death of their loved one. But should they step out of the city, they are considered fair game, and can be killed with no penalty. So they are to remain there until the death of the current High Priest, which could be decades.

There is, of course, a certain moral logic to this system. The Torah seems to be attempting to strike a balance between compassion for the unintentional killer and empathy for the aggrieved family. On the one hand, this is just a case of bad luck, and this guy doesn't deserve to die. But on the other hand, he took a human life! How can he just continue to walk around freely, a constant reminder that his victim lies in the ground? So we give him the option of protection from society's rage, but only within a certain kind of exile.

Still, how strange that the Torah should take such great pains to set aside entire cities for this one situation. Did this really happen so often? How many accidental killers could there be? And yet the Torah proscribes these Cities of Refuge no less than three separate times: a brief allusion to them back in Exodus (*21:13*), here in the Book of Numbers, and then again in Deuteronomy (*19:1-13*). Clearly, this is important.

And then the legal discussion in the Talmud (*Makot 9b-11a*) goes on to add forty-two more cities of refuge. The rabbis of the Talmud also mandated the construction of direct roads to the cities, which were to be clearly marked. The killers were provided two escorts on the road, to ensure their safe passage. Precautions are taken to make sure the cities are near a water supply, that they have sufficient marketplaces, and sizable populations. There are even stories that the mother of the High Priest would feed and clothe the killers, so they would not be inclined to pray for the death of her son.

*

But the most surprising allowance of all is given to a scholar who becomes an accidental killer:

A student who goes into exile is joined in exile by his teacher.

תלמיד שגלה מגלין רבו עמו

This poor teacher! Bad enough that the student has swung an axe wildly enough to have landed in all this trouble – but now his innocent teacher has to go, too? What is the justification for this? The rabbis derive the rule from the wording of a verse in Deuteronomy (4:42):

"He can flee to one of these cities and live" **– which means, provide him with *whatever* he needs to live.**

וחי עביד ליה מידי דתהוי ליה חיותא

It is a powerful statement about the nature of Torah. These cities are meant to keep the killers alive. So they have to have everything they need to survive. What does a student need to live? To learn Torah. So the teacher has to go, too.

And what if the teacher is the one who accidentally kills? There the ruling is even more extreme:

Rabbi Yochanan said: A teacher who goes into exile is joined by his entire *yeshiva* (his entire school).

א"ר יוחנן הרב שגלה מגלין ישיבתו עמו

Imagine: You go off to school, full of excitement, to study with a great rabbi, along with hundreds of other eager young scholars. You study, you learn, you slowly grow wiser. Life is good. One day, tragedy strikes. The rabbi was out chopping wood when the axe handle flew off and...now he has to flee to the nearest City of Refuge.

And you – and all of your hundreds of classmates – are going, too. To stay in the city for good. Until the death of the High Priest.

Now how do the rabbis justify *this*?! The students need their teacher, sure. They need Torah to live, and their teacher is the only one who can provide that lifeline. But the teacher? The teacher already knows the Torah! What does the teacher need the students for?

The answer may be found a little further down on the same page of Talmud, where we find a famous maxim of Rabbi Yehuda HaNasi's:

Much Torah have I learned from my teachers, more from my colleagues, and from my students most of all.

הרבה תורה למדתי מרבותי ומחבירי יותר מהם ומתלמידי יותר מכולן.

So teachers *do* need their students for that life-giving learning experience – more, even, than the students need their teacher. In fact, the whole environment of the study hall is one great immersive experience, all of which is essential, and all of which will have to be transported to the City of Refuge if any one member suddenly has to flee.

*

There is, however, possibly a deeper reason why the rabbis made such major provisions, specifically for Torah scholars, in the laws of the City of Refuge. A hint of it can be found when – again on that same page of Talmud – the rabbis express surprise that a great scholar would ever be the victim of such terrible circumstances. Wouldn't the merit of his Torah study protect him from such an unlucky occurrence?

It's an interesting bit of theological speculation, but even more interesting is the language they use to describe this metaphysical protection:

Rabbi Yochanan said: From where can we show that the words of Torah provide refuge?

א"ר יוחנן: מנין לדברי תורה שהן קולטין?

Refuge. In Hebrew, the words of Torah are '*koltin*' (קולטין) from the very same root as the City of Refuge, the '*Ir Miklat*' (עיר מקלט). The rabbis are describing their own enterprise, Torah study, with language borrowed from this refuge for killers on the run.

On some level, then, they seem to identify with these social outcasts. It's no wonder that they would allow for the transport of an entire *yeshiva* to the City of Refuge – for the *yeshiva* itself is a kind of City of Refuge!

*

In making this link, perhaps the rabbis were inspired by the model of the Torah itself, which places criminals together with the Levites – the lowest members of the social order with the highest. For there is something shared about their experiences of apartness. And that apartness applies to the rabbis as well.

These scholars were often people who had left society to seclude themselves in a world of pure thought, hermetically sealed from the outside world, and protected from distraction. There is, for the soul who is called to this kind of extreme lifestyle, something profoundly life-giving – perhaps even life-saving – about the practice of sacred study.

But it is also a kind of prison, a form of self-imposed isolation. And over time, it can lead to a form of social alienation, as the purity and intensity of this pious immersion becomes increasingly wrapped up in the fear that if one wanders too far out of the *yeshiva* there will be great danger.

This kind of refuge from the world may provide serene escape and profound spiritual growth, but it is no way to live one's whole life. No one wants to be trapped in the City of Refuge forever. There may be great wisdom in creating separate spaces in our society for people to flee to when they have no other choice. They may need to stay there for a long time, and they may even come to love it. But let them not forget that their exile was taken in response to a crisis. Let them not come to think that the City of Refuge – as nurturing as it may be – is their home.

*

Perhaps that is why the term of exile ends with the death of the High Priest. In order for one extreme end of society to rediscover life in the middle, the other extreme must also fade away. In order for us to be able to live fully in the world, something sacred has to die.

V

Deuteronomy

CHAPTER 44
THEY MIGHT BE GIANTS – Parshat Devarim

This land was once filled with giants. But they died out, slowly, over the centuries, until there was only one left – the great and mighty Og. And now he, too, is gone.

So we read in this week's parsha, in the description of the battles that the Israelites fought as they approached the land of Canaan:

Only Og, King of Bashan was left of the remaining *Rephaim*. His bed, a bed of iron, is now in Rabbah of the Ammonites; it is nine cubits long and four cubits wide. *(Deut. 3:11)*

כִּי רַק עוֹג מֶלֶךְ הַבָּשָׁן נִשְׁאַר מִיֶּתֶר הָרְפָאִים הִנֵּה עַרְשׂוֹ עֶרֶשׂ בַּרְזֶל הֲלֹה הִוא בְּרַבַּת בְּנֵי עַמּוֹן תֵּשַׁע אַמּוֹת אָרְכָּהּ וְאַרְבַּע אַמּוֹת רָחְבָּהּ בְּאַמַּת־אִישׁ.

There are three words in the Torah that are sometimes translated as "giants" – *Rephaim, Nephilim,* and *Anakim* – and all of them will be relevant to our story eventually. But, for now, let's stay with this verse.

This is the only place in the Torah that makes reference to Og's size – though only indirectly, through the description of this "bed." The cubit measurement here would come out to approximately 14 feet by 6 feet; and if it was roughly proportional, then Og must have been at least 10 feet tall.

Now that's a big bed by anyone's standards, but the **Rashbam** tells us that the unusual word for bed here – *eres* (ערש) – actually means crib!

His bed **– a child's crib, for when he was a baby.**

הנה ערשו – עריסה של קטן כשהיה תינוק

So if this was Og's bed when he was a baby, there's no telling how massive he became eventually! (The **Ramban** adds that the bed had to be made of iron, and not the standard wood, so that it wouldn't break under Og's weight.)

These are some of the technical attempts to prove Og's gigantic stature. But much more interesting are the many strange stories of Og the Giant recorded in the Talmud and Midrash. Taken together, they constitute one of the most fascinating legends in rabbinic literature. Og is a shadowy figure who seems to always have been around, and – according to the rabbis – keeps popping up at key moments in the Torah's narrative.

Why are the rabbis so obsessed with Og? What does he represent? And where does the legend of Og begin?

*

To answer those questions, let's start with the battle that Moses is describing in our parsha, and work our way back. This battle took place in the Book of Numbers, and while we hear about the start of the conflict – *"King Og, of Bashan, with all his people, came out to Edrei to engage them in war" (21:33)* – and its conclusion – *"They defeated him and his sons and all his people, until no remnant was left of them and they took possession of his country" (21:35)* – there is no detailed account of the battle itself. So the Talmud steps in to tell the story. And it is a wild one:

There is a legend about the rock that Og, King of Bashan, tried to throw at Israel. He said, "How large is the camp of Israel? Three parasangs (*approx. 10 miles*). I will go and uproot a mountain three parasangs wide and throw it on them and kill them!

He went and uprooted the mountain and hoisted it up over his head. But the Holy Blessed One sent ants, which dug holes in the mountain, and it collapsed around Og's neck. He tried to cast it off, and gnashed his teeth from side to side, but he could not get it off…

Then Moses, whose height was ten cubits, took an axe ten cubits long, and jumped ten cubits into the air, and struck Og in the ankle, and killed him. *(Berachot 54b)*

אבן שבקש עוג מלך הבשן לזרוק על ישראל גמרא גמירי לה אמר מחנה ישראל כמה הוי תלתא פרסי איזיל ואיעקר טורא בר תלתא פרסי ואישדי עלייהו ואיקטלינהו

אזל עקר טורא בר תלתא פרסי ואייתי על רישיה ואייתי קודשא בריך הוא עליה קמצי ונקבוה ונחית בצואריה הוה בעי למשלפה, משכי שיניה להאי גיסא ולהאי גיסא ולהאי גיסא ולא מצי למשלפה...

משה כמה הוה עשר אמות שקיל נרגא בר עשר אמין שוור עשר אמין ומחייה בקרסוליה וקטליה.

Mountain-tossing! Ants to the rescue! Wow. And how is Moses suddenly ten cubits tall? That's about fifteen feet. Looks like we've got another giant on our hands!

To make some sense of this fantastic tale, we'll need more information. The only other thing about Og we read in the Torah itself is that God said to Moses:

Do not fear him, for I will deliver him and all his people into your hands. ***(Num. 21:34)***

אַל תִּירָא אֹתוֹ כִּי בְיָדְךָ נָתַתִּי אֹתוֹ וְאֶת כָּל עַמּוֹ

Why, the *Midrash Tanchuma* asks, is Moses particularly afraid and in need of reassurance? And they answer:

For no one mightier than him had ever stood in the world. For *"Only Og, King of Bashan was left of the remaining Rephaim." (Deut. 3:11)* He remained from those mighty ones that Amraphel and his troops had killed. As it says, *"They struck the Rephaim at Ashterot-karnaim." (Gen. 14:5)* But he was the survivor among them, like the pit of an olive, that survives the olive press. As it says, *"And a survivor came and brought news to Abram the Hebrew." (Gen. 14:13)* That survivor was Og. *(Tanchuma, Chukat 55:1)*

שלא עמד גבור בעולם קשה הימנו, שנאמר: כי רק עוג מלך הבשן נשאר מיתר הרפאים (דברים ג, יא). והוא נשאר מאותן הגבורים שהרגו אמרפל וחבריו, שנאמר: ויכו את רפאים בעשתרות קרנים (בראשית יד, ה). וזה פסלת שלהם כפריצי זיתים הפליטים מתוך הגפת, שנאמר: ויבא הפליט ויגד לאברם וגו' (שם פסוק יג), זה עוג.

So there was once a race of giant men, in the days of Abraham, and they were destroyed. But Og was too tough to kill – he survived as all his compatriots fell. He even came and told Abraham that his relative Lot had been captured in the war. So Moses is afraid of him not just because he seems invincible, but also – as **Rashi** explains:

Moses was afraid to fight him, because of the merit he earned for what he did for Abraham.

שהיה משה ירא להלחם, שמא תעמד לו זכותו של אברהם.

Og's good deed has given him extra merit in God's eyes, Rashi explains, and therefore earned him divine protection. Og is suddenly not just a monster. Yes, he is massive, and terrifying... but there is also something righteous in him.

Now, there is another tradition that also identifies Og as the "survivor" who brought news to Abraham. But in this version, what he had survived was not just the war. Take a look at this passage from the Talmud, again attempting to explain why Moses feared Og so much:

[Moses] thought, maybe the merit of our father Abraham will stand with him, for it says, *"And a survivor came and brought news to Abram the Hebrew." (Gen. 14:13)* Rabbi Yochanan said: this was Og, who survived the generation of the flood. *(Talmud, Niddah 61a)*

אמר שמא תעמוד לו זכות של אברהם אבינו שנאמר (**בראשית יד, יג**) ויבא הפליט ויגד לאברם העברי ואמר רבי יוחנן זה עוג שפלט מדור המבול.

The flood?! We thought only Noah and his family survived the flood. But no! Og managed to make it through somehow, even as the entire world was being destroyed. What did he do? Did he just swim for forty days? Was he so tall that the water did not drown him? Another midrash – this time *Pirkei d'Rabbi Eliezer* – gives an even stranger answer:

"All existence on earth was blotted out..." (Gen. 7:23)* Except for Noah and all who were with him on the Ark, as it says, *"Only Noah remained, and those with him on the Ark."* And except for Og, King of Bashan, who sat on a rung of one of the ladders on the Ark, and swore to Noah and his sons that he would be a servant to them forever. So what did Noah do? He drilled a hole in the Ark and would stick out food for Og every day. And so Og also remained, as it says, *"Only Og, King of Bashan was left of the remaining Rephaim." (Deut. 3:11) (Pirkei d'Rabbi Eliezer 23:8)

ונמחו כל היקום שבארץ שנאמר וימח את כל היקום אשר על פני האדמה, חוץ מנח וכל אשר אתו בתבה שנאמר וישאר אך נח ואשר אתו בתיבה, וחוץ מעוג מלך הבשן שישב לו על עץ אחד מן הסולמות של התיבה ונשבע לנח ולבניו שיהיה להם עבד עולם מה עשה נח נקב חור אח' בתיבה והיה מושיט לו מזונו בכל יום ויום ונשאר גם הוא שנ' כי רק עוג מלך הבשן וגו'.

So now, Og's story goes back to the days *before* the flood. And not only was he connected to Abraham, but he forged some kind of eternal pact with Noah. Think of it: the whole point of that story was that only one righteous family survived – and now we learn that, of all people, Og was there, too!

But there is one piece of this account that doesn't fit. In this version, what do we make of this last verse the Midrash quotes, the one we started with up top, that only Og was *"left of the remaining Rephaim."* Earlier, we thought that meant he survived an attack against the Rephaim. But where were the Rephaim *before* the flood? Rashi answers that question for us, revealing the final piece of Og's origin story:

"The remaining Rephaim,"* refers back to what it says in Genesis: *"And the Nephilim were upon the earth." (Rashi on Gen. 14:13)

וזהו מיתר הרפאים, שנאמר הנפלים היו בארץ וגו'

Remember how there are three words for giants in the Torah? Well, the first one to appear is *'Nephilim,'* and that reference takes us to one of the strangest passages in Genesis:

It was then, and also afterwards, that the *Nephilim* were upon the earth – when divine beings came and cohabited with the daughters of humans, who bore them offspring. They were the ancient mighty ones, the men of renown. *(Gen. 6:4)*

הַנְּפִלִים הָיוּ בָאָרֶץ בַּיָּמִים הָהֵם וְגַם אַחֲרֵי כֵן אֲשֶׁר יָבֹאוּ בְּנֵי הָאֱלֹהִים אֶל בְּנוֹת הָאָדָם וְיָלְדוּ לָהֶם הֵמָּה הַגִּבֹּרִים אֲשֶׁר מֵעוֹלָם אַנְשֵׁי הַשֵּׁם.

These giants, it seems, were more than just enormous men. They were divine beings. In fact, the word, *'nephilim'* (נפילים), means, 'fallen,' and many suspect that this refers to fallen angels. The *Targum Yonatan*, for example, says that among them was the fallen angel, Shemchazai. And the Talmud – in the very last clue of our story – tells us that Og was the grandson of Shemchazai.

So Og was not just ancient; he was primordial. He goes all the way back, almost to the beginning. And he was not just a giant; he was partly divine. Partly, that is, but not all. Og may have had angelic parentage, but he was not himself an angel. He was some kind of blend: in some ways just like us, and in some ways otherworldly.

*

That is the long and twisted story of Og.

But we still have not answered any of the questions of what it all means? What is it about this giant that keeps him coming back? What role does the story of Og play in our own story?

The key to understanding all of this, I believe, can be found in one line from the Book of Numbers. It appears in the infamous story of the spies who are sent to scout out the Land of Canaan – that promised land that is supposed to flow with milk and honey. They are expected to bring good tidings. But when they come back, their report is... not so good.

They bring back some of the fruit of the land, which is gigantic. That seems like a good sign of abundance. But then, they tell of great dangers. The nations who dwell there are powerful. The cities are large and fortified. And, above all, they warn, "we saw the *Anakim* there."

Remember '*Anakim*'? That was our third world for 'giants,' along with *Rephaim* and *Nephilim*. And the spies make this connection explicit:

All the people we saw there are men of great size. We saw the *Nephilim* there – the *Anakim* come from the *Nephilim* – and we looked like grasshoppers to ourselves, and so we were in their eyes. *(Num. 13:32-33)*

וְכָל הָעָם אֲשֶׁר רָאִינוּ בְתוֹכָהּ אַנְשֵׁי מִדּוֹת. וְשָׁם רָאִינוּ אֶת הַנְּפִילִים בְּנֵי עֲנָק מִן הַנְּפִלִים וַנְּהִי בְעֵינֵינוּ כַּחֲגָבִים וְכֵן הָיִינוּ בְּעֵינֵיהֶם.

So the Anakim come from the Nephilim. These giants come from those mysterious giants back in Genesis, just as Og was descended from those same angelic beings. It seems that all the giants in the Torah are related.

But the strangest thing about this verse isn't how the Anakim looked. It is the last phrase, about how the *spies* looked. For the spies don't just say that "we looked like grasshoppers to them." They say, "we looked like grasshoppers to *ourselves* ... and so we were in their eyes."

The fruit, the cities, the people – everything and everyone looked overwhelmingly big to the Israelites – because in their own self-perception, they were so small. The Anakites may indeed have been people of great stature, but God certainly doesn't think they are unbeatable. To the spies, however, they are simply giants. More, even – they are the legendary Nephilim, the kind of giants that possess supernatural powers, the kind of giants that take the daughters of men.

But then, when you feel like a tiny insect, every person you come across is a giant.

The persistence of Og in our collective story, then, is a testament to our persistent feeling of smallness. Giants haunt us because we fundamentally do not believe that we are big enough, or strong enough, to survive.

That is why, in the crazy story of Og and the mountain, God sends *ants* to save the day – as if to say, even the smallest creatures on earth have the power to defeat a giant. And that is why, perhaps, Moses is then suddenly 15 feet tall. At first he was afraid of Og, just as the spies were afraid of their giants. But when one arrives at a place of confidence in one's own stature in the world, then one walks tall like everyone else.

Og is gone, but there will always be giants in the world. So long as we are small in our own eyes, there will always be some new, oversized monster, threatening to annihilate us. To defeat giants, we must begin to see ourselves as normal-sized. And then, remarkably, the giant begins to shrink.

Maimonides, the great rationalist, held that Og was:

Twice the size of most other people, or a little bit more. This is undoubtedly rare in the human race, but in no way impossible. *(Guide to the Perplexed 2:47)*

Yes, he was big. But he wasn't inhuman.

That confusion has been with us from the start. All of the stories we've seen have this element of uncertainty in them. Is Og human, or not? Is he righteous, or evil? Is he our friend, or our enemy?

We remain suspicious, nervous, wary of everyone around us. We are always worried that the giant will come back. But the truth is, we are not really afraid of how big the giant is. We are afraid, have always been afraid, of how small we are.

CHAPTER 45

THE LIFE YOU SAVE - Parshat Va'etchanan

You do not have to die for God... most of the time.

That is one of the overarching principles regulating the system of Jewish Law. In a religion full of rules, *Pikuach Nefesh*, or, "preservation of life," is the concept that any of those rules can be broken to save a life – yours or someone else's. So if I stick a gun to your head and say, "Here, eat this bacon cheeseburger, or I'll kill you!" – you may feel free to take a bite. In fact, you'd be *required* to. The preservation of life is your primary obligation.

This override function in the legal system is derived from a verse in Leviticus, which states:

You shall keep My rules and My laws, which a person shall perform, and live by them – I am the Eternal. *(Lev. 18:5)*

וּשְׁמַרְתֶּם אֶת חֻקֹּתַי וְאֶת מִשְׁפָּטַי אֲשֶׁר יַעֲשֶׂה אֹתָם הָאָדָם וָחַי בָּהֶם אֲנִי ה'.

The Talmud (*Sanhedrin 74a*) emphasizes the phrase, "live by them," and understands it to mean that you should keep the laws as long as you can *live* by them, but not to the extent that you would *die* by them. Even earlier, the Mishnah (*Yoma 8:4*) states that you can eat on Yom Kippur if you are deliriously sick, or break the Sabbath to save someone buried under rubble in an accident.

There are, however, some exceptions. In particular, the Talmud lists three cardinal rules that cannot be broken, even under the threat of death: Idolatry, Incest, and Murder. So if I stick the gun to your head again, and say, "Worship the sun or die!" or "Sleep with your sister or die!" or "Kill Steve or die!" – then you are supposed to choose death.

But for the most part, this principle of *Pikuach Nefesh* applies broadly, across the whole of Jewish practice. And it isn't just operative as a response to some threat, but to any situation that might be construed as life-saving. Organ donation, for example, though it ostensibly violates the precept of doing yourself no bodily harm, is permitted by most Jewish authorities under the rule of *Pikuach Nefesh*.

This precept contributes legal weight to the general philosophical sense that "life" is a supreme value in Judaism: we celebrate human life and condemn martyrdom, our focus is on life in this world rather than what happens in the afterlife, and we are fiercely committed to our own survival as a people. These are all Jewish cultural hallmarks that have been informed and bolstered by the principle of *Pikuach Nefesh*. Yes, Judaism cares about life.

*

But is that good enough?

That is a question that *Rabbi Naftali Tzvi Yehuda Berlin* (the "Netziv"), asks, implicitly, in reflecting on this week's *parsha*. The Netziv was the last great head of the Volozhin Yeshiva, in 19th century Lithuania, and his commentary on the Torah – **HaEmek Davar** – is a modern classic of the genre, but his volume on Deuteronomy is particularly stunning.

His comments come at the beginning of the fourth chapter of Deuteronomy. The first major section of the book – a kind of long introduction in which Moses recounts the whole journey through the desert – is over. Now Moses is turning to deliver to the people the inspirational speech of a lifetime. And in his first line, we encounter a verse that is reminiscent of everything we've discussed so far:

And now, O Israel, listen to the rules and laws that I am teaching you to perform, so that you will live… ***(Deut. 4:1)***

וְעַתָּה יִשְׂרָאֵל שְׁמַע אֶל הַחֻקִּים וְאֶל־הַמִּשְׁפָּטִים אֲשֶׁר אָנֹכִי מְלַמֵּד אֶתְכֶם לַעֲשׂוֹת לְמַעַן תִּחְיוּ...

Rules and laws to perform, "*so that you will live.*" That sounds a lot like our verse back in Leviticus. But this presents a bit of a problem. Because according to a fundamental interpretive principle in *parshanut*, the Torah speaks in a language of economy. That is, nothing is extra, not even a word. So what is the purpose of *another* verse telling us to perform the laws so that we will live? We've already learned the principle of *pikuach nefesh* from an earlier verse. So this verse must – according to this interpretive assumption – be here to teach us something else. And the Netziv offers us a remarkable possibility of what that might be:

So that you will live… **"Life" in many places means the joy of the soul, the pleasure it receives when it arrives at its complete fullness. The**

general principle is that any spiritual feeling increases life. So the life-force of every person depends on the feeling of pleasure that comes from knowledge and glory. This is much greater than the life-force of an animal, that feels only pleasures like eating and drinking and such things.

If it happens that a person loses or destroys his spiritual feelings, and becomes immersed only in the desire for food and such things, then he becomes like an animal. And then he cannot be truly called a "Living Person." For he has wasted his potential to truly live well.

So it is that when a Jew serves God faithfully, he takes great pleasure, and feels the life-force from his service. But a Jew who loses this form of pleasure is considered dead, for he has destroyed the potential life-force within him…

Someone who has been able to rise up on the path of life, and to begin to understand and feel the pleasure of clinging to God, is then able to add much more life-force than someone who has not had this feeling…

And Moses is saying that listening to these rules and laws – which is immersing oneself in learning – brings about the greatest life-force possible.

משמעות חי כ״פ הוא עליזת הנפש ועונג שמשיג בהגיעו לתכלית שלימותו. והכלל דכל הרגש רוחני מוסיף חיות וכמו שחיות האדם תלוי במה שמרגיש עונג הדעת והכבוד והוא מרובה יותר מחיות הבהמה שאינה מרגשת עונג אלא באכילה ושתיה וכדומה.

ואם יקרה אדם שמאבד ומשחית הרגשותיו הרוחניים וישקיע עצמו והרגשו רק בתאות אכילה וכדומה ה״ז נחשב כבהמה ואינו נקרא אדם חי שהרי מאבד מה שהי׳ בכחו לחיות בטוב.

כך העובד את ה׳ באמונה מתענג ומרגיש חיות מזה העבודה ומי מישראל שמאבד הרגשה נעימה זו נקרא מת. שהרי הוא משחית חיות שהיה בכחו...

אמנם מי שזכה לעלות באורח חיים למעלה למשכיל להרגיש עונג מדביקות בה׳ הוא מוסיף עוד חיות הרבה ממי שלא הגיע לזה ההרגש...

ואמר משה דשמיעת החקים והמשפטים שהוא עסק התלמוד יביא לידי חיות היותר אפשר...

So the Torah, according to the Netziv, is repeating the injunction to "live by" these laws, not simply to re-emphasize the principle of *pikuach nefesh,* but to take the mandate to preserve life to the next level. The idea that the law can be broken to save a life has been well established. The question now is: What kind of lives are we saving?

We have come to take great pride in the humanist quality of Judaism's emphasis on the importance of everyday life. But how do we fill those days? With eating and drinking? Yes, of course. But is that all? Physical pleasures are indeed celebrated in Jewish tradition as gifts from God. But they are not the highest pleasures.

Have we immersed in Torah, cultivating the pleasures of the mind? Have we clung to God, and felt the sweet pleasures of the soul? What are the untapped potentials in our life-force?

Our obsession with the preservation of basic, physical life is understandable. We are a people who have had to struggle to survive. And so survival has become like a national ethos for us.

But we have been so busy surviving that we have forgotten how to live.

And this is exactly the state that our ancestors must have been in, at the conclusion of their long journey. They had escaped from slavery and then wandered for forty years in the desert, plagued by hunger, and always guarding against enemy attacks. It took all they had just to survive.

But now, as they prepare to finish their journey, and enter into the land where they will build a real society, they must be reminded that life is more than mere survival. So Moses tells them again that the Torah is meant to be *lived.*

Yes, yes, they know, they've heard this idea before – they can break any law to save a life. No, but this time, he means something more: the Torah has not come just to preserve life, but to perfect it.

In that same spirit, just three verses later, Moses then adds this line:

And you, who cling to the Lord your God, *you* are all alive today. ***(Deut. 4:4)***

וְאַתֶּם הַדְּבֵקִים בַּה' אֱלֹהֵיכֶם חַיִּים כֻּלְּכֶם הַיּוֹם.

This is the verse that we chant together every week on Shabbat, right before we begin the reading of the weekly parsha. For in that moment, when we unscroll the Torah and begin to immerse ourselves in the words that have sustained us throughout our long journey, we remember once again what it means to truly live.

CHAPTER 46

THERE WAS A CROOKED MAN – Parshat Eikev

We begin with a word.

The word is the title of our parsha: *Eikev* (עקב). It is taken, following the custom, from the most prominent word in the first verse of the *parsha*. However, in this particular *parsha*, the word is prominent specifically because we are not quite sure what it means.

So here is that first verse (and I will leave the word untranslated for now):

And *EIKEV* you heed these laws, to guard them, and perform them, and the Eternal your God will guard the covenant and the kindness that God swore to your ancestors. ***(Deut. 7:12)***

וְהָיָה עֵקֶב תִּשְׁמְעוּן אֵת הַמִּשְׁפָּטִים הָאֵלֶּה וּשְׁמַרְתֶּם וַעֲשִׂיתֶם אֹתָם וְשָׁמַר ה' אֱלֹהֶיךָ לְךָ אֶת הַבְּרִית וְאֶת הַחֶסֶד אֲשֶׁר נִשְׁבַּע לַאֲבֹתֶיךָ.

The message is reasonably clear. We are to keep the laws. God will fulfill the promises made to our ancestors. But what is this "*eikev*"? *If* we keep the laws? *Because* we keep them? *Take care* to keep them? Perhaps – various translations may follow one or another of these options. But there are easier ways to say those things. This word is uncommon, and seems to have been chosen deliberately, to communicate a particular message. To fully understand the verse, we will have to decode the precise meaning of its leading word.

The classical commentators all attempt answers, each of which helps to lend a different nuance to the word. **Rashi**, always our first stop, starts us off with the following:

And **'eikev'** ***you heed*** **– That is, if you heed the minor commandments, which a person usually tramples over with his heels.**

והיה עקב תשמעון – אם המצות הקלות שאדם דש בעקביו תשמעון

Rashi is reminding us that the word, *eikev*, can also mean 'heel' – as in, the bottom of the foot. In fact, that is the meaning in its first usage, in the Garden of Eden story, when we are told that the snake strikes "at the heel" (תשופנו עקב). So, Rashi presumes, something about its usage here must be alluding to heels. But what could feet have to do with the message of following the laws? So he suggests that we are being warned not to trample over with our heels – that is, to carelessly violate – those laws that seem to be of lesser importance.

Rashi's answer does some important semantic work for us. The connection of *eikev* to the heel is intriguing. But then again, a cautionary note to keep one's heel from "trampling over minor commandments" seems like an overly specific focus for a verse that goes on to speak of the fulfillment of God's covenant with our forefathers. And anyhow, if minor commandments were the Torah's true concern, why wouldn't it just say so more explicitly? Rashi's version of *eikev* is interesting, but it doesn't fit the actual context of the passage very well.

So we move on to the other great father of the classical commentators, the **Ibn Ezra**, who offers us another connotation of the word *eikev*:

Eikev **– This means, "the end reward," as in, *"forever, to the end –* לעולם עקב."** ***(from Psalms 119:112)***

עקב – כמו לעולם עקב שכר באחרונה

The idea of a final reward does seem to fit the general message of verse: If you keep the laws, then the fulfillment of the covenant and the kindness of God will be your reward in the end. But again, this translation is a bit difficult to read into the verse itself. One would need to add some extra words to form a grammatically correct sentence:

And the end reward, ***IF*** *you heed these laws and guard them, and perform them,* ***WILL BE THAT*** *the Lord your God will guard the covenant and the kindness that God swore to your forefathers.*

This is perhaps less of a stretch than Rashi's reading, but it is still a fairly inefficient translation. Reading *eikev* as "end reward" requires us to adjust the verse in other ways to make sense of the cause and effect of the two clauses: if you do this, then God will do that.

Finally, then, we turn to the third great luminary in the elite trifecta of classical commentators, Rabbi Moses Nachmanides – the **Ramban**. He begins by referencing yet another usage of the word *eikev*, and the connotation of this one is much easier to read into the verse itself:

The meaning of *eikev* is "because of – בעבור," as in *"[I will make your heirs as numerous as the stars of heaven, and assign to them all these lands…] BECAUSE OF the fact that Abraham heeded my voice, [and kept my charge: My commandments, My laws and My teachings.]" (Gen. 26:5)*

עקב כמו בעבור וכן עקב אשר שמע אברהם בקולי (בראשית כו ה)

Not only does this translation, "because of," make the most sense in our verse itself, but the earlier usage in Genesis provides the closest contextual parallel to our passage that we have seen so far. Abraham heeded the commandments, so God will fulfill the covenant; so, too, we should heed the laws so that God will deliver on the same promises first made to our forefather. The Ramban's explanation seems to work much better than Rashi's or Ibn Ezra's.

Yet, it quickly becomes clear that though he offers us a third understanding of the word *eikev*, he does not mean to leave the first two behind. The Ramban is writing a century after Rashi and Ibn Ezra, and is well aware of the work they've done so far. And he cites them both immediately after he has given his own definition:

And Rashi wrote, "If you heed the minor commandments, which a person usually tramples over with his heels".... And [Ibn Ezra] said, "*Eikev* – means, 'the end reward'"... And all of this is correct. For in Hebrew we call the beginning of something the "head" (*rosh* – ראש)... and so we call the end of something the "heel."

וכתב רש"י אם המצות הקלות שאדם דש בעקביו תשמעון... והמפרשים אמרו כי טעם "עקב" שכר באחרית וכן בשמרם עקב רב (תהלים יט יב) ... ונכון הוא כי יקראו בלשון הקדש תחלת כל דבר בלשון "ראש"... וכן יקראו אחרית כל דבר "עקב"

The Ramban has not only affirmed the interpretations of both of his predecessors, he has also managed to synthesize them. For the "heel," he explains, is one way of referring to the "end." And so just as we might speak of the "head of the year," so we can refer to the end of the year its "heel," in Hebrew, the way in English we might speak of the "tail of the year."

But why is the Ramban doing all this work to validate the other possible meanings of the word *eikev:* "heel" and "end reward"? Hasn't he already provided us with a better understanding: "because of"? It must be that he wants to retain all of these connotations, and put them together in order to give the fullest explanation of the verse.

But in what way can these three distinct meanings all be connected? Behold the textual brilliance of the Ramban, as he continues:

So, in my opinion, the language of *eikev* always refers to twists and turns… as in the verse, "[Esau said], *"Is that why he was named Jacob, so that he could turn me away these two times?! First he took away my birthright, and now he has taken away my blessing!" (Gen. 27:36)*

וכן על דעתי כל לשון עקיבה גלגול וסבוב ... ויעקבני זה פעמים (בראשית כז לו)

The Ramban is now pointing us to probably the most important usage of this word root in the Torah, but one just obscured enough by its form that we might have overlooked it: *eikev* is the basis for the name Jacob, the third of the forefathers: *Ya'akov* (יעקב). And, in line with Rashi's explanation above, the naming of Jacob comes from the word for "heel." For when Isaac and Rebecca's two twins Esau and Jacob are born, we read:

The first one emerged, all red and hairy, and they called him Esau. And after this, came his brother, who was holding onto the heel of Esau. So they called him 'Jacob.' *(Gen. 25:25-26)*

וַיֵּצֵא הָרִאשׁוֹן אַדְמוֹנִי כֻּלּוֹ כְּאַדֶּרֶת שֵׂעָר וַיִּקְרְאוּ שְׁמוֹ עֵשָׂו. וְאַחֲרֵי כֵן יָצָא אָחִיו וְיָדוֹ אֹחֶזֶת בַּעֲקֵב עֵשָׂו וַיִּקְרָא שְׁמוֹ יַעֲקֹב.

Jacob, in other words, means, "The Heel-grabber." Esau is technically the older brother, and so the inheritor to the covenant. But from his very first moment, Jacob was trying to pull himself forward and drag his brother back, to twist the inheritance away from him. And this heel-grabbing will come to symbolize Jacob's interaction with his brother from then on. Jacob will twist the birthright away from Esau by exchanging it for food when Esau is starving. And Jacob will disguise himself as Esau in order to steal their father's favored blessing. These are the two incidents that Esau refers to when he says Jacob, *"has turned me away these two times."* More literally, Esau might have been saying, *"he has grabbed at my heel these two times, and so twisted the lineage in his favor."*

And this is what the Ramban means when he says that *eikev* always refers to twists and turns, and that the allusions to "heels" and to "end rewards" are relevant, along with his own interpretation of *eikev* – "because of." All three connotations are important aspects of the full meaning of the word. Put together, they mean something like:

You will receive the end reward because of your grabbing the heel.

In other words, you will inherit the covenant of your forefathers, but it will come to you unexpectedly, even illicitly, by way of a series of twists and turns, many of which will be brought about through your own guile.

The Ramban then makes this implication even more explicit by highlighting the contrast between the name Jacob and the other names Jacob will one day receive: 'Israel' and 'Jeshurun,' both of which come from the root *yashar*, which means 'straight':

Therefore, they called Jacob, "Jeshurun" – because the opposite of 'twisted' is 'straightened.' Whereas the back of the leg is called the heel, and so when *"his hand was holding on to the heel of Esau,"* they called him by this incident because he was crooked.

ולכן יקראו יעקב "ישורון" כי היפך העקוב מישור. וכן אחורי הרגל שנקרא עקב וידו אוחזת בעקב עשו (בראשית כה כו) יקראנו כן בעבור היותו מעוגל.

Jacob did become the third patriarch, the inheritor of the covenant, but he arrived at his "reward" through crooked channels, through twists and turns. He was not born with the birthright; he had to grab for it, and wrestle it away from his brother. In the course of his life, he did not always conduct himself in the most upright way: he was a man who bargained, played tricks, and fled the scene in the middle of the night. And then, when the time came to pass on the birthright, he kept twisting the lineage, playing favorites, choosing the younger son over the older. He walked a crooked path, but he managed to straighten it as he went, and finally, he ended up with the reward. He was born Jacob the Bent, but he would be remembered as Jeshurun, or Israel – the Straightened One.

And so it will be with the Children of Israel. Our journey through history will not be straightforward. We will have to struggle and strive, to grab on to what we can to survive. We will learn to deal and trade, to reason and fast-talk our way out of danger, and sometimes, when there is no other choice, to flee from our enemies. We are the scrappy youngest child, the weakling, who came out all twisted and tangled up. We are the unlikeliest of people to make it all the way to the end of time. But we will make it. For we will learn to straighten out our crooked journey as we go.

So, following the explanation of the Ramban:

And because of your heeding these laws, to guard them, and perform them, the Lord your God will guard the covenant and the kindness that God swore to your forefathers.

But also:

And because of your constantly grabbing the heel, and forcing your way forward, against all odds, you will ultimately receive the reward.

We will get there, in the end, by hook or by crook.

CHAPTER 47

THE CHILDREN OF BELIAL - Parshat Re'eih

It is one of the most disturbing commandments in the Torah: The Case of the Condemned City (עיר הנידחת).

We are told in this week's parsha that when it becomes clear that an entire city in the Land of Israel has been overtaken by idolatry, they are to be wiped out completely:

Strike down the inhabitants of the town with the sword. Destroy it, and everything in it; put even the animals to the sword. Gather all its goods in the central square and burn the town and everything in it like a sacrifice to the Eternal your God. It shall remain in everlasting ruin, never to be rebuilt. (*Deut. 13:16-17*)

הַכֵּה תַכֶּה אֶת יֹשְׁבֵי הָעִיר הַהִוא לְפִי חָרֶב הַחֲרֵם אֹתָהּ וְאֶת כָּל אֲשֶׁר בָּהּ וְאֶת בְּהֶמְתָּהּ לְפִי חָרֶב. וְאֶת־כָּל שְׁלָלָהּ תִּקְבֹּץ אֶל תּוֹךְ רְחֹבָהּ וְשָׂרַפְתָּ בָאֵשׁ אֶת הָעִיר וְאֶת כָּל שְׁלָלָהּ כָּלִיל לַה' אֱלֹהֶיךָ וְהָיְתָה תֵּל עוֹלָם לֹא תִבָּנֶה עוֹד.

The savagery of this punishment is unparalleled in the Torah. An entire city, burned to the ground. Men, women, and children – and even animals! – slaughtered without mercy. It's enough to make you want to just tear this page out of the Bible.

And rabbinic tradition nearly does just that. First, they establish all kinds of prerequisites for carrying out this punishment, making it highly unlikely that such a thing could ever occur. To be fair, they are playing off the words of the Torah itself, which prefaced the above passage with an insistence that:

You shall inquire, and investigate, and interrogate thoroughly... (*v. 15*)

וְדָרַשְׁתָּ וְחָקַרְתָּ וְשָׁאַלְתָּ הֵיטֵב...

The tripled verbiage here seems to suggest extreme caution. But then the rabbis take those hesitations a step further, declaring boldly that:

The Condemned City never happened and never will happen. (*Talmud, Sanhedrin 71a*)

עיר הנדחת לא היתה ולא עתידה להיות.

This is one of only three cases that receives this unusual treatment; it is written out of existence, relegated to the realm of the purely theoretical. And perhaps that is for the best.

But before we let the Condemned City fade from our memory entirely, there is one strange detail that calls for a bit of exploration, and perhaps will help us understand what had gone so wrong there to begin with. For the inhabitants of this city are not simply described as idolaters. They seem to have a very particular form of worship:

If you hear it said that in one of the cities the Eternal your God is giving you to dwell in, that the people have become Children of Belial, and have subverted the residents of the city, saying, *"Come, let us worship other gods..."* (*vv. 13-14*)

כִּי תִשְׁמַע בְּאַחַת עָרֶיךָ אֲשֶׁר ה' אֱלֹהֶיךָ נֹתֵן לְךָ לָשֶׁבֶת שָׁם לֵאמֹר. יָצְאוּ אֲנָשִׁים בְּנֵי בְלִיַּעַל מִקִּרְבֶּךָ וַיַּדִּיחוּ אֶת יֹשְׁבֵי עִירָם לֵאמֹר נֵלְכָה וְנַעַבְדָה אֱלֹהִים אֲחֵרִים...

Hold on there. "Children of Belial"? Who or what is this *Belial*? Is this the name of a god? It certainly sounds like it. Or perhaps it refers to a particular form of strange worship – some kind of necromancy or black magic. What legend lies behind this mysterious name? What strange tales of the occult are we about to uncover?

*

Ah, but Jewish commentary gives us nothing so dramatic. **Rashi** tells us that *belial* is not a name at all, but a compound word: '*bli – ol*', meaning, 'without – yoke.' In other words, these people are unrestrained by obligation. They do what they want. In fact, most translations do not even use the word, '*belial*.' They simply say, "lawless people," or just "scoundrels." But it this usage seems a bit odd. Why have a separate compound word for this description that could easily have been made with the two short words we already know? And why describe these people as *"The Children of..."* lawlessness?

Rabbeinu Bachya gives an even weaker version of the same kind of interpretation. He says it may mean, '*b'lo – al*', meaning 'not – going up.'

These folks will never rise up toward God. Still others suggest, *'bli – ya'al,'* or, 'without – worth.'

Is this getting tiring? One gets the impression that these commentators are trying a bit too hard, and that no one really knows what this word really refers to. But why not just go with what it looks like – a name? Only the **Ibn Ezra** ventures this suggestion, but even he seems rather uncertain:

Belial **– A name. Though there are those who say it is a compound word.**

בליעל – שם, ויש אומרים שהיא מלה מורכבת.

That's as strong a suggestion as we get that *belial* might refer to someone specific. But if so, who would it be?

*

If we leave the classical Jewish canon, we start getting some scintillating suggestions. Belial is mentioned in several of the Dead Sea Scrolls, in language like this:

You made Belial for the pit, angel of enmity; in darkness is his domain, his counsel is to bring about wickedness and guilt. All the spirits of his lot are angels of destruction, they walk in the laws of darkness; toward it goes their only desire. *(The War Scroll)*

Here Belial is an angel, who has been created by God to rule over darkness, and who seems to command a host of other angels. Then, in early Christian writings, Belial is given even more power. Here a description of him from a book called, *'The Ascension of Isaiah'* (a sort of long-form Christian midrash on the prophecies of Isaiah):

And Manasseh turned aside his heart to serve Belia[l]; for the angel of lawlessness, who is the ruler of this world, is Belia[l], whose name is Matanbuchus. (*2:4*)

Now Belial is ruler of this whole world. And now he is collecting other names: Matanbuchus. By the time we get to the Latin Vulgate translation of the Bible, Saint Jerome will add one more:

And bringing two men, sons of the devil (*belial: diaboli*), they made them sit against him: and they, like men of the devil, bore witness against him before the people. (*from the translation of I Kings 21:13*)

The Devil himself! That, according to Christian tradition, is who has been haunting this condemned city. That is who these heretics worshipped. And that is who must be purged through death and fire.

*

Now why did Jewish tradition never go this way?

Of course, the obvious answer is that we simply don't have the same concept of "The Devil." We do, however, have plenty of angels and demons floating around in midrashic literature. Yet here, in the story of the Condemned City – where the explicit crime is idolatry and we might expect a particular emphasis on strange forms of worship – nearly all the commentators avoid any trace of supernaturalism and stick to a strictly moral interpretation of *belial*. It is lawlessness; godlessness; worthlessness – but it is not sorcery or witchcraft. Why is it so clear in Jewish tradition that following *belial* is an ethical violation, rather than a theological heresy?

I believe the answer to that question is actually quite close at hand. For while there are twenty-seven occurrences of the word *belial* in the whole of the Hebrew Bible, the only other mention it receives in the Torah itself is right here in our parsha, two chapters later. But this time it appears in a totally different context. It is the source text for the commandment to give *tzedakah* (charity) to the poor. And we are famously told to:

Open your hand to him and lend him whatever he needs. ***(Deut. 15:8)***

כִּי פָתֹחַ תִּפְתַּח אֶת יָדְךָ לוֹ וְהַעֲבֵט תַּעֲבִיטֶנּוּ דֵּי מַחְסֹרוֹ אֲשֶׁר יֶחְסַר לוֹ.

But there is a potential problem here, which the Torah addresses right away. Jewish law mandates that all loans are forgiven every seven years. The Torah anticipates that people will be less likely to loan to the poor toward the end of this cycle, knowing they may not be repaid. To combat this tendency, in the next verse, this stern warning is issued:

Beware, lest you have a thought of *belial* in your heart, and say, "The seventh year of remission is approaching," so that you are wicked to your needy kinsman and give him nothing. (*15:9*)

הִשָּׁמֶר לְךָ פֶּן יִהְיֶה דָבָר עִם לְבָבְךָ בְלִיַּעַל לֵאמֹר קָרְבָה שְׁנַת הַשֶּׁבַע שְׁנַת הַשְּׁמִטָּה וְרָעָה עֵינְךָ בְּאָחִיךָ הָאֶבְיוֹן וְלֹא תִתֵּן לוֹ וְקָרָא עָלֶיךָ אֶל ה' וְהָיָה בְךָ חֵטְא.

Here is *belial* again. But it is no foreign god. It is no cultish worship. He is not haunting you from out there somewhere.

Belial is in your heart. It is your selfishness. Your greed. Your lust for wealth, and the cruelty you will show to the most needy. You will defy the Torah and you will defy God in order to keep what you have all to yourself. *Belial* is no angel up in the heavens, or down in hell. *Belial* is as human and terrestrial a thing as could be.

But, of course, it goes both ways. These two reference points inform one another. If the idolatrous children of *belial* in the condemned city are to be understood as *ethically* corrupt, then the thought of *belial* in the heart of the one who refuses to give must be, on some level, an *idolatrous* thought.

The rabbis of the Talmud, never missing a beat, make exactly that connection:

Rabbi Yehoshua ben Korcha says: Whoever turns away his eyes from one who asks for charity is considered as if he were worshipping idols. For it is written here, "*Beware, lest you have a thought of* belial *in your heart*," and there, "*the people have become children of* belial*.*" Just as in that case the sin is idolatry, so in this case the sin is idolatry. *(Bava Batra 10a)*

רבי יהושע בן קרחה אומר כל המעלים עיניו מן הצדקה כאילו עובד עבודת כוכבים כתיב הכא (**דברים טו, ט**) השמר לך פן יהיה דבר עם לבבך בליעל וכתיב התם (**דברים יג, יד**) יצאו אנשים בני בליעל מה להלן עבודת כוכבים אף כאן עבודת כוכבים

You, who hoarded your money – you worshipped a god of greed. You, who let the poor go hungry – you let a devil into your heart. You, who turned your eyes away from your brother's outstretched hand – you are the true heretic.

And we will burn your city down.

CHAPTER 48

KINGS OF FLESH AND BLOOD – Parshat Shoftim

Monarchy is one of the most fiercely debated topics in all of Jewish law and literature.

On the one hand, we have a long and storied tradition of kings ruling over ancient Israel – chief among them King David, a paragon of passion and piety, and one of the great heroes of the Hebrew Bible. Even our concept of the messiah is traditionally understood not as some supernatural being, but a human king whose reign will usher in an era of utopian peace.

On the other hand, from the very start, there have been vociferous objections to the appointment of a king over Israel. At the people's first call for a king, the prophet Samuel is outraged, and delivers a fiery warning of the dangers they should expect from human power: *He will conscript your sons into his army and take your daughters as his personal attendants; he will seize your land and your flocks; and eventually, he will make you his slaves...*

The day will come when you cry out because of the king whom you yourselves have chosen; and the Eternal will not answer you on that day. ***(I Samuel 8:18)***

וּזְעַקְתֶּם בַּיּוֹם הַהוּא מִלִּפְנֵי מַלְכְּכֶם אֲשֶׁר בְּחַרְתֶּם לָכֶם וְלֹא יַעֲנֶה ה' אֶתְכֶם בַּיּוֹם הַהוּא.

But the people are insistent. They must have a king, *"to rule over us like all other nations."* And God tells Samuel to give them what they want – though God, too, seems deeply disappointed:

Heed the demand of the people, everything they have said to you. For it is not you they have rejected; it is Me they have rejected as their king. ***(I Sam. 8:7)***

שְׁמַע בְּקוֹל הָעָם לְכֹל אֲשֶׁר יֹאמְרוּ אֵלֶיךָ כִּי לֹא אֹתְךָ מָאָסוּ כִּי אֹתִי מָאֲסוּ מִמְּלֹךְ עֲלֵיהֶם.

For that is the real theological issue at the heart of the Jewish debate over the merits of monarchy: Ideally, God should be our one and only king. We should instinctively reject all human authority, all "kings of flesh and blood" (as the classic rabbinic phrasing goes), and recognize only (as Jewish liturgy sometimes describes God) the "King of kings." Wasn't that, after all, the central lesson of the Exodus?

*

Yet there is also good textual reason to assume that Jewish tradition explicitly sanctions – and perhaps even mandates – the appointment of a king over Israel. As a matter of *parshanut*, the debate centers on the specific wording of the following verses in *Parshat Shoftim*:

When you come into the land that the Eternal your God has given you, and have taken possession of it, and settled in it, and you say, "I will place upon me a king, like all the nations around me." Then place upon yourself a king, one whom the Lord your God will choose from amongst your brothers; you must not place a foreigner upon you, one who is not your brother." ***(Deut. 17:14-15)***

כִּי־תָבֹא אֶל־הָאָרֶץ אֲשֶׁר ה׳ אֱלֹהֶיךָ נֹתֵן לָךְ וִירִשְׁתָּהּ וְיָשַׁבְתָּה בָּהּ וְאָמַרְתָּ אָשִׂימָה עָלַי מֶלֶךְ כְּכָל־הַגּוֹיִם אֲשֶׁר סְבִיבֹתָי. שׂוֹם תָּשִׂים עָלֶיךָ מֶלֶךְ אֲשֶׁר יִבְחַר ה׳ אֱלֹהֶיךָ בּוֹ מִקֶּרֶב אַחֶיךָ תָּשִׂים עָלֶיךָ מֶלֶךְ לֹא תוּכַל לָתֵת עָלֶיךָ אִישׁ נָכְרִי אֲשֶׁר לֹא אָחִיךָ הוּא.

There are many ambiguities in this short passage, some of which are concealed by the English translation. The primary question the commentators have is whether these lines are meant to give *permission* to appoint a king, or to *command* such appointment. Is this a conditional directive, dependent on whether or not you say, *"I will place upon me a king"*? That would mean that if you do not ask for a king, there is no need for one. Or are these verses telling us we are to appoint a king whether we want one or not?

To make interpretive matters more challenging, the first word, which we have translated as 'when,' in the Hebrew is *'ki'* (כי), which could also mean 'if.' One can easily see that the choice between these two meanings makes a big difference in our understanding of the law. A passage that begins with the word 'if' can be read as entirely conditional: if you ask for a king, then you will have one; if not, then you won't. Whereas the word 'when' more strongly suggests that this should and will happen.

Those parsing the Hebrew carefully will also note that the beginning of the second sentence, which we have translated as, "then you shall place upon yourself," is actually written in an emphatic form of the verb: *'som tasim'* (שום תשים). The repetitive sound here may indicate an imperative: "*som tasim*" – "place, you must place!" But then again, as we just said, even that imperative might be only activated by the conditional: "*If* you ask for one, then *you must place* one upon you."

So we can see the difficulty the commentators are faced with. *Can* we have a king, or *must* we? And even if we are *allowed* to opt out of kingship, does that mean we should? There are strong opinions on either side, and the implications are quite serious, for they speak to the greater question of whether or not having a king is a good thing at all.

*

This debate was already playing out in the Talmud, with Rabbi Yehuda declaring the appointment of a king as a mandatory act upon entering the land of Israel, while Rabbi Nehorai argued that the passage in Deuteronomy was only written, *"to speak to the murmurers"* in the book of Samuel *(Sanhedrin 20b)*.

The figure who most solidly codifies the kingship into a legal imperative is the great medieval philosopher, **Moses Maimonides** ("The Rambam"). He states, in no uncertain terms, in the opening of his "Laws of Kings and Wars":

Israel is commanded with three things upon entering into the Land: 1.) to appoint for themselves a king... 2.) to destroy the descendants of Amalek... and 3.) to build the Temple... And the appointment of the king comes first... *(Mishneh Torah, Hilkhot Melakhim u'Milchamot 1:1-2)*

שלוש מצוות נצטוו ישראל בשעת כניסתן לארץ: למנות להם מלך... ולהכרית זרעו של עמלק... ולבנות להם בית הבחירה... מינוי מלך קודם.

There you have it: the establishment of the kingship is not only mandatory, but primary among the laws that regulate the formation of a new society in the land of Israel. Maimonides does briefly consider the episode in the Book of Samuel, where God seems not to approve of the request for a king, but concludes that this is only because the people had the wrong motivations in that case; they wanted to oust Samuel and to imitate the nations around them, not to fulfill the commandment. In his typical fashion, Maimonides selects the opinion of Rabbi Yehudah in the Talmud as conclusive, and leaves the other position out. Over time, the authority of Maimonides' legal code grew stronger and stronger, and by now, it is generally taken as a matter of accepted law that the appointment of a king is one of the 613 commandments.

However, throughout the medieval period, this question was still very much unresolved, and many interpreters preferred the second opinion in the Talmud, the one given by Rabbi Nehorai, that the appointment of a king is an unfortunate concession. Among them is one of the greatest Jewish political thinkers, and a prolific Biblical commentator, Don Yitzchak Abarbanel ("The **Abarbanel**"). He considers the position of Maimonides, and all the various arguments for kingship, and then writes:

Even if we admit that the presence of a king is a useful and necessary thing for a nation, to establish and maintain its society – still, for the nation of Israel this is not the case. For them it is not necessary at all.

אף שנודה היות המלך דבר מועיל והכרחי בעם לתקן הקבוץ המדיני ושמירתו, מה שהוא, הנה בעם ישראל איננו כן כי אינו צריך ולא הכרחי להם.

Why is Israel distinct from all the other nations in this way? Abarbanel lists the primary functions of a king: to fight wars for the people; to establish guidelines and rules of conduct for a well-functioning society; to punish those who commit acts of treachery but are able to escape legal prosecution. Some will argue that a nation needs a king to perform these functions. But that argument does not apply to the nation of Israel. For they turn instead to God to assist them in their battles, to give them clear instructions on how to run their society, and to punish the wicked.

What, then, does Abarbanel make of the passage in *Parshat Shoftim* that could be read as an instruction to appoint a king? Here is his reading:

Listen, this is the explanation of the passage on kingship, and whether or not it is truly a commandment. When it says, *"When you come into the land that the Eternal your God has given you, and taken possession of it and settled in it, and you say, 'I will place upon me a king, like all the nations around me,'"* this is not a commandment at all. For God does not command them to ask for a king. This is, rather, a foretelling of the future, for it speaks of *after* you are in the promised land, and *after* the conquest and all the wars, and *after* the distribution of land (for it says *"you have taken possession of it and settled in it") – then* God is saying, I know you will be ungrateful for all the good I have done when you say, *"I will place upon myself a king."* It is not because you need one to fight wars with other nations or to conquer the land. For it is already con-

quered! Rather, you wiljust want to be like the other nations, who have appointed kings. And this is foolishness…

שמע פי׳ פרשת המלך וענין המצוה כפי אמתתה, הנה באמרו כי תבאו אל הארץ אשר ה׳ אלהיך נותן לך וירשתה וישבת בה ואמרת אשימה עלי מלך ככל הגוים אשר סביבותי אין בזה מצוה כלל כי לא צוה הש״י שיאמרו זה וישאלו מלך, אבל הנה הוא הגדת העתיד, יאמר אחרי היותכם בארץ הנבחרת, ואחרי הכבוש והמלחמות כלם ואחרי החלוק וזהו אמרו וירשתה וישבת בה אני ידעת ישתהיו כפוים טובה כשתאמרו מעצמכם אשימה עלי מלך לא מפני ההכרח להלחם עם העממים ולכבוש את הארץ כי כבר היא נכבשת לפניכם כי אם להשתוות עם האומות הממליכי׳ עליהם מלכים, ובזה מהסכלות...

Abarbanel has cleverly undone Maimonides' legal formulation through a careful reading of the verses. For Maimonides made it clear that the appointment of a king should be the first act of state business upon entering the land. Only then should the nation move to conquer its enemies and build the Temple. But the Torah seems to speak of people who are calling for a king *after* they have conquered and settled the land. So they clearly do not need a king for the functional reasons we listed above. Indeed, God has already done that work for them. Instead, the Abarbanel argues, they want a king in order to become a nation like all other nations, to submit to the cult of nationalism that turns the state into an object of veneration – with the king, as a pseudo-deity, at its head.

This was the problem Samuel and God were worried about to begin with. They warned that the appointment of a monarch is, inherently, a rejection of Divine authority. For only God has absolute power. When we give such powers to a human being, with all their mortal desires, we can only expect the worst: *He will conscript your sons into war, and your daughters into his personal service. He will seize your land and your flocks. And eventually, he will make you his slaves.*

*

But what was it that caused Abarbanel to so forcefully reject the interpretation of Maimonides? It may well have been a simple divergence in the interpretation of textual ambiguities. That, in turn, may have been driven by a deeper disagreement over political and theological principles.

One cannot help but wonder, however, if biography also had something to do with it. For, as it happens, Abarbanel's remarkable life story is one that intersected regularly with actual kings. Along with his plentiful intellectual gifts, he also had a superb command of financial matters, and so was recruited at a young age by King Afonso V of Portugal, to serve as his treasurer. Abarbanel proved quite adept at this task, and became close enough to the king that he was occasionally able to act as an advocate for the Jewish community.

However, when King Afonso died, his successor, King John II – like the Pharaoh of old – forgot all that Abarbanel had done for the country, and quickly accused him of conspiracy. Abarbanel managed – like Moses of old – to flee the country before he was killed, but not before the king seized his entire family fortune.

In his new home in Spain, he once again rose quickly, and became close to King Ferdinand and Queen Isabella. But when that country became obsessed with purging itself of Jews, he was forced to flee once again. From Venice, he attempted, with great sums of money he had collected, to persuade the Spanish monarchy to allow the Jews to stay. Legend has it that he was nearly successful when suddenly, Torquemada – the Grand Inquisitor himself – personally intervened, bursting into the royal chamber and throwing a crucifix down in front of the king and queen like a gauntlet. The expulsion continued and all remaining Jews were either forcefully converted or executed.

So the Abarbanel knew a thing or two about kings and queens, and how well they could be trusted to protect their people.

One can imagine him in his final years, in the study of his second exilic home in Venice, working away at his commentary, and coming to the passage on kingship in Deuteronomy. What did it mean? Was it conditional or imperative? Are we supposed to appoint a king? Should we try to be like all the nations around us? Or are we only to accept the authority of the one above, the King of all kings? The words in front of him could be read either way.

He sat and reflected for a time, perhaps. He looked back at the book of Samuel. He read over what Maimonides had written before him.

He dipped his quill in ink, and wrote the following words:

But what need have we for intellectual arguments? For experience trumps theory. Just look and see how it is, in lands governed by kings…

ומה לנו להביא על זה טענות שכליות והנה הנסיון גובר על ההקש, הביטו וראו הארצות שהנהגתם על ידי המלכים...

CHAPTER 49
THE CURSE OF THE HANGING MAN – Parshat Ki Teitzei

Oh, Rashi.

Rashi – Rabbi Shlomo Yizchaki, of 11th century France: so cryptic, so laconic, so casually brilliant. He is the most famous of the classical Torah commentators, and for good reason. His work is both concise and comprehensive – usually just offering us a few words, but words laden with enough meaning that later scholars continue to grapple with them for centuries, slowly unpacking all the nuances and coded references. Indeed there have been over 300 commentaries on Rashi's commentary (what are called "supercommentaries").

And Rashi has done it again this week. He has left us with a short piece of writing (though long by his standards) – just forty-three words – that took me days to work through. I turned it over and over, in fascination and frustration, like trying to put together a jigsaw puzzle missing a piece.

But I think I got it. So I'm going to attempt to take you through this one comment of Rashi's, slowly, so you can appreciate all the twists and turns and the greatness of this quiet *parshanut* giant.

*

We begin our investigation with a man hanging from a tree.

Parshat Ki Teitzei – the most law-filled reading in the Torah – gives us the following regulation for capital punishment:

If a man is guilty of a capital offense and is put to death and you hang him on a tree, you must not let his corpse remain on the tree overnight, but must bury him on that same day. For a hanging body is a curse to God – you shall not defile the land that the Eternal your God is giving you as an inheritance. ***(Deut. 21:22-23)***

וְכִי יִהְיֶה בְאִישׁ חֵטְא מִשְׁפַּט־מָוֶת וְהוּמָת וְתָלִיתָ אֹתוֹ עַל עֵץ. לֹא תָלִין נִבְלָתוֹ עַל־הָעֵץ כִּי קָבוֹר תִּקְבְּרֶנּוּ בַּיּוֹם הַהוּא כִּי קִלְלַת אֱלֹהִים תָּלוּי וְלֹא תְטַמֵּא אֶת אַדְמָתְךָ אֲשֶׁר ה' אֱלֹהֶיךָ נֹתֵן לְךָ נַחֲלָה.

The intention of this rule seems relatively clear. Although the Torah does allow for the death penalty, it cautions us against relishing in the punishment by leaving the body up as a display. The hanging corpse is an affront to human dignity, and also – says the verse – a curse to God.

But Rashi is perplexed by that phrasing: "a curse to God." God may not approve of this barbaric practice, but how is God "cursed" by it? So Rashi begins by redefining the word for 'curse' here – *klalah* – as follows:

For a hanging body is a curse to God – meaning, it is an *insult* to the King, for a person is made in God's image, and Israel are God's children.

כי *קללת אלהים תלוי* – זלזולו של מלך הוא, שאדם עשוי בדמות דיוקנו, וישראל הם בניו.

Okay, this much of the commentary we can at least understand – whether or not we sign on to the theology. We were made in God's image – that we know from the creation story in Genesis – and so when our bodies are left hanging in disgrace, it is as if God's own image is disgraced. It is unclear exactly how literally Rashi takes the idea of the human form as an actual representation of the image of God – that seems rather anthropomorphic – but in any case, the parallel between the two means that degrading a corpse is like insulting God. Hence, a hanging body is a curse to God.

That seems like enough of an explanation. I would have been satisfied with that answer. But then Rashi, continues, with a parable he borrows from Rabbi Meir, in the Talmud, Tractate Sanhedrin *(46b)*:

A parable. There were two twins who looked exactly alike. One was made a king, while the other was arrested for robbery and hanged. Then whoever saw him would say, "The King is hanging!"

משל לשני אחים תאומים שהיו דומים זה לזה, אחד נעשה מלך ואחד נתפס ללסטיות ונתלה, כל הרואה אותו אומר המלך תלוי.

We might well ask why Rashi needed this extra imagery at all. What does this add to his first point, about the hanging body being an insult to God because we are made in God's image?

But more than that, it isn't entirely clear who is who in the analogy. Is God the twin who was made a king, and the criminal is the other twin? In which case, when people see him hanging, do they think it is actually God dangling there?! Or is God the parent of both twins, one of whom is a good boy – fit to become the next king – and one of whom is very bad? So then, when the bad twin is hanged, people mistakenly think it is the good twin – the future king – who has committed this terrible crime.

In other words, do we take the hanging man down in order to save God's reputation, or our own? And in either case, are we really so worried about a case of mistaken identity? We began by speaking of the "curse" of a hanging, and now it seems we are also concerned about the confusion it might cause.

*

If all that weren't dizzying enough, Rashi throws one final thought into his commentary:

Every instance of the word *klalah* in scripture is some kind of belittling or insult, as in *(I Kings 2:8)*, [when David says,] "and he insulted me outrageously." (*kilelani klalah*)

כל קללה שבמקרא לשון הקל וזלזול, כמו (מלכים א ב') "והוא קללני קללה נמרצת."

Now, this is a curious move. First of all, it is not true that every instance of this word means "insult." Some of the most prominent usages mean, straightforwardly, "curse" – as in, the opposite of a blessing. If that were not the case, why would we have translated our verse as "a curse to God," to begin with?

But much more interesting is the context of the example verse that Rashi chooses. This is taken from a passage at the beginning of the Book of Kings. That book opens with King David nearing the end of his life, and the question of who will be his successor. Presumably that question has already been answered by God, who has chosen Solomon to be the next king – the one who will finally build the temple in Jerusalem.

But as David lay weak on his deathbed another of his sons, Adonijah, makes a move for the kingship:

Adonijah son of Haggit went about boasting, "I will be king!" He provided himself with chariots and horses, and an escort of fifty men running before him. *(I Kings 1:5)*

וַאֲדֹנִיָּה בֶן חַגִּית מִתְנַשֵּׂא לֵאמֹר אֲנִי אֶמְלֹךְ וַיַּעַשׂ לוֹ רֶכֶב וּפָרָשִׁים וַחֲמִשִּׁים אִישׁ רָצִים לְפָנָיו.

Adonijah is actually the older son, with some reasonable claim to the throne, and so he manages to get priests and the commander of the army on his side. He even hosts a great sacrificial feast, announcing his ascendance to the throne. But when this news is reported to King David he will have none of it, and quickly moves to officially appoint Solomon as the new king, before all the people.

As quickly as Adonijah has attempted to steal the throne, it is snatched back from him, and he must admit defeat and humble himself before Solomon. At first it seems that the brothers make peace, but eventually Adonijah offends Solomon and Solomon has him killed.

Now we could go on and on with the drama here. But turning back to our Rashi, what is so striking about the reference to these scenes in the Book of Kings is that the story sounds strangely similar to the very last thing Rashi has mentioned – the parable of the two twin brothers. Remember: one son was the king, one was a thief. And the thief was eventually caught and killed for his treachery.

Rashi did not have to mention either of these things: not the parable, nor the quote from the Book of Kings. But the parallel between the two is so strong, and mentioned in such quick succession, that we must ask what Rashi is trying to say here. Why is the story of Solomon and Adonijah like the parable of the twins? And – let's not forget, we're still in Deuteronomy – what does all this have to do with the hanging man?

The jigsaw puzzle is there in front of us, but we're still missing that final piece. And that's all that Rashi gives us. The comment is over.

*

Almost. Rashi doesn't tell us anything more, it's true. But King David does. Remember that Rashi's example of the usage of *klalah* to mean 'insult' came from David speaking to Solomon. We've already looked at the larger context in which the scene takes place. But who is it that David is saying *"insulted me outrageously"*? He gives a name: Shimi ben Gera. And if we go back to David's story in the Book of Samuel, we can find his encounter with this man, who indeed insults him outrageously:

As King David was approaching Bachurim, a member of Saul's clan—a man named Shimi son of Gera—came out from there, hurling insults as he came. He threw stones at David and all King David's courtiers, while all the troops and all the warriors were at his right and his left. And these are the insults that Shimi hurled: "Get out, get out, you criminal, you villain! The Eternal is paying you back for all your crimes against the family of Saul, whose throne you seized. The Eternal is handing over the throne to your son Absalom; you are in trouble because you are a criminal." ***(II Samuel 16:5-8)***

וּבָא הַמֶּלֶךְ דָּוִד עַד בַּחוּרִים וְהִנֵּה מִשָּׁם אִישׁ יוֹצֵא מִמִּשְׁפַּחַת בֵּית שָׁאוּל וּשְׁמוֹ שִׁמְעִי בֶּן גֵּרָא יֹצֵא יָצוֹא וּמְקַלֵּל. וַיְסַקֵּל בָּאֲבָנִים אֶת דָּוִד וְאֶת כָּל עַבְדֵי הַמֶּלֶךְ דָּוִד וְכָל הָעָם וְכָל הַגִּבֹּרִים מִימִינוֹ וּמִשְּׂמֹאלוֹ. כֹּה אָמַר שִׁמְעִי בְּקַלְלוֹ צֵא צֵא אִישׁ הַדָּמִים וְאִישׁ הַבְּלִיָּעַל. הֵשִׁיב עָלֶיךָ ה׳ כֹּל דְּמֵי בֵית שָׁאוּל אֲשֶׁר מָלַכְתָּ תַּחְתָּיו וַיִּתֵּן ה׳ אֶת הַמְּלוּכָה בְּיַד אַבְשָׁלוֹם בְּנֶךָ וְהִנְּךָ בְּרָעָתֶךָ כִּי אִישׁ דָּמִים אָתָּה.

The themes here again strongly parallel those in the Solomon and Adonijah story. David, too, had his claim to the throne questioned. For David, too, had taken it from an older King, at God's direction. And here, though David is the legitimate king, Shimi ben Gera is suggesting that his kingship is a mistake and that he is actually a criminal.

David and Saul. Solomon and Adonijah. The good twin and the bad twin. The king and the criminal. All these pairs are in conflict, and all are easily confused with one another. And the confusion isn't really a matter of who looks like whom. It is a question of who is really in power, and who is an enemy of the state – who is legitimate and who is illegitimate.

And in each case we know, more or less, the answer: David, Solomon, the good twin. These are the rightful kings.

Or are they? Not everyone is so sure. Are *we* really so sure? If we look at the stories long enough, we can start to see the other side. Was Saul robbed of the kingship? Shimi ben Gera thought so. Was Adonijah? He was the older son.

Who is it there on the tree: the criminal, or the rightful king? As we stare at the body, hanging in the wind, whoever it is, we begin to wonder if this was really a just execution.

For all human power is suspect. Any state's right to kill or imprison its citizens ought to make us uncomfortable. For only God can truly say who shall live and who shall die. Perhaps this or that leader claims he or she has God's approval. But are we really so sure? But for a shift in circumstances, a twist of fate, perhaps this king would be a criminal, and this man hanging before us would be free. Should anyone, after all, ever be hanging so gruesomely from a tree? When human beings take upon themselves the authority to execute one another, isn't that always – on some basic level – an insult to God?

We must at least ask these sorts of questions of ourselves. The Torah, even as it sanctions capital punishment, forces us to ask how comfortable we are using this power. And Rashi, in just forty-three words, forces us to ask these questions throughout the rest of our history – even of our greatest leaders. Even of King David.

Oh, Rashi. You've done it again.

CHAPTER 50

THE HOLY TONGUE - Parshat Ki Tavo

During the first half of the 13th century, the Holy Roman Emperor Frederick II conducted a series of experiments on young children, in order to discover the language of God. He would take an infant and have it imprisoned from birth, with hardly any human contact, in order to see if the growing child would naturally begin to speak the language first given to Adam and Eve. The monk Salimbene of Parma writes, in his *Chronicles*, that Frederick ordered nurses, *"to suckle and bathe and wash the children, but in no ways to prattle or speak with them; for he would have learnt whether they would speak the Hebrew language, which had been the first..."*

This disturbing experiment would be repeated, two centuries later, by James IV of Scotland, who sent two children to be raised on an island by a mute woman. *"Some sayes they spak guid Hebrew,"* writes Robert Lindsay, in *The Cronicles of Scotland*, though he seems rather dubious that this could have been the case.

Where did Frederick and James get such a notion – that there was a primary language at all, and that it was probably Hebrew? Likely, they took their cue from a literal reading of Genesis, Chapter 11, verse 1 – the opening of the Tower of Babel story – in which we read that:

The whole earth had one language, and shared words.

וַיְהִי כָל הָאָרֶץ שָׂפָה אֶחָת וּדְבָרִים אֲחָדִים.

The Bible says that once upon a time, everyone spoke the same language. And the Bible is written in Hebrew. So, one might presume, *that* was the language that everyone spoke. And since no other language had been mentioned before this, Hebrew must have been the only language on earth from the time of Adam and Eve on – until after the Tower of Babel had been built and God came down and "scrambled their language" and scattered them throughout the world. *(vv. 7-8)*

In Rabbinic literature, however, the story of language development is not so straightforward. In fact, there is a sharp debate in the Talmud over exactly what it means that, "the whole world had one language."

Rabbi Elazar and Rabbi Yochanan disagreed. One said that they spoke seventy languages, and the other said that they spoke the language of the Great One: The Holy Tongue. ***(Jerusalem Talmud, Megilah 10a)***

ר' לעזר ור' יוחנן חד אמר שהיו מדברים בשבעים לשון וחורנה אמר שהיו מדברין בלשון יחידו של עולם בלשון הקודש.

Rabbi Yochanan seems to share Frederick's assumption that the first language must have been Hebrew – commonly referred to in ancient Jewish literature as the "Holy Tongue." But Rabbi Elazar's opinion is harder to understand: "they spoke seventy languages." How then, can the earth have been "of one language"? My great namesake, Rabbi Menachem Mendel Kasher, explains, in his **Torah Shleimah**, that:

This means that everyone understood the language of his fellow, even though their words were "singular," in that each one had his own language.

שפה אחת שהיה כל אחד מבין שפת חבירו, אע"ג שדברים מיוחדים שלכל א' היה לשון משלו

Rabbi Elazar, then, does not seem to believe that there was a primary language, but instead that a certain degree of language diversity was always a feature of human life.

But where does he get the number seventy?

That seems to come from an ethnological table in the previous chapter, where Noah's grandchildren are listed as the founders of the nations of the world. There are seventy of those descendants, and so, a tradition develops that there were seventy founding nations in the world after the flood.

But what about *before* the flood? Would even Rabbi Elazar have to admit that in the prehistoric days of Adam and Eve there was only one language for all humankind – since after all, we all descend from that primeval pair?

Not necessarily. An intriguing comment of **Rashi**'s in this week's *parsha* draws from an alternate vision of our linguistic origins. As we near the end of the Torah's narrative, Moses begins to recount and write down everything that has happened. And this process is described (both here in *Parshat Ki Tavo*, and earlier, in the first *parsha* of Deuteronomy) with the unusual language of *be'er* (באר), a word related to 'well' – as in, a well of water. This suggests there was some great depth to the kind of communication Moses was engaged in. In both instances of this usage, Rashi says the same thing:

Moses expounded (be'er) this Torah (Deut. 1:5) **– That is, he explained it in seventy languages.**

באר את התורה – בשבעים לשון פרשה להם.

... and again:

[Moses wrote all the words of the Torah] most distinctly (be'er heiteiv) (Deut. 27: 8) **– That is, in seventy languages.**

באר היטב – בשבעים לשון.

So, it seems that for Moses to fully clarify and record the depth of the Torah, he must do so in seventy languages. This seems to be a reference to the seventy nations of the world. Moses must articulate the message of the Torah in every one of the languages that resulted from the scattering at Babel in order to give it full expression.

But the *Midrash Tanchuma,* which Rashi is drawing from in these comments, goes back even further in its account of the seventy languages:

The Holy Blessed One said: behold – the First Person, Adam, who had not been taught anything, how do we know that he spoke seventy languages? For it says, *"And Adam called [all the animals] names." (Gen. 2:20)* It does not say Adam called each animal 'a name,' but 'names.' And now you, Moses, who said, *"I am not a man of words,"* at the end of this forty years after leaving Egypt, you will begin to explain this Torah in seventy languages. As it says, *"and Moses expounded (be'er) this Torah."*

אמר לו הקדוש ברוך הוא, והרי אדם הראשון שלא למדו בריה, מנין היה יודע שבעים לשון, שנאמר: ויקרא להם שמות (בראשית ב, כ). שם לכל הבהמה אין כתיב כאן, אלא שמות. ואתה אומר, לא איש דברים אנכי. בסוף ארבעים שנה שיצאו ישראל ממצרים, התחיל מפרש התורה בשבעים לשון, שנאמר: באר את התורה הזאת.

In this account, when Moses renders the Torah in seventy languages, he is not merely opening it up to the nations of the world, but reconnecting it back to the primary forms of expression. For the first human language was not Hebrew, nor any one single language. We were born into linguistic diversity. A return to our natural state will not simplify our modes of communication, but complexify them. There is no one holy tongue, but instead a primordial, cacophonous babble.

*

Now this is a message that some in the tradition simply cannot swallow. One of the sharpest responses to Rashi's "seventy languages" comment comes from the 19th century German rabbi, Yaakov Tzvi Mecklenburg, in his **HaKtav v'HaKabbalah**. He writes:

Rashi, borrowing from our rabbis, says that Moses explained the Torah in seventy languages. But they cannot mean that he wrote it in the languages of the other nations! For what would be the purpose of that for Israel?! No, the rabbis would not change their language so that it could be spoken by some other nation. Rather, it is the way of the rabbis to refer to 'intention' with the word 'language'... and so, too, here: "seventy languages," is "seventy intentions."

לשון רש"י מרבותינו בשבעים לשון פירשה להם. אין כוונתם על לשונות שאר העמים, כי מה תועלת היה להם לישראל מזה, וגם לרבותינו לא שנו את לשונם לדבר בשפת אומה אחרת, אבל דרך רבותינו לקרוא הכוונה והמכוון במאמר במלת לשון... וכן כאן בשבעים לשונות ר"ל בשבעים כוונות.

Rabbi Mecklenburg does not accept the idea that the Torah is simply being translated by Moses. So he instead takes Rashi to mean that Moses delivered the Torah with seventy different connotations – the same message, in the same language, but each time spoken with different nuances and implications. He compares this process to the well-known rabbinic maxim that there are "seventy faces to the Torah." Moses was illuminating them all.

What motivates Rabbi Mecklenburg to suggest such a (lovely but) far-fetched reading of Rashi? Well, first of all, he simply cannot seem to fathom the possibility that the Torah might be available for study and engagement by all peoples. The only question that concerns him is the Torah's "purpose for Israel."

Secondly, it must be noted, he was clearly a passionate Hebraicist. His commentary, *HaKtav v'HaKabbalah*, is one of the most linguistically-oriented works in the genre. Nearly every comment is an in-depth explanation of the roots of a particular Hebrew phrasing. A work like that is the product of a person convinced that an analysis based on the power and depth of the Hebrew language, alone, is capable of uncovering all the hidden layers of meaning in the Torah. Why would we ever need a translation?

But I suspect that Rabbi Mecklenburg was also driven by a vision he shared with Rabbi Yochanan – and perhaps also the Emperor Frederick and King James of Scotland – of discovering a pure, original, Holy Tongue. These men were obsessed with the idea of a primary language because it was something akin to the code of the universe. If they could learn the language of God, they could understand how the world was created through its words – and they could enter into dialogue with the Creator. It was that potential that excited these linguistic purists.

*

There is another vision of the power of language, however, that emerges in response to that same piece of Rashi's commentary – a very different, but equally exciting vision. It is well-expressed by the 18th century Hassidic Master, Rabbi Levi Yitzchak of Berdichev. *"Why is the Torah expounded here in seventy languages?"* he asks in his masterwork, the **Kedushat Levi.** He first points out that the Torah itself contains fragments of Aramaic, Greek, and some African languages. So even the original text, it seems, is not linguistically "pure." And then he explains:

And the reason for this is that the language of every nation is the life-force of that nation. Hebrew, the Holy Tongue, is the distinct language of Israel. And indeed, they heard first the Torah at Mount Sinai in the Holy Tongue. But the Holy Blessed One, who sees from beginning to end, saw that Israel would have to be in exile, and so for this reason wrote into the Torah the languages of all nations. So that, through this, they would have the ability to hold on to the life-force of each one, through the language of the Holy Torah, in order for Israel to be able to survive in exile.

וחד טעם הוא, כי הלשון של כל האומות הוא החיות מן האומה ולשון הקודש הוא של ישראל לבד. ובאמת ישראל שמעו התורה בסיני רק בלשון הקודש והקדוש ברוך הוא המביט מראשית אחרית שראה שישראל צריכין להיות בגלות לזה כתב בתורה לשון של שאר אומות שעל ידי זה יהיה להם אחיזה בחיות שלהם שהוא הלשון בהתורה הקדושה בכדי שישראל יוכל להיות להם תקומה בגלות.

According to this understanding, every language represents a life-force – an entire culture. Just as the Holy Tongue created a new reality for Israel in the great moment of Revelation – so, too, does every language create a whole, unique world. And we, a wandering people, will find ourselves, in the course of history, living in all of those worlds.

How will we survive? How will we, so foreign and estranged, find a foothold in terrain so alien to us?

In this mystical vision, then, we can find our place in the world – in every world – through our Torah. For our Torah – singular, particular, distinct in its form of expression – has been embedded with every other language in the world. Somewhere in our own tradition, we can find a point of intersection with every other culture we encounter.

Deep, deep down in the well of our own sacred script, we will draw forth a living connection to all of humanity. We will learn to speak, like the First Person, a language of seventy tongues.

CHAPTER 51
CHOP WOOD, DRAW WATER – Parshat Nitzavim

"You stand here, today, all of you, before the Eternal your God."

Thus Moses begins the last section of the great oratory that makes up the Book of Deuteronomy. He has recounted the history of their long journey. He has delivered heaps of new laws meant to help them establish a working society in this new land across the Jordan. And now he pauses, looks out over the crowd, scans the faces, and says, "Here you are. All of you."

So who is this "all of you"? Who is standing there, ready to become the Nation of Israel? Who is in our community?

Moses begins to list distinct groups of people. First the officials: the heads of the tribes, the elders, the legal authorities.

Then the members of the family unit: the men, women and children.

And finally, *"the stranger within your camp"* – for Deuteronomy has made constant mention of our obligations toward the stranger – reminding us, again and again, *"for you were strangers in Egypt."*

But then Moses calls out two further categories of people, seemingly at random:

From your wood-chopper to your water-drawer. ***(Deut. 29:10)***

מֵחֹטֵב עֵצֶיךָ עַד שֹׁאֵב מֵימֶיךָ.

What a strange phrase! Why single out these particular laborers? And what is it about these groups that has not been covered by any of the categories we have heard so far?

Rashi has an answer to these questions, and it's a pretty clever one:

From your wood-choppers to your water-drawers **– This teaches us that in the days of Moses some Canaanites came to convert, just as the Gibonites came in the days of Joshua. For this is what is said about the Gibonites:** ***"And they also acted cunningly…" (Josh. 9:4)*** **So Moses made them wood-choppers and water-drawers.**

מחטב עציך **– מלמד שבאו כנעניים להתגייר בימי משה כדרך שבאו גבעונים בימי יהושע, וזהו האמור בגבעונים (יהושע ט') "*ויעשו גם המה בערמה*", ונתנם משה חוטבי עצים ושואבי מים.**

Rashi has found another place, later in the Bible, when wood-choppers and water-drawers come up again. In the Book of Joshua we read that the Gibonites approached the tribes of Israel, claiming to be a distant people who had journeyed to join the Israelites out of admiration. Israel agrees to accept the Gibonites, but later discovers they had been lying and were actually a local enemy tribe, just seeking security from the Israeli attack.

Joshua could not kick them out – he'd already made a promise to them – but he did condemn them to this curse:

Your descendants shall always be servants – wood-choppers and water-drawers – for the House of my God. *(Josh. 9:23)*

וְלֹא יִכָּרֵת מִכֶּם עֶבֶד וְחֹטְבֵי עֵצִים וְשֹׁאֲבֵי מַיִם לְבֵית אֱלֹהָי.

There are those specific groups again: wood-choppers and water-drawers. And here they are meant to represent positions of servitude, assigned as a punishment for deception. So Rashi reads this context backwards, into Deuteronomy, and assumes our wood-chopper and water-drawer were also converts from the local population.

But there are a number of problems with this explanation. First, it's disgraceful to think that Moses would have given new converts the most demeaning jobs in the community, and then called that out in front of everyone. (In the Book of Joshua, remember, the Gibonites had lied their way in; here, the Canaanites seem to be sincere converts.) Secondly, Moses' phrasing, *"from your wood-chopper to your water-drawer,"* suggests that there is a distinction between the two groups – in fact, that they represent a spectrum, from one end to the other – whereas the meaning of these tasks drawn from the Book of Joshua is simply that there are both lowly positions, similar to one another.

Finally, and perhaps most difficult from a narrative perspective, this interpretation forces us to see the earlier Book of Deuteronomy referencing the later Book of Joshua. It is as if what Moses is saying made no sense on its own, at the time, and only came to have meaning once the story of the Gibonites was explained by Joshua, in the future. That is an awkward way to think of these opening phrases in Moses' great speech.

Would the people there have even understood what Moses was talking about?

What would be ideal, instead – from a *parshanut* perspective – is if there were prior instances in the Torah of these categories, and Moses was hearkening backwards to reference an earlier context. And, even better – while we're wishing – would be if each of these two roles were mentioned only one other time previously, so that we knew exactly where to draw a connection. And, best of all would be if the two earlier mentions of wood-choppers and water-drawers were very different, so that we could understand some distinction between the two.

Well, good news, *parsha* nuts. It turns out that all that is *exactly* what we find when we look backwards in the Torah. There is exactly one other mention of a wood-chopper, and one other mention of a water-drawer. And they appear in very different contexts, indeed.

*

Our wood-chopper can be found just a few chapters back in Deuteronomy, in *Parshat Shoftim*, in the description of a case of involuntary manslaughter:

When someone goes with his fellow into the woods to chop wood; as his arm swings the axe to cut down a tree, the axe-head flies off the handle and strikes the other so that he dies. Then the first one must flee into one of the cities [of refuge] and live there. ***(Deut. 19:5)***

וַאֲשֶׁר יָבֹא אֶת רֵעֵהוּ בַיַּעַר לַחְטֹב עֵצִים וְנִדְּחָה יָדוֹ בַגַּרְזֶן לִכְרֹת הָעֵץ וְנָשַׁל הַבַּרְזֶל מִן הָעֵץ וּמָצָא אֶת רֵעֵהוּ וָמֵת הוּא יָנוּס אֶל אַחַת הֶעָרִים הָאֵלֶּה וָחָי.

The cities of refuge, mentioned several times in the Torah, are designated centers of asylum for those who have committed a terrible act of violence *accidentally*. They are being pursued by the outraged family of the deceased, but can find safety in these cities of refuge. If they leave this sanctuary, however, they no longer have the protection of the law. And the classic case of this kind of exile from the community is the anonymous wood-chopper.

*

Our water-drawer, meanwhile, is a far more famous character. There are several stories in the Torah of women going to get water from a well. But only one of them uses the specific language of 'drawing' – *shoeiva*

(שואבה). It is the tale of Abraham's servant, traveling in search of a wife for Isaac. Here he tells what happened:

I came today to the spring and I said, "Eternal, God of my master Abraham, if You would please grant success to me on my way. As I stand by the spring of water, let the young woman who comes out to draw and to whom I say, 'Please, let me drink a little water from your jar,' and who answers, 'You may drink, and I will also draw for your camels' – let her be the wife whom the Eternal has decreed for my master's son." I had scarcely finished praying in my heart, when Rebecca came out with her jar on her shoulder, and went down to the spring and drew... ***(Gen. 24:42-45)***

וָאָבֹא הַיּוֹם אֶל הָעָיִן וָאֹמַר ה׳ אֱלֹהֵי אֲדֹנִי אַבְרָהָם אִם יֶשְׁךָ נָּא מַצְלִיחַ דַּרְכִּי אֲשֶׁר אָנֹכִי הֹלֵךְ עָלֶיהָ. הִנֵּה אָנֹכִי נִצָּב עַל עֵין הַמָּיִם וְהָיָה הָעַלְמָה הַיֹּצֵאת לִשְׁאֹב וְאָמַרְתִּי אֵלֶיהָ הַשְׁקִינִי נָא מְעַט מַיִם מִכַּדֵּךְ. וְאָמְרָה אֵלַי גַּם אַתָּה שְׁתֵה וְגַם לִגְמַלֶּיךָ אֶשְׁאָב הִוא הָאִשָּׁה אֲשֶׁר הֹכִיחַ ה׳ לְבֶן אֲדֹנִי. אֲנִי טֶרֶם אֲכַלֶּה לְדַבֵּר אֶל לִבִּי וְהִנֵּה רִבְקָה יֹצֵאת וְכַדָּהּ עַל שִׁכְמָהּ וַתֵּרֶד הָעַיְנָה וַתִּשְׁאָב...

Rebecca. The second of the great Matriarchs. She is the first water-drawer. And it was through her water-drawing that she showed herself to be a righteous woman, worthy of God's covenant. She was then a foreign woman, but because of her kindness to travelers – and even their beasts of burden – she would become the mother of Israel.

*

A wood-chopper and a water-drawer. The refugee and Rebecca. Here we have two members of the people of Israel – one nearly a prisoner, and the other nearly royalty. And perhaps this disparity is part of what Moses is referencing: *from* your wood-chopper *to* your water-drawer – from the bottom to the top, from the most wretched to the most exalted.

But there are also things that these two people have in common. Both are leaving their homes – one to enter into our community, and the other to flee from it. And both are recognized to be people of pure intention. The wood-chopper is guilty of manslaughter, but we know he meant no harm. So he will have to temporarily leave the place he is from, but he will not be cut off from the people of Israel. The water-drawer is at first a suspicious character, an outsider, but she soon reveals an inner essence so admirable that we beg her to leave the place she is from and come join our people.

These, then, are two perfect examples for Moses to use to define the boundaries of the congregation that stands before him. Who is in our community? Who will be counted among the people of Israel?

The case of the wood-chopper teaches us that no one among us can ever be cut off, no matter what they do, so long as we know them to be pure of heart. The case of the water-drawer teaches us to seek out the righteous among the nations, and ask them to join us.

Can a Jew ever be excommunicated? When should an outsider be welcomed into the congregation? On one side of the community we have the question of whom we would drive out, and on the other side the question of whom we will let in? And the answer to both of those questions, Moses suggests, is determined not by status, but by character.

For we are to be a people of righteousness, who love justice and revere compassion. Our mother is a foreigner, and our brother is a refugee. They stand with us here, today, and we stand with them.

CHAPTER 52

THE HIDDEN FACE OF GOD – Parshat Vayeilekh

It was the worst thing we had ever heard.

Of all the terrible curses that have been threatened so far in the Book of Deuteronomy – and there have been plenty – this, says **Rashi**, was the worst:

I will hide My face from them on that day, because of all the evil that they have done by turning to other gods. *(Deut. 31:18)*

וְאָנֹכִי הַסְתֵּר אַסְתִּיר פָּנַי בַּיּוֹם הַהוּא עַל כָּל הָרָעָה אֲשֶׁר עָשָׂה כִּי פָנָה אֶל אֱלֹהִים אֲחֵרִים.

Well now, honestly, that doesn't sound *so* bad. Not when compared to all the threats of death and destruction that have come before it. Some real horrors. We've seen descriptions of plagues and famine, of mothers eating their young. Could the simple hiding of God's face really be worse than that?

But that's what Rashi says, in his commentary over in the book of Isaiah, when the prophet Isaiah uses similar phrasing:

I will wait for the Eternal, who *hides His face* from the House of Jacob, and I will hope for Him. *(Isa. 8:17)*

וְחִכִּיתִי לַה' הַמַּסְתִּיר פָּנָיו מִבֵּית יַעֲקֹב וְקִוֵּיתִי לוֹ.

Rashi hears that phrase, remembers our verse in Deuteronomy, and says:

There is no prophecy more difficult than the one Moses said then: "I will hide My face from them on that day…" *(Deut 31:18)*

אין לך נבואה קשה כאותה שעה שאמר משה (דברים ל"א:י"ח) ואנכי הסתר אסתיר פני ביום ההוא.

No prophecy more difficult! This was the hardest thing of all, to think that God would hide the Divine face from us.

And indeed, that phrase – *Hester Panim* (הסתר פנים), the 'Hiding of the Face' – has come to hold an ominous place in traditional Jewish parlance, representing the seeming absence of God in the midst of great tragedy. The Holocaust, notably, is often referred to as a time of *Hester Panim*. In this usage the term suggests not just that God is hiding from view, but is mercilessly denying us salvation, just when we need it most.

That is precisely the interpretation of the phrase given by the **Ibn Ezra**:

I will hide My face **– So if they call to me, I will not answer.**

הסתר אסתיר – שאם יקראו אלי לא אענם.

...and the **Sforno**:

I will hide my face **... from saving them.**

אסתיר פני... מהצילם.

This kind of hiding is, indeed, the worst punishment of all. For it indicates a potential relief from all the other punishments, and then this relief is deliberately denied. What a terrifying image of God – almost as if God felt a kind of malice toward us!

The **Chizkuni** has a slightly gentler approach. He says that the hiding of God's face:

...is done out of love. Like a person whose child has sinned, who says, "Just don't lash him in front of me!" because he loves him so.

זו היא דרך חבה כאדם שחטא לו בנו ואומר להלקותו שלא בפניו מתוך שאוהבו.

In this reading, the hiding is not born of anger, but affection. It does not represent God's unwillingness to alleviate our suffering, but God's own pain at having to witness it.

Still, this is not a good situation for us to be in. God may be hiding God's face out of more tender motivations, but the end result is a feeling of abandonment. The Hidden Face is always, on some level, a bad sign.

*

There is, however, another way of understanding the whole phenomenon of divine hiddenness. The Book of Proverbs contains the following saying:

The glory of God is a hidden thing. The glory of kings is a knowable thing. ***(Prov. 25:2)***

כְּבֹד אֱלֹהִים הַסְתֵּר דָּבָר וּכְבֹד מְלָכִים חֲקֹר דָּבָר.

Here, the hidden nature of God appears to be a part of God's essence – almost a good thing – made all the more sacred by its obscurity.

Now, the poetic style of Proverbs makes it easy to dismiss its aphorisms as mere rhetorical flourish. But really, isn't this formulation of God's hiddenness much closer to everything we've seen so far in the Torah's narrative?

When, for example, Moses begged God, *"Please, show me your glory!"* God replied:

You cannot see My face, for a person cannot see Me and live! ***(Exodus 33:20)***

וַיֹּאמֶר לֹא תוּכַל לִרְאֹת אֶת פָּנָי כִּי לֹא יִרְאַנִי הָאָדָם וָחָי.

The hiding of God's face, then, is not a punishment. It is simply a description of the vast distance between our powers of perception and the true nature of God's essential being. We cannot see God's face, for if we did, we would lose our separateness and cease to exist. It would kill us. In that sense, the true punishment would be not the hiding, but the *revealing* of God's face.

In like manner, even when recalling the greatest moment of direct experience of the presence of God, the revelation on Mount Sinai, we are told to remember to:

Be very careful – for you saw no visual image on the day that the Eternal spoke to you at Horeb out of the fire – not to make for yourselves a sculptured image in any likeness of the form of a man or a woman. ***(Deut. 4:15)***

וְנִשְׁמַרְתֶּם מְאֹד לְנַפְשֹׁתֵיכֶם כִּי לֹא רְאִיתֶם כָּל תְּמוּנָה בְּיוֹם דִּבֶּר ה׳ אֲלֵיכֶם בְּחֹרֵב מִתּוֹךְ הָאֵשׁ. פֶּן תַּשְׁחִתוּן וַעֲשִׂיתֶם לָכֶם פֶּסֶל תְּמוּנַת כָּל סָמֶל תַּבְנִית זָכָר אוֹ נְקֵבָה.

Revelation itself is a testament to the impossibility of seeing God in any form. The truest encounter with God is the one that shows that God is fundamentally hidden.

And then the first two of the Ten Commandments, the first utterances of the revelation, play out precisely this dialectic. The first is: *"I am the Eternal, your God."* In other words, this is Me, here I am, in the purest form you will ever witness. But that knowledge immediately prompts the second commandment:

You shall have no other gods before Me. (*literally, "upon my face"* – על פני)

לֹא יִהְיֶה לְךָ אֱלֹהִים אֲחֵרִים עַל פָּנָי.

And how does one refrain from placing other gods "upon God's face"? The commandment continues: by not making *"for yourself a sculptured image, or any likeness of what is in the heavens above..."*

To commit idolatry, to corrupt one's service of God, is to put a face on it. The visual image of God is a heresy, because God must remain forever hidden. God is – in God's true essence – unknowable, incomprehensible, and invisible. This is the very core of our faith.

One rabbi in the Talmud sums that notion up brilliantly when reflecting on our original "Hidden Face" passage from Deuteronomy:

"I will hide My face from them."* Rabbi Bardela bar Tavyumi said in the name of Rav: To whomever 'hiding of the face' does not apply, is not one of 'them.' *(Chagigah 5b)

והסתרתי פני מהם אמר רב ברדלא בר טביומי אמר רב כל שאינו בהסתר פנים אינו מהם.

That is, to be one of them, one of the Children of Israel, means to have God's face hidden from you. It is definitional. That is who we are. We are the people who believe that God's face is hidden.

But if that is so, then how do we make sense of the language of "cursing" in our parsha?

I will hide My face from them on that day, because of all the evil that they have done by turning to other gods. *(Deut. 31:18)*

וְאָנֹכִי הַסְתֵּר אַסְתִּיר פָּנַי בַּיּוֹם הַהוּא עַל כָּל הָרָעָה אֲשֶׁר עָשָׂה כִּי פָנָה אֶל אֱלֹהִים אֲחֵרִים.

God's face is being hidden, "*because* of the evil that they had done by turning to other gods." If God's hiddenness is integral to God's being, if it is even a good thing – how can it be described as a punishment?

The key to this verse may be found in a nuance in the Hebrew language. Because the word for "turning" (*panah* / פנה) – is directly related to the word for "my face" – *panai* (פני).

There is a bit of wordplay here, such that the verse can actually be read:

I will hide *My face* (פני) from them on that day, because of all the evil that they have done, by *making a face* (פנה) of other gods.

In this reading the hiding of God's face is not so much a punishment as it is a lesson. It is as if to say, "I see you, desperately longing to see the face of God. So you do what you think it takes. You go following other gods, who promise to show their faces. Or you create images of the faces of new gods. You want to know God intimately, to actually see God, face to face. So I must hide My face, again, on that day – to remind you that the true nature of God is forever hidden."

This hiddenness is no curse. It is the very glory of God.

CHAPTER 53

A ROCK AND A HARD PLACE – Parshat Ha'azinu

Moses has rocks on the brain.

Parshat Ha'azinu is only one chapter long, almost all of it in the form of a poem delivered by Moses to the Children of Israel. In the previous chapter, God told Moses that his time had come to die. So, as one of his final acts he writes down a poem, gathers together the elders of the community, and teaches it to them.

Ha'azinu is written in one of the classical forms of Biblical poetry: parallelism. The poem is laid out in two columns, every verse a couplet made up of two parallel lines. Each half of the verse expresses the same basic idea, but each one uses different (but thematically similar) words in order to subtly shift the meaning from one column to the next. So, for example, the opening verse is:

Give ear, O heavens, let me speak; Let the earth hear the words I utter! ***(Deut. 32:1)***

הַאֲזִינוּ הַשָּׁמַיִם וַאֲדַבֵּרָה; וְתִשְׁמַע הָאָרֶץ אִמְרֵי פִי.

Both sections of the verse announce Moses' desire to speak; but in the first he is addressing the heavens, and in the second, the earth. So, when taken as a unit, the rhetorical point is that Moses is speaking to *all* of creation, both the upper and lower realms – but acknowledging some important difference between the two.

Every verse in the poem has this interplay of two similar images that both build on, and distinguish themselves from, one another. In this way, every word in the poem gains emphasis and echo from some other word in the poem.

*

But there is one word in *Ha'azinu* that is uniquely prominent: 'rock' – *tzur* (צור), in Hebrew. The word appears again and again throughout the poem. The first instance is especially powerful, for the rock is used as a metaphor for God:

The Rock! His deeds are perfect, for all of His ways are justice; A faithful God, never false, just and righteous is He. ***(Deut. 32:4)***

הַצּוּר תָּמִים פָּעֳלוֹ כִּי כָל־דְּרָכָיו מִשְׁפָּט; אֵל אֱמוּנָה וְאֵין עָוֶל צַדִּיק וְיָשָׁר הוּא.

The metaphor becomes explicit when "The Rock" in the first half of the verse appears as "a faithful God" in the second, suggesting that God is like a rock precisely because God is solid, steady, and dependable – in a word: faithful.

The word "rock," then, has already been given a major spotlight: it has been paralleled with God, and so it provides strong visual imagery for evoking one of God's qualities. But Moses is by no means done with rocks in *Ha'azinu*. He will mention the word seven more times throughout the poem. Let's lay them all out, to feel the full effect:

He nursed them with honey from a boulder; and oil from the crag of the ***rock. (v. 13)***

וַיֵּנִקֵהוּ דְבַשׁ מִסֶּלַע; וְשֶׁמֶן מֵחַלְמִישׁ צוּר.

He forsook the God who made him; and spurned the ***Rock*** **of his support.** ***(v.15)***

וַיִּטֹּשׁ אֱלוֹהַּ עָשָׂהוּ; וַיְנַבֵּל צוּר יְשֻׁעָתוֹ.

You neglected the ***Rock*** **that begot you; Forgot the God that brought you forth.** ***(v. 18)***

צוּר יְלָדְךָ תֶּשִׁי; וַתִּשְׁכַּח אֵל מְחֹלְלֶךָ.

If not that their ***Rock*** **had sold them; The Eternal had shut them down.** ***(v. 30)***

אִם לֹא כִּי צוּרָם מְכָרָם, ה׳ הִסְגִּירָם.

For our ***Rock*** **is not like their** ***rock*****; and our enemies are criminals.** ***(v. 31)***

כִּי לֹא כְצוּרֵנוּ צוּרָם; וְאֹיְבֵינוּ פְּלִילִים.

He will say, "Where is their god? The *Rock* in whom they sought refuge." ***(v. 37)***

וְאָמַר אֵי אֱלֹהֵימוֹ; צוּר חָסָיוּ בוֹ.

So now we have in our poem, in addition to parallelism, another classic Biblical literary device – what **Martin Buber** called the '*leitwort*:' a key word that repeats itself throughout one passage, as a way of emphasizing the significance of that word without stating it explicitly.

*

What, then, is the significance of the 'rock' for Moses? Well, if we look back at his life, it is clear there was one rock in particular that most affected his fate. And Moses has plenty of reason to be ruminating on that rock at this moment. For both Moses' impending death and his ban from entering the Land are punishments he received, quite unexpectedly, for striking a rock.

In the Book of Numbers the people were once again complaining about the long journey and their thirst. So God told Moses and Aaron to "speak" to the rock and order it to produce water. But Moses, furious with the people for their insolence, instead strikes the rock with his staff. The rock does produce water. But afterwards, God is furious with Moses:

The Eternal said to Moses and Aaron, "Because you did not trust Me enough to affirm My sanctity in the sight of the Israelite people, therefore you shall not lead this congregation into the land that I have given them." ***(Num. 20:12)***

וַיֹּאמֶר ה׳ אֶל מֹשֶׁה וְאֶל אַהֲרֹן יַעַן לֹא הֶאֱמַנְתֶּם בִּי לְהַקְדִּישֵׁנִי לְעֵינֵי בְּנֵי יִשְׂרָאֵל לָכֵן לֹא תָבִיאוּ אֶת הַקָּהָל הַזֶּה אֶל הָאָרֶץ אֲשֶׁר נָתַתִּי לָהֶם.

The commentators are shocked, as Moses himself must have been. For this seemingly minor transgression, Moses – the great leader who has served God devotedly, and given so much of himself to liberate the people – will not be allowed into the promised land... just for striking a rock?!

Whether or not there was something else Moses was being punished for – a lack of faith or a loss of temper, perhaps – the fact is that the course of his life, and the timing of his death, were forever altered because of this one moment with one rock. It must have seemed to him so unfair.

What makes the severity of this punishment even more baffling is that there was an earlier incident when the people were complaining of thirst, back in the Book of Exodus, and there, God told Moses *explicitly* to strike the rock:

Pass before the people, and take the elders of Israel with you, and take in your hand your staff, with which you struck the Nile, and go. And I will be standing before you, there at the rock of Horeb. Then strike the rock, and water will come forth from it, and the people will drink. ***(Exod. 17:5-6)***

עֲבֹר לִפְנֵי הָעָם וְקַח אִתְּךָ מִזִּקְנֵי יִשְׂרָאֵל וּמַטְּךָ אֲשֶׁר הִכִּיתָ בּוֹ אֶת הַיְאֹר קַח בְּיָדְךָ וְהָלָכְתָּ.
הִנְנִי עֹמֵד לְפָנֶיךָ שָּׁם עַל הַצּוּר בְּחֹרֵב וְהִכִּיתָ בַצּוּר וְיָצְאוּ מִמֶּנּוּ מַיִם וְשָׁתָה הָעָם.

So God has already established a procedure of striking a rock to produce water. But when nearly the same scene repeats itself in the Book of Numbers, God changes the directions slightly – speak to the rock instead of hitting it. And when Moses, caught up in the moment, acts out of instinct or habit and deviates from the exact directive, his punishment is swift and devastating.

How often Moses must have thought back to this moment! How often must he have pictured that damned rock! He must have cursed his own failure. But surely he also wondered, as so many of our sages have, whether the punishment really fit the crime. Was God justified in taking from him the privilege of crossing the Jordan, just for changing "speak to the rock" to "strike the rock"?! And doesn't God's verdict appear especially unjust if we consider that God had told him once before to "strike the rock" in language that was otherwise nearly exactly the same? Can Moses really be faulted for missing that one shift in wording?

It bears noting, however, that there was one other important difference in the words from these two scenes. For we have so far been talking about 'rocks' here and 'rocks' there. But in fact, it is only in the first scene, from Exodus, that God tells Moses to strike "the rock" – *v'hikita ba'tzur* (והכית בצור). Whereas in the later scene, from Numbers, God tells Moses and Aaron to speak to "the boulder" – *v'dibartem el hasela* (ודיברתם על הסלע). Here is the whole instruction God gives:

Take the staff, and gather the congregation, you and your brother Aaron. And speak to the *boulder* before their eyes, and it will give forth water. Thus you shall produce water for them from the *boulder*, and quench the thirst of the congregation and their beasts. ***(Num. 20:8)***

קַח אֶת הַמַּטֶּה וְהַקְהֵל אֶת הָעֵדָה אַתָּה וְאַהֲרֹן אָחִיךָ וְדִבַּרְתֶּם אֶל הַסֶּלַע לְעֵינֵיהֶם וְנָתַן מֵימָיו וְהוֹצֵאתָ לָהֶם מַיִם מִן הַסֶּלַע וְהִשְׁקִיתָ אֶת הָעֵדָה וְאֶת בְּעִירָם.

Speak to the boulder. Produce water from the boulder. Here God never uses the word 'rock' (*tzur*), as God did before. Now, of course, a boulder (*sela*), is a kind of rock. We might say that the difference in wording is insignificant. But as the wording has changed, so has the instruction, and so the subtle shift in language might have been a way of indicating to Moses to listen carefully and to note that task had changed as well. But Moses missed the change. He heard "rock," he remembered striking the rock before, and so he struck the rock again.

And he has been thinking about it ever since.

So when he writes his final poem (which, recall, is addressed to the heavens *and* to the earth – to the people *and* to God) the word which has been torturing him, the word he heard when he should have heard something else, the word that does not stop echoing in his head – spills out all over the page.

There is, however, one exception to Moses' constant repetition of the word 'rock' (*tzur*). For, if you look again at all the verses we listed above, you will see that our word for 'boulder' (*sela*), also makes an appearance:

He nursed them with honey from a *boulder*; and oil from the crag of the *rock*. *(v. 13)*

וַיֵּנִקֵהוּ דְבַשׁ מִסֶּלַע, וְשֶׁמֶן מֵחַלְמִישׁ צוּר.

This is the only time in the poem that the 'rock' is not a metaphor for God. And what is the "rock" compared to here, in the parallel structure of the poem? A "boulder." The rock and the boulder perform a similar function – sustaining the people in the desert – just as they did in the actual narrative of the Torah. They are distinct, of course, but essentially the same. In fact, **Rashi** comments, later on in the poem:

Every 'rock' mentioned in scripture is a 'boulder.' *(Rashi on v. 31)*

כל צור שבמקרא לשון סלע.

As a matter of semantics, these terms are indistinguishable.

Yet eight times Moses mentions a 'rock' in this poem. Eight times. And only once, he slips in a boulder. Did you catch it? Did you see the shift? If you did not notice, then you are just like Moses himself. You heard the word 'rock' again, because you'd heard it before. And come on – they mean the same thing anyway.

So did Moses mean to bury the boulder amidst all the rocks? Was it his way of saying – to God, to us, to himself – "We're only human. We miss things. We make mistakes."

Every line in this poem has subtle distinctions, tiny shifts in wording that point to shifts in meaning. Did you catch them all? Could anyone but God, whose "deeds are perfect," ever understand all these little nuances? Is it really fair to lose everything you've ever dreamed of over such a small misunderstanding?

If that is the question Moses is asking, then God has an answer. In the last verses of the chapter, the poem ends. Moses tells the people to take his words to heart. And then God addresses Moses directly:

You shall die on the mountain that you are about to ascend, and shall be gathered to your kin, as your brother Aaron died on Mount Hor and was gathered to his kin; for you both broke faith with Me among the Israelite people, at the waters of Merivat-Kadesh in the wilderness of Zin, by failing to uphold My sanctity among the Children of Israel. You may view the land from a distance, but you shall not enter it – the land that I am giving to the Children of Israel. ***(Deut. 32:50-52)***

וּמֻת בָּהָר אֲשֶׁר אַתָּה עֹלֶה שָׁמָּה וְהֵאָסֵף, אֶל עַמֶּיךָ. כַּאֲשֶׁר מֵת אַהֲרֹן אָחִיךָ בְּהֹר הָהָר וַיֵּאָסֶף אֶל עַמָּיו. עַל אֲשֶׁר מְעַלְתֶּם בִּיבְּתוֹךְ בְּנֵי יִשְׂרָאֵל בְּמֵי מְרִיבַת קָדֵשׁ מִדְבַּר צִן עַל אֲשֶׁר לֹא קִדַּשְׁתֶּם אוֹתִי בְּתוֹךְ בְּנֵי יִשְׂרָאֵל. כִּי מִנֶּגֶד תִּרְאֶה אֶת הָאָרֶץ וְשָׁמָּה לֹא תָבוֹא אֶל הָאָרֶץ אֲשֶׁר אֲנִי נֹתֵן לִבְנֵי יִשְׂרָאֵל.

God seems to know exactly what Moses is asking. And the answer, one last time, is no. No, you cannot cross over. What's said is said, what's done is done. Words are precise, and they matter.

Firm, unyielding, impenetrable. Like a rock.

CHAPTER 54

MOURNING MOSES – Parshat V'zot HaBrakha

When Moses died, yes, we wept for him. Of course we did. But not, shall we say ... excessively.

One of the last verses in the Torah records our period of mourning as follows:

And the Children of Israel cried for Moses on the plains of Moab for thirty days, and then they ended the days of crying and mourning Moses. ***(Deut. 34:8)***

וַיִּבְכּוּ בְנֵי יִשְׂרָאֵל אֶת מֹשֶׁה בְּעַרְבֹת מוֹאָב שְׁלֹשִׁים יוֹם וַיִּתְּמוּ יְמֵי בְכִי אֵבֶל מֹשֶׁה.

Thirty days of crying. That seems like a good long time. Surely we honored well the passing of our greatest teacher.

But both **Rashi** and the **Ibn Ezra**, our two greatest medieval commentators, notice a disparity. For when Moses' brother, Aaron the High Priest, died, back in the book of Numbers, the language of mourning was slightly more emphatic:

And the whole congregation saw that Aaron had passed, and the whole House of Israel wept for Aaron for thirty days. ***(Num. 20:29)***

וַיִּרְאוּ כָּל הָעֵדָה כִּי גָוַע אַהֲרֹן וַיִּבְכּוּ אֶת אַהֲרֹן שְׁלֹשִׁים יוֹם כֹּל בֵּית יִשְׂרָאֵל.

The *whole* congregation. The *whole* House of Israel. Not just "the Children of Israel," which could have referred to just some of us. The weeping that followed Aaron's departure somehow seems to have been more fully and collectively felt.

And though the period of mourning here is the same – thirty days – the Torah doesn't go out of its way to say that *"they then ended the days of crying,"* as it did with Moses. It is as if they could have kept crying for Aaron all year – whereas with Moses, once they were done, they were done.

What could account for this emotional gap? How could we have given Moses any less of our grief than we found for Aaron. If anything, it should have gone the other way! Moses was the real hero. He was our liberator, our guide through forty years of wandering and, above all, our teacher – the one who gave us the laws by which we live our lives. We owed him everything. So how could Aaron's death have been the greater tragedy?

*

Rashi and Ibn Ezra give two very different answers. Rashi finds a hint in the language of the "Children of Israel" – which in Hebrew takes the male form – that Moses may not have served all the people equally:

"The Children [or 'Sons'] of Israel cried for Moses" **– That is, the men. But for Aaron, who sought to bring peace not only between men, but between a woman and her husband, it says,** ***"the whole House of Israel"*** **– the men** ***and*** **the women.**

בני ישראל – הזכרים, אבל באהרן מתוך שהיה רודף שלום ונותן שלום בין איש לרעהו ובין אשה לבעלה נאמר (במדבר כ, כט) "כל בית ישראל" – זכרים ונקבות.

In Rashi's reading, Moses was less attentive to domestic conflicts than he was to civil disputes. He was concerned with the general public welfare, but allowed suffering to take place behind closed doors. Aaron, meanwhile, realized that families also sometimes needed intervention, for terrible abuse could take place inside the home, where women were often most vulnerable. So when Aaron died, everyone mourned, for *he* had the sensitivity to care for them all.

If Rashi's interpretation contains an implied critique of Moses, the Ibn Ezra's does just the opposite. In fact, he understands the extra crying for Aaron as a form of tribute to Moses:

The whole House of Israel [mourned] Aaron out of respect for Moses.

ובאהרן כל בית ישראל בעבור כבוד משה.

In other words, Moses was our leader – so his tragedy was our tragedy, his loss was our loss. The whole congregation went into mourning as a way of showing solidarity with the man we revered most. If this display of grief appeared even greater than the one for Moses' own death that is because it contained the added layer of a nation's solemn attempt to comfort its chief.

*

The earliest rabbinic interpretation of the verse, from the midrashic collection *Avot d'Rabbi Natan*, echoes Ibn Ezra in depicting the great mourning of Aaron as an identification with Moses. But whereas Ibn Ezra suggested a formal national mourning as a kind of ceremonial display of honor, *Avot d'Rabbi Natan* imagines a much more instinctive response to Moses' grief:

It says, *"the whole House of Israel wept for Aaron for thirty days,"* for anyone who witnessed Moses sitting and weeping, how could they not also weep?! *(Avot d'Rabbi Natan 12:4)*

לכך נאמר ויבכו את אהרן שלשים יום כל בית ישראל שכל מי שרואה משה רבינו שיושב ובוכה מי לא יבכה.

It was impossible not to cry. Moses had just lost his beloved brother and closest confidant. He was devastated. He collapsed to the floor, like a broken man, and began to weep. And he wept, and wept, and wept. The sobbing that erupted from him was terrible and raw; it cut through the air around him and pierced the ears of all who could hear.

And if you saw Moses mourning his brother that month you were witness to a living manifestation of pure pain. One look and you felt the pain yourself. You immediately began to cry along with him; you could not help yourself. It was a mourning so profound and so potent that it swept through the nation like a contagion. Soon we were all crying.

So why did we not cry as hard when Moses himself died? Because – following the logic of this midrash – we did not have Moses there to model the crying for us. We observed the requisite period of mourning – thirty days – just as we had for Aaron. We knew the formal process, for Moses had taught us the laws of mourning. But we were missing the *feeling* of loss, the experiential quality of mourning. That, Moses had taught us as well – by example – but we had forgotten it as soon as he departed.

For it is relatively easy to pass on the laws and rituals of a tradition, but it is much harder to preserve the emotional and spiritual experiences that those laws were meant to contain. Our memory of those feelings can fade over time until all we have left is the formal ritual – hollowed out, empty.

Moses, come back. Teach us again how to cry, so that we might finally mourn you as we should have.

נשלם ספר פרשנות בעזר יוצר כל יצורים

Biographical Notes on the Commentators

Abarbanel

Rabbi Don Yitzchak ben Yehudah Abarbanel (*Portugal, 1437 – Venice, 1508*) led one of the most eventful lives of all the classical commentators. From a young age, he showed great talent in financial matters, and was recruited by King Alfonso V of Portugal to serve as the royal treasurer. When Alfonso died, his successor, John II, accused Abarbanel of conspiring against the crown, and he was forced to flee to Spain. There he once again rose to political prominence, and then, once again, had to flee during the 1492 expulsion. This time he went to Naples, yet again entered the service of the king, and fled yet again when the French conquered the city. Remarkably, along this rocky road, he managed to write one of the most comprehensive Biblical commentaries of the medieval period. A late-medieval commentator, Abarbanel often summarizes the positions of his predecessors before offering his own. His commentary is particularly distinguished by the excellent questions he lays out at the beginning of every chapter, which are as likely to be quoted as his answers. In a genre defined by asking good questions, being known for them is a badge of great honor.

Cited in chapters: 26, 39, 48

Avivah Gottlieb Zornberg

One of the greatest contemporary commentators on the Torah, Dr. Avivah Gottlieb Zornberg (*Scotland, 1944 – Israel, present*) brings an academic expertise in literature and psychology to her study of *parshanut* to offer a lyrical, postmodern journey into the unconscious of the Torah.

Cited in chapter: 6

Ba'al HaIkarim

Rabbi Yosef Albo (*Spain, 1380-1444*), like Maimonides, was a philosopher who never wrote a formal work of Torah commentary. He is remembered for his work *Sefer HaIkarim* ('The Book of Fundamentals'), in which argued that the core beliefs of Judaism came down to just three things: God, Revelation, and Reward & Punishment. The book contains many interpretations of the Torah, which brought him into dialogue with the *parshanim*, who often referred to him as the *Ba'al HaIkarim*.

Cited in chapter: 39

Ba'al HaTurim

Rabbi Yaakov ben Asher (*Germany, 1269 – Spain, 1343*) was called the *Ba'al HaTurim* (The Master of Columns) after his most famous work, the *Arba'ah Turim* (The Four Columns), a magnificent summary of Jewish Law that paved the way for the Shulchan Arukh. But he also wrote not one, but two commentaries on the Torah. The one printed in most editions of *Mikraot Gedolot* is the shorter of the two, known as *Remizei Ba'al HaTurim* – 'The Hints of the Master of Columns.' That title is telling, for the commentary mostly focuses on hints, allusions, and other linguistic clues that point to hidden layers of mystical and symbolic meaning. The *Ba'al HaTurim* is famous for his *gematria* (adding up the numerical value of Hebrew letters), his deriving acronyms from the first or last letters of words in a verse, and especially for his encyclopedic ability to find all the places in the Bible where a particular word or phrase is used. I think it's fair to say that his is the most fun of all the classical commentaries.

Cited in chapters: 14, 26

Bekhor Shor

Rabbi Yosef ben Yitzchak Bekhor Shor *(France, 1145-1195)* was a true man of letters. He was known especially for his commentary on the Bible, but he was also a Tosafist, a member of the schools that composed one of the hallmark commentaries on the Talmud, and a *paytan*, a composer of liturgical poetry. He also seems to have been well acquainted with Christian thinkers – whom he often polemicizes against. He even cites (and then rejects) Saint Jerome once in his commentary on the Psalms (which, incidentally, I also did once in this book).

Cited in chapters: 7, 32, 39

Chizkuni

Rabbi Chizkiah ben Manoach's (*13th century France*) commentary on the Torah, a standard inclusion in *Mikraot Gedolot*, does contain many original interpretations, but it is largely a collection of earlier commentary. He says in his introduction (written entirely in verse): "To find commentaries on the Five Books, I sailed to every port; And indeed I found commentaries, twenty of every sort!" He might therefore be considered the first serious compiler of *parshanut*.

Cited in chapter: 52

Gur Aryeh

Rabbi Yehuda Loew ben Betzalel (*Poland, 1520 – Prague, 1609*), the "Maharal of Prague," is probably best known from the legend that he created a *Golem* (a kind of Jewish Frankenstein) to defend the Jews of Prague against attacks based on blood libel. But he was in fact one of the greatest Jewish philosophers in history, a prolific scholar who wrote on all areas of Jewish thought. His first book, the *Gur Aryeh*, was a supercommentary on Rashi, though it nicely displays the Maharal's own unique approach to Torah interpretation. It the first work of *parshanut* I fell in love with, and is still probably the one I have spent the most time poring through.

Cited in chapter: 39

HaEmek Davar

Rabbi Naftali Tzvi Yehuda Berlin (*Russia, 1816 – Poland, 1893*), known (by his initials) as "The Netziv," was the last head of the famous Volozhin yeshiva in Lithuania, and his commentary, *HaEmek Davar*, is based on a weekly class he gave there. He was famous for a comprehensive knowledge of rabbinic literature and his commentary surely displays that prowess. But it also displays a remarkable sensitivity to the inner life of human emotions and a keen awareness of his political and social reality. It is his ability to offer novel readings of well-trodden passages, above all, that makes his work a modern classic of *parshanut*.

Cited in chapters: 2, 6, 10, 39, 45

HaKtav v'HaKabbalah

The title of Rabbi Yaakov Tzvi Mecklenburg's (*Germany, 1785-1865*) commentary on the Torah, *HaKtav v'HaKabbalah* – 'The Written and the Received' – speaks directly to Mecklenburg's intention for the book, which he states in the introduction: "to demonstrate the indivisibility of the written Torah and the oral Torah." The need to do so came in response to the Haskalah and Reform movements that were emerging in

Germany at the time. The commentary is particularly sensitive to the nuances of the Hebrew language, attempting to show how the words of the Torah itself indicate the legitimacy of classical rabbinic interpretation.

Cited in chapters: 39, 50

Ibn Ezra

Second only to Rashi on any list of the most classic Torah commentators, Rabbi Abraham Ibn Ezra (*Spain, 1089-1167*) was the other commentator included in the very first *Mikraot Gedolot* ever printed. He lived in his native Spain for much of his life, distinguishing himself there as a poet. But in 1137, for reasons unknown, he left and began three decades of traveling – moving from country to country, community to community, and supporting himself through the donations of wealthy patrons. It is during this itinerant period that he produced his famous Biblical commentaries. He has been described as a polymath, for along with the classics of rabbinic literature, he was well-versed in philosophy, astronomy, and mathematics – all of which make appearances in his eclectic commentary. But language was his primary passion, and his comments are most often grounded in the intricacies of Hebrew grammar and semantics. He championed the *pshat*, the simple, literal meaning of the text, and – unlike Rashi – tended to avoid midrashic interpretations of the text (except in matters of law). He led a difficult life, losing several children, and often suffering from poverty and illness. In fact, it was during one such illness that he vowed, if he recovered, to write a commentary on the Torah. And so, his pain led to our great gain.

Cited in chapters: 1, 2, 3, 7, 18, 19, 30, 32, 33, 35, 39, 46, 47, 52, 54

Kedushat Levi

The first published Hassidic book was organized around the weekly *parshot*, setting a template for what would become the primary form of Hassidic writing. But many of the early works seem to be using the form of Torah commentary as a forum to sing the praises of the Ba'al Shem Tov or to push a particular theological vision. It is Rabbi Levi Yitzchak of Berdichev (*Poland, 1740-1809*) who writes the first truly masterful Hassidic work of *parshanut*. It is indeed full of Hassidic theology, but it also asks serious questions of the verses of the Torah and grounds its theological interpretations in the language of the text.

Cited in chapters: 39, 50

Kli Yakar

Rabbi Shlomo Ephraim ben Aaron Lunschitz (*Poland, 1550 – Prague, 1619*) served as Rosh Yeshiva in Lvov and then as the Rabbi of Prague. As famous rabbis of that city go, Lunschitz is usually overshadowed by the legendary Maharal of Prague. But when it comes to Torah commentary, it is Lunschitz's *Kli Yakar* that takes center stage, having become a standard inclusion in many editions of *Mikraot Gedolot*. On those pages, it serves as a contrast to the other classical commentaries; for if medieval *parshanut* was characterized by reason, precision, and literalism, the *Kli Yakar* represents a return to the midrashic style: symbolic, creative, and linguistically playful. The commentary is in constant search of spiritual meaning and full of penetrating psychological insight and, in that sense, it anticipates and paves the way for the Hassidic commentaries that will follow.

Cited in chapters: 14, 27

Maimonides

The most well-known of all Jewish thinkers, and perhaps the greatest mind of the Middle Ages, Rabbi Moshe ben Maimon's (*Spain, 1135 – Egypt, 1204*) mastery of Jewish law and his attempt to synthesize rationalist philosophy with religious tradition left Jewish thought forever changed. He did not write a running commentary on the Torah, but his interpretations of Biblical verses appear throughout his writings. It is a testament to his towering influence that even though he never composed a formal work of Torah commentary, he is one of the most cited medieval thinkers in this book.

Cited in chapters: 8, 24, 35, 39, 44, 48

Martin Buber

One of the great Jewish thinkers of the 20th century, Martin Buber (*Austria, 1878 – Israel, 1965*) was especially well known for his philosophy of dialogue, which he describes in his famous essay, 'I and Thou.' He was also, however, a noted Biblical scholar and commentator, and even completed a translation of the Bible into German.

Cited in chapters: 22, 53

Meshekh Chokhmah

Rabbi Meir Simcha HaKohen (*Lithuania, 1843 – Lativa, 1926*) was well known for his commentaries on the Talmud and Maimonides' *Mishneh Torah*, but it is in his commentary on the Torah that we discover some of his most inventive thinking. His novel interpretations are often surprising and sometimes even radical. While he served as the rabbi of the non-Hassidic community in Dvinsk, he befriended his Hassidic counterpart, the Rogatchover Gaon, and one sees in their dialogue a blurring of the intellectual lines between the two communities. For just as the Rogatchover was a revered Talmudist, so has the *Meshekh Chokhmah* sometimes been described as a Hassidic commentary for non-Hassids.

Cited in chapters: 21, 39

Nechama Leibowitz

In 1942 Nechama Leibowitz (*Latvia, 1905 – Israel, 1997*), a European immigrant to mandate Palestine, began sending out her *gilyonot* (worksheets) with questions on the weekly *parsha* to a select group of students. They would send back their answers and she would personally review them and send back her notes. These sheets began to circulate and gain popularity throughout Israeli society, and were eventually published as essays on the *parsha*, with specific focus on the *parshanim*. Leibowitz became the major figure responsible for reviving interest in *parshanut* in the 20th century. Famously humble, when asked about her methodology, she replied, "I have no *derekh* (method)... I only teach what the commentaries say. Nothing is my own." We might well respond, paraphrasing Rabbi Akiva: all that we have belongs to her.

Cited in chapter: 22

Netivot Shalom

Rabbi Shalom Noach Berezovsky (*Belarus, 1911 – Israel, 2000*) served as the Slonimer Rebbe and helped to reestablish the Slonimer Hassidic dynasty in Israel after the Holocaust. His commentary on the Torah, *Netivot Shalom*, is a kind of encyclopedia of Hassidic thought, often citing earlier masters and summarizing key theological concepts. It is written in a clear, easy Hebrew, and is an excellent introduction to Hassidut.

Cited in chapter: 35

Or HaChayim

Rabbi Chayim ben Moshe Ibn Attar (*Morocco, 1696 – Jerusalem, 1743*) is one of a handful of Jewish thinkers who are by custom referred to as *HaKadosh* – 'The Holy.' That is a fitting description of his famous commentary on the Torah, the *Or HaChayim* ('The Light of Life'), for it is indeed a work constantly in pursuit of the theme of holiness in the Torah. The *Or HaChayim* asks the classic questions of *parshanut*, but his answers come in the form of spiritual lessons, often drawn from Kabbalah. No wonder that his commentary became particularly beloved among the Hassidim. In fact, legend has it that the moment Ibn Attar died, the Ba'al Shem Tov exclaimed, "The light from the West has gone out!"

Cited in chapter: 39

Rabbeinu Bachya

Rabbi Bahya ben Asher ibn Halawa (*Spain, 1255 – 1340*) was a celebrated preacher in Zaragosa, Spain, but apparently lived in total poverty. In the introduction to his commentary, he calls himself "a wretched soul" who suffered all kinds of trials and tribulations. He also says that he was reluctant to write a commentary at all: "How will I muster the right words? For I know nothing! How will I give insight when I stumble over every idea? I am a fool among men, and not a person of any understanding." But his commentary quickly proves him to be, quite the contrary, a profoundly brilliant and creative thinker. It is elegantly divided into four levels of analysis: *"The Simple Path"* (דרך הפשט), *"The Path of Midrash"* (דרך המדרש), *"The Path of the Intellect"* (דרך השכל) – which was meant to show how the Torah is compatible with reason and the worldly sciences, and *"The Path of Light"* (דרך האור) – which is really the path of mysticism. Indeed, Rabbeinu Bachya is known for being one of the first to explicitly incorporate Kabbalah into his commentary.

Cited in chapters: 27, 38, 39, 47

Ramban

Rabbi Moshe ben Nachman, or, 'Nachmanides,' (*Spain, 1194 – Jerusalem, 1270*), is widely considered to be one of the most brilliant Jewish medieval thinkers. He was a giant of Jewish law, philosophy, and mysticism, and wrote voluminously on a wide array of subjects. In 1263, as the Chief Rabbi of Catalonia, he was summoned by king's order to defend Judaism in a public debate with Pablo Cristiani, a Jewish convert to

Christianity. Nachmanides seems to have won the debate handily, but the embarrassment of his victory prompted further persecution. Eventually, he fled to Israel, and settled in Jerusalem, where he spent the last three years of his life writing his commentary on the Torah, the work for which he is best known. It is one of the great masterpieces of the genre, managing to develop an entire philosophy of religion out of his commentaries. He also directly engages Rashi, the Ibn Ezra, and Maimonides (often openly disagreeing with them) and thus, in a sense, can be considered to have founded the discourse of *parshanut*.

Cited in chapters: 1, 7, 11, 12, 27, 29, 30, 39, 44, 46

Rashbam

Rabbi Shmuel ben Meir (*France, 1085-1158*) was Rashi's grandson, but his commentary could not have been more different than his ancestor's. Where Rashi's commentary injects the wild interpretations of the midrash into the Biblical narrative, the Rashbam's is known for its strict adherence to the *pshat*, the plain and simple meaning of the text. In fact, in his commentary *(on Gen. 37:2)*, he says he used to argue with Rashi about this, and his grandfather admitted to him that if he had more time he would have written another commentary, one more like the Rashbam's. Now that's the kind of comment only a grandchild could get away with.

Cited in chapters: 7, 10, 23, 44

Rashi

"Rashi" is the acronym of Rabbi Shlomo Yitzchaki (*France, 1040-1105*), the undisputed King of the Commentators. His commentary is a standard accompaniment to printed editions of the Torah, and has itself inspired over 300 works of supercommentary. It is largely based on the midrashic tradition of rabbinic interpretation, which drew out connections in the Biblical text and then used them to construct all kinds of fantastic backstories and hidden meanings. Rashi mastered this sprawling tradition, then sifted through it and selected out key fragments, and then deftly edited them together and inserted them back into the text with his commentary. He was able to synthesize and condense an enormous literature into a concise, running commentary, one which brings all the wildness of the midrash back into the Bible. Legend has it he worked as a vintner, though one wonders where he could have found the time to make wine given that in addition to his work on the Torah, he also managed to produce the defining commentary on the entire Talmud.

Cited in chapters: 1, 2, 3, 4, 5, 6, 7, 9, 11, 12, 13, 14, 15, 16, 17, 18, 19, 23, 25, 27, 29, 30, 31, 32, 39, 40, 41, 42, 44, 46, 47 49, 50, 51, 52, 53, 54

Samson Raphael Hirsch

Rabbi Shimson Raphael Hirsch (*Germany, 1808-1888*), was a leader of the early Orthodox movement in Germany, a staunch defender of rabbinic law, and a vociferous critic of Reform Judaism. At the same time, he preached a philosophy of merging Torah with worldly sensibilities (*Torah Im Derekh Eretz*), spoke in eloquent German, and dressed in the manner of German clergy of the time. So he was at once a modernist and a traditionalist, and his commentary – also written in German – reflects that tension. It is a passionate philosophical defense of the enduring relevance of Torah, which he presents as a rational system of values and ethics designed to promote human thriving.

Cited in chapters: 30, 35, 39

Sforno

After the great works of medieval Torah commentary, Rabbi Ovadiah Sforno (*Italy, 1475-1550*) might be thought of as the first great commentator of the Renaissance. He studied philosophy and medicine in Rome, and became friendly with leading Christian thinkers of the time. His commentary also clearly reflects the influence of the Italian Renaissance, imbued as it is with humanist values and a poet's feel for language.

Cited in chapters: 1, 26, 39, 52

Sfat Emet

Rabbi Yehudah Aryeh Leib Alter (*Poland, 1847-1905*) was the third Gerrer Rebbe, and wrote one of the later masterpieces of Hassidic Torah commentary. The spiritual poetry of Alter's writing is so gorgeous that one sometimes forgets what a keen and precise reader of text he was. He was obsessed with the "spark of animating life-force that can be found in all things," and his commentary turns again and again to this theme.

Cited in chapter: 39

Siftei Chakhamim

Rabbi Shabtai ben Yosef Bass (*Poland, 1641 – Germany, 1718*) was a scholar and printer who was obsessed with Hebrew books. He published a landmark bibliographical manual, *Siftei Yeshenim,* listing and categorizing over 2,200 works. His supercommentary on Rashi, *Siftei Chakhamim,* true to his style, is actually a concise summary of many previous supercommentaries. It is included in most editions of *Mikraot Gedolot.*

Cited in chapter: 11

Torah Shleimah

Rabbi Menachem Mendel Kasher (*Poland, 1895 – Israel, 1983*) was the editor of the *Torah Shleimah,* an ambitious attempt to compile all the midrashim on every verse in the Torah and list them alongside the text of Torah itself, in the fashion of *Mikraot Gedolot.* If that weren't impressive enough, he also wrote an accompanying commentary, which not only showcases his astounding erudition, but also contains many unique interpretations of its own. I have long searched for a family connection to this great Torah scholar whose name I share; but so far, I am sad to say, I cannot claim him as my ancestor. Still, it's nice to end with a Kasher.

Cited in chapter: 50

About the Author

Rabbi David Kasher grew up bouncing back and forth between the Bay Area and Brooklyn, hippies and Hassidim – and has been trying to synthesize these two worlds ever since. After graduating from college at Wesleyan University in 1998, he studied for several years in yeshivot in Israel before heading off to rabbinical school at Yeshivat Chovevei Torah. He was ordained there in 2007, and returned to Northern California, where he became the Senior Jewish Educator at Berkeley Hillel. While he was there, he completed a doctoral degree at Berkeley Law, where he focused on the comparative study of religious and secular legal cultures. He then became part of the founding team at Kevah, a non-profit specializing in Adult Jewish Education, where he worked from 2012 to 2018, and developed the Kevah Teaching Fellowship. He has served on the faculty of Berkeley Law, the Wexner Heritage Program, Reboot, and the BINA Secular Yeshiva, and also taught courses at Pardes, SVARA, The Hartman Institute, AJR, and HUC.

Rabbi Kasher is a teacher of nearly all forms of classical Jewish literature, but his greatest passion is Torah commentary, and he spent five years producing the weekly ParshaNut blog and podcast exploring the riches of the genre. In 2018, he began work as an Associate Rabbi at IKAR, a non-denominational spiritual community in Los Angeles, where he now teaches a weekly parsha class and has a new parsha podcast called 'Best Book Ever.' In the summer of 2023, Rabbi Kasher will be joining the faculty at Yeshivat Hadar.

He previously published an essay, 'Eating Our Way from Justice to Holiness,' in *Kashrut and Jewish Food Ethics* (Academic Studies Press, 2019), and completed a translation of *Avot d'Rabbi Natan* for Sefaria. This is his first book.

Visit us at *www.quidprobooks.com.*

Made in the USA
Middletown, DE
02 May 2023

29878737R00176